The Battle of Minden 1759

1759

The Impossible Victory of the Seven Years War

The Battle of Minden 1759

1759

The Impossible Victory of
the Seven Years War

Stuart Reid

Frontline Books

THE BATTLE OF MINDEN 1759
The Miraculous Victory of the Seven Years War

This edition published in 2016 by Frontline Books,
an imprint of Pen & Sword Books Ltd,
47 Church Street, Barnsley, S. Yorkshire, S70 2AS

ISBN: 978-1-47384-733-0

For more information on our books, please visit
www.frontline-books.com,
email **info@frontline-books.com**
or write to us at the above address.

Printed and bound by CPI Group (UK) Ltd, Croydon, CR0 4YY [TBC]

Typeset in 10/13 Palatino

Contents

Introduction

His Serene Highness Prince Ferdinand was taken by surprise. A French attack had been expected, and indeed it had been deliberately invited. A massive trap was prepared and his army ordered to stand-to in readiness. Yet when the French actually moved forward across the Bastau stream in the very early hours of the morning of 1 August 1759 no warning reached him. Not until 03.00 hours, when it was almost too late, was he roused and told that the French were already driving in his outpost line. The battle of Minden had begun without him and his well-conceived plan at first seemed to be in tatters. Fortunately, in the still uncertain light of dawn the French fumbled their chance and their offensive momentarily ground to a halt as they recognised their peril. As the Allied columns hurried forward on to what would shortly become the battlefield, a thoroughly impatient Prince Ferdinand, scrambling to regain the initiative, sent off a rider with an urgent verbal order for 'General Spörcken to advance with the regiments he had, with drums beating, and attack whatever he might encounter.'

It was a very soldierly order and yet a fateful one too, which unexpectedly turned an uncertain beginning into a famous victory. Yet Ferdinand, seeing the British and Hanoverian infantry storm forward with more zeal than discretion, denied then and afterwards having sent the order and instead tried in vain to halt them.

Any author venturing on to the North German plain in search of what really happened at Minden inevitably does so in the shadow of Sir Reginald Savory's magisterial *His Britannic Majesty's Army in the Seven Years War*, which covered the entire conflict from its fumbling beginning to its exhausted end. A word or two of justification is therefore called for in introducing this new study of the battle.

While Savory's title was both correct and entirely appropriate, it was also literal in covering the operations of all of King George's soldiers in Germany, who were very largely his own Hanoverian subjects and their Hessian, Brunswick and Prussian allies and hired auxiliaries, amongst whom the British contingent played a comparatively small part.

Yet Minden once ranked high in the pantheon of British battles that won the Empire, and for a good reason. In contemporary public relations terms it was one of a trio of battles fought in 1759 which established Britain's ascendency over France for a generation: At Quebec, in September of that year, James Wolfe won all of Canada for the British Crown; in a no less dramatic running battle fought in a November storm at Quiberon Bay the French fleet was wrecked; while at Minden in August French ambitions in Europe had arguably been stopped dead in their tracks. Yet Minden is now very largely forgotten, save by the descendants of those few British regiments that fought there. Indeed, from a British perspective, it was not a particularly large battle. In marked contrast to Waterloo in 1815 where half the British Army appeared to be present and were led by the great Duke of Wellington to boot, only twelve British regiments (and the ever ubiquitous Royal Artillery) served at Minden under the command of a German general!

Yet now, in an age of coalition warfare where national armies such as those of Waterloo have given way to regimental-sized battle-groups and brigades committed, largely for political reasons, to multi-national task forces under international leadership, the battle of Minden once again has a familiar resonance and indeed a relevance to the present day.

This, therefore, is a book as much about the British Army and its curious road to Minden as it is about the extraordinary victory which two British infantry brigades won there. It is a story which had its unlikely origins in North America, and in Germany in a battle on the Weser which saw both sides running away from each other. It is also a story which for the British Army began with a series of futile amphibious operations against the French coast. These were launched not with any realistic strategic goal, but rather to serve a now familiar political one of visibly contributing to the Allied war effort whilst at the same time gingerly avoiding any serious commitment or real expenditure. Predictably, the futility of 'breaking windows with guineas' was underlined by the disaster which ended the policy, but by that time some of the officers and men involved, sick of what they called buccaneering, had managed to find themselves a real war in Germany.

Stuart Reid
Whitley Bay, 2015

List of Maps

Chapter 1

Hastenbeck and the Fall of Cumberland

At the mid-point of the eighteenth century the eastern seaboard of what is now the United States comprised a patchwork of English colonies stretching from New Hampshire in the north to Georgia in the south and westwards inland as far as the Allegheny mountain chain. To the south and west of these colonies were Spanish Florida and French Louisiana, while to the north Canada was also part of New France. Linking the thinly spread French colonies and outposts were the Mississippi and Ohio rivers, which at once served as a vital corridor from Great Lakes all the way down to the Gulf of Mexico, a springboard for exploration and trade further to the west – and at one and the same time a barrier to the westward expansion of the British colonies.

The key to severing that corridor was the future site of Pittsburgh. At the time it was unsettled and simply known as the Forks of the Ohio, but by attempting to seize the Forks in 1754 a young George Washington turned a remote border dispute into a shooting war. Ironically he had no thought of provoking the French but was intent on pre-empting the neighbouring British colony of Pennsylvania which also had designs upon the area. At first it was hoped in both London and Versailles to keep this local difficulty safely at arms-reach, but inevitably the conflict escalated as both powers shipped substantial reinforcements of regular soldiers across the Atlantic. In a naval operation off the Grand Banks in 1755 some of those French reinforcements were intercepted by the Royal Navy, and to that there was no answer but open war.

Unfortunately the British government had failed to anticipate that its aggressive policy in North America might provoke a European conflict and was totally unprepared when it happened. When the French responded to the threat to its colonies by making preparations for a cross-Channel invasion, they inspired widespread panic for there were very few troops in England to stop them.

There were the various regiments of Horse Guards and Footguards stationed in London, but the latter were at best capable of mustering just a single infantry brigade. Otherwise, out of fifty-one ordinary marching regiments of foot then paid for by the Crown, only fifteen battalions were actually stationed in England at the time and not all of them were fit for service. Some of the others formed part of the permanent garrison of Ireland; but the rest were far away in the Americas, in the West Indies and in the Mediterranean garrisons of Gibraltar and Minorca. There was still the Royal Navy of course, but its officers were uncomfortably aware that in certain wind conditions it was impossible to blockade the port of Dunkirk. Should the French then come out they could have an army landed on the Kentish beaches, or even within the Thames Estuary, with little interference.

An increase in the strength of the Army was hurriedly authorised and even a long moribund county militia was once again sanctioned by Parliament, but it would take time to recruit, organise and train these new soldiers. In the meantime, the French were sagely thought unlikely to wait. Reinforcements had to be sought elsewhere. The first to be called upon for help were the Dutch. There was a long-standing defensive alliance with Holland going back to the days of William of Orange and Dutch troops had come to Britain's aid before. Unfortunately this time the Dutch politely declined to intervene. Britain was considered to be the aggressor and alone answerable for the consequences of her actions.

Fortunately, the King himself then stepped into the breach. Although King George II and his father before him had worn the British Crown for over forty years, they still remained Prince Electors of the entirely separate German state of Hanover. Consequently the King immediately consented to release a substantial portion of his Hanoverian Army for the defence of his British dominions.

This was all well and good, and with the addition of a contingent from the neighbouring state of Hesse-Kassel which was hired directly into British pay, a comfortable total of twenty-one battalions of well-trained German infantry was found to defend England's beaches. Unfortunately the threatened French invasion was a chimera; a diversion masking an all too real expedition mounted against the British-held Mediterranean island of Minorca. This operation, commanded by the Duc d'Richelieu, was not only swift and successful in itself, but led to the scapegoating and dismissal of the military governor who failed to hold the fortress, Thomas Fowke, and to the equally vindictive execution of Admiral Byng who had failed to rescue him. Even that victory, however, was not the limit of French ambition. Rather than risk the uncertain Channel crossing, Versailles now considered the possibilities of turning the French Army towards Germany and a suddenly vulnerable Hanover.

Indeed as recently as April 1755, France's then ally, King Frederick of Prussia, had cynically suggested just such a move. The alliance between France and Prussia was, however, a defensive one and in any case was due to expire shortly. Moreover, notwithstanding Frederick's kind invitation to make use of his conveniently situated fortress of Wesel as a base of operations, such a move would inevitably cast France as the aggressor. Just as the Dutch had declined to help Britain, there would then be no obligation on the part of Prussia to assist the French. As a counter-proposal, Versailles then rather ingeniously suggested that if Frederick himself were to seize Hanover, France would reciprocate by invading the Austrian Netherlands (modern Belgium) on his behalf. Frederick was not unsympathetic to this idea, but thought it wise to decline. A war with Austria was already all but inevitable, but now he was becoming aware of another growing threat in the form of Russia.

Whilst there is no denying existing Russian hostility or the personal animosity displayed by the Czarina Elisabeth towards Frederick himself, this was in part a fruit of British diplomacy. All too aware of the threat to Hanover posed by Prussia, British gold was offered to neutralise it. On 30 September 1755, Russia undertook to maintain an army of 55,000 men on the eastern borders of Prussia in return for an annual subsidy from Britain of £100,000, rising to £500,000 per year in the event of war. With that assurance in place, Frederick himself was then approached through the good offices of the Duke of Brunswick, and formally requested not to intervene in the present crisis. The request was accompanied by a rather veiled reference to the possible involvement of Russia should Frederick choose not to offer any guarantees that the neutrality of Hanover would be respected. Slightly puzzled, he in turn sought clarification as to exactly what was being hinted at.

Seldom can such a diplomatic overture have been answered as this one was. Brunswick obtained from London the full text of the Russian agreement and presented it to Frederick! At one and the same time this was accompanied by a polite suggestion that a formal British and Prussian understanding over Hanover might be to their mutual advantage. Frederick was being very openly blackmailed, but he immediately recognised that a friendly Hanover (and British gold) offered far more security than a French alliance when Versailles already had an agenda of its own. He therefore had little hesitation in agreeing, and, on 16 January 1756, the Convention of Westminster was signed. Through this Britain and Prussia entered into a defensive alliance and pledged to jointly resist the entry of foreign armies (i.e.; those of France and Russia) into Germany.

For over two centuries European diplomacy and warfare had been underpinned by a deadly rivalry between Bourbon France and Hapsburg Austria. Now that was completely overturned and to their mutual astonishment, the two enemies suddenly found themselves thrown into an uneasy alliance. In return for a promise of Austrian neutrality in the war with Britain (and Hanover), France agreed in a treaty signed at Versailles on 1 May 1756 to similarly respect the neutrality of the Austrian Netherlands. So far so good, but the treaty included a clause obliging each to come to the assistance of the other with 28,000 men if attacked.

At the very outset of the last war back in 1741 Frederick of Prussia had seized the coal-rich Hapsburg province of Silesia and grimly held on to it ever since. The conclusion of peace with Prussia, first in 1742 and again by the Treaty of Dresden in 1745, was regarded by the Hapsburg Empress Maria Theresa merely as a breathing space. It was no more than an opportunity to repair and modernise her armies, recruit new allies and prepare for a renewed conflict to recover both the lost lands and Austrian prestige. With the signing of the Treaty of Versailles the last piece was in place. If called for, 28,000 French soldiers were hardly going to alter the balance of power in Central Europe. Of far greater value to Austria, however, were the guarantees concerning Belgium and the removal of the Bourbon threat to Maria Theresa's Italian possessions. No longer would the Empress have to fight a war on three fronts. Instead all her energies would be devoted to the war against Prussia.

Accordingly, plans were laid for an attack on Prussia in the autumn of 1756 by the combined forces of Austria, Saxony and Russia. Unfortunately it soon became apparent that this timetable was going to be overly ambitious. Possibly hampered by the loss of the British subsidy, the Russians were behindhand with their mobilisation and admitted they would not be ready in time. Even Austria's own preparations were unaccountably slow. Thus the decision was taken to postpone the offensive until the spring. Frederick, in possession of a good army which was already fully mobilised, decided to strike first and invaded Saxony on 28 August 1756.

4

Thus began the Seven Years War. Whilst a renewed conflict between Austria and Prussia over possession of Silesia was all but inevitable, it was ultimately George Washington's ill-starred expedition to the Forks of the Ohio which brought Britain and France into that war.

The War Begins

It is easy to sympathise with the Hanoverian authorities at this point for they had no interest in either facet of the war. Indeed, on the one hand as a constituent state of the German *Reich* or empire they had a clear duty to provide a contingent of troops for the *Reichsarmee*, in order to assist the Empress in her war against Prussia. Yet at one and the same time, because their Elector also happened to be the King of Great Britain, Hanover was being menaced by the Empress's ally, France. Notwithstanding the alliance with Frederick, it was little wonder that over the next few months the overriding preoccupation of the Hanoverian ministers should be to attempt to secure the Electorate's neutrality.

However, the defeat of the Saxons and the subsequent movement of Prussian troops into the Hapsburg province of Bohemia provided Austria with the justification to request French intervention. France duly agreed to honour her obligations and this ready acquiescence very conveniently masked preparations for her own project of invading Hanover. Nevertheless neither movement could now take place until the spring. Hanover was thus offered an uncovenanted respite, but to Frederick's mingled frustration and dismay his allies' mobilisation continued to be plagued by indecision and delay.

In late November he optimistically estimated that the combined Hanoverian and Hessian forces would amount to some 35,000 men once their troops returned from England. In addition he thought a further 5,000 men might be obtained from Brunswick, and even a wholly unrealistic 4,000 more from Saxe Gotha. In addition, if circumstances allowed, he also thought he might be able to contribute up to 10,000 of his own Prussians to the Allied force. This ought to be adequate to match the French army; which he assumed for no very good reason would likewise amount to about 50,000 men.

He also reckoned the French were unlikely to move before the middle of March. Since Wesel with its Prussian garrison of six battalions then ought to be able to hold out for at least a month, this would allow his allies ample time to move forward from their concentration areas and form an Army of Observation. This was to take post behind the River Lippe, running due west from the Teutoburgerwald to the Rhine and so forming a useful barrier against any army moving north towards Hanover.[1]

The term 'Army of Observation' was a significant one, very much beloved of cautious generals and political gentlemen in the eighteenth century. It was an army carefully calculated to be small enough to avoid any imputation of aggressive behaviour, but at the same time strong enough to inhibit the enemy's own operations. With overt hostilities not yet broken out in the west, it was arguably the wisest policy to adopt at the time, but it foundered on two important points. First the all-important troop concentrations failed to be carried through in a timely fashion. Still pre-occupied by the threat of a seaborne invasion, the British government would only consent to release the German troops stationed in England as and when each individual battalion could be replaced by a British one. In fact, the last Hessian battalion did not return home until the middle of May 1757! Quite naturally this continuing shortage of troops inspired the Hanoverian ministers to try once more to seek an accommodation with Austria and thereby restrain France. Equally naturally, in the meantime, they were also careful not to offer any provocation by hastening their own mobilisation. Fearing the worst, by early January an increasingly worried Frederick was reduced to drawing up contingency plans to evacuate the fortress of Wesel in order to at least save its garrison and its guns.

Had France remained quiet at this point, Frederick's attempts to secure his vulnerable right flank might have collapsed. Instead, Versailles maladroitly intervened with a number of demands. The fortress of Hameln was to be handed over to the Austrians, roads and bridges between the Weser and the Elbe were to be maintained in good order at Hanoverian expense – in order to facilitate the movement of French and Imperial troops to the Prussian Front – and Hanoverian troops were not to move from place to place without consent. This was too much and so Georg, the Prince Elector of Hanover, was at last reluctantly at one with his other persona, King George II of Britain, in going to war with France.

Now that the decision had been taken, a commander needed to be appointed. *Generalleutnant* Ludwig von Zastrow of the Hanoverian Army was all of seventy-seven years old and no-one was under any illusions as to his utter incapacity. Other names were suggested as a matter of course, but at this stage the obvious and indeed only realistic candidate was the Elector's favourite son, William Augustus, Duke of Cumberland. In many ways, although very reluctant, the Duke was ideally suited for the job. The very fact of his being a prince of the blood lent him the necessary authority not only to deal with the recalcitrant Hanoverian ministers but to meet on equal terms with the other rulers who were providing troops for his army. He was also an experienced soldier who had won the Battle of Culloden and commanded the Allied army in Flanders during the last war. If he had not met with the success his hard work deserved, that might be attributed to his misfortune in facing the legendary *Marechal* de Saxe. Since then, and just as importantly, he had proven himself a very capable administrator as Captain-General of the British Army. On 30 March 1757, Cumberland therefore received his orders, which inter alia made it absolutely clear that although he was to command the grandly titled 'Army of his Britannic Majesty', he was doing so as a Hanoverian general, not a British one, and that as such he was to report through the Hanoverian minister in London, Baron Münchhausen. The distinction was subtle, but it was to be a significant one. For the most part Cumberland's orders were sufficiently vague and imprecise as to allow him considerable latitude in his interpretation of them. He was effectively given a free hand, yet at the heart of the orders was an unequivocal stipulation which must have caused great uneasiness in Frederick of Prussia's mind had he learned of it:

> The Position and Operations of Our Army must however be directed to Our Chief Aim. This is: not to act offensively, neither against the Empress Queen, nor any other Power, but merely protect Our own Dominions, those of the King of Prussia in Westphalia, and those of the LandGrave of Hesse, from hostile invasions of Foreign Troops, and repulse force by force.
>
> If, therefore, it is observed that the Crown of France has no Views of penetrating into Westphalia, but that the said Crown's sole intent is, to send an Assistance of Troops into Bohemia, it is not in such a case Our intention, that Our Army marches against them, and oppose them.[2]

In other words, both Elector and ministers were still hoping to the last to avoid hostilities. Cumberland's role was strictly limited to the immediate defence of Hanover, Hesse-Kassel and the Prussian possessions of Wesel and Geldern. If the French refrained from attempting to cross the Lippe, he was to sit tight and watch them go by as they marched east join the Austrians. Frederick, in short was to be sold down the river if that would spare Hanover.

Not that it mattered. Just five days before Cumberland received those fateful orders, the first shots were fired when some French hussars appeared before Geldern and the second of Frederick's strategic assumptions was dramatically overturned. Not only had his allies failed to mobilise in good time, but the French were coming on in far greater numbers than anyone had anticipated. Back in November Frederick calculated they would have something in the region of 50,000 men; instead they were double that number, comprising no fewer than 135 infantry battalions and 143 squadrons of cavalry, commanded by the Prince de Soubise.

The Road to Hastenbeck

Worse still, the Army of Observation was not yet concentrated and indeed some units were still in England. Far from equalling the French, as Frederick had optimistically calculated, it may only have mustered little more than a third of their number. Little wonder then that Wesel was evacuated on 12 March; its heavy guns shipped down the Rhine to neutral Holland and thence by sea back to Prussia, whilst the six battalions of fusiliers forming its garrison headed for Lippstadt, about fifteen miles west of Paderborn.[3] There they were ordered by Frederick to hold on until reinforced, and Cumberland, who arrived at the mouth of the Elbe on 14 April, was accordingly urged to close up on the place. By way of encouragement, Frederick's emissary, *Generalleutnant* von Schmettau, informed Cumberland that if he could maintain his position on the Lippe for six weeks, some further Prussian reinforcements might be spared. It was a forlorn hope. The French, having already crossed the Rhine and occupied Wesel, then seized Münster on the 24th. This in turn forced the evacuation of Lippstadt, but by 1 May Zastrow, still in operational command of the Hanoverian army, had closed up to Bielefeld, in the Teutoburger Wald. Together with the Prussians he mustered a total of twenty squadrons of cavalry and twenty-seven battalions of infantry, but resisting the temptation to strike at the momentarily unsupported French advance guard, he sat tight to await the Duke.

As it was, Cumberland arrived at Bielefeld two days later on 3 May, but by then the French main body, now under the Comte d'Estrées, was closing in and next day some Hanoverian foraging parties were surprised by French light troops under the celebrated partisan leader Johann Christian Fischer. A polite exchange of courtesies then followed as the rival generals each enquired as to the other's intentions. Invited to step aside and so preserve Hanoverian neutrality, Cumberland very properly declined. For his part d'Estrées was aware that a Prussian victory outside Prague on 6 May raised the possibility of a negotiated settlement even at this late stage.

8

If Prussia and Austria made peace, France would not fight on alone. In the event, although the Austrians had been badly defeated Frederick's own losses were so heavy as to prevent him taking Prague itself. The war was to go on and d'Estrées received impatient instructions from Versailles to resume his advance and drive Cumberland across the Weser.

The French advance resumed on 21 May, but it was a leisurely business averaging only about five miles a day. Cumberland was still in a defensive position on the forward slopes of the Teutoburger Wald, and it was not until 12 June that the French actually began closing up on the Hanoverian outposts. If Cumberland had a particular fault it was a peculiarly British one of being unable to properly handle cavalry and to conserve them as a battlefield asset rather than as a means of finding and observing the enemy, while simultaneously screening the positions and movements of his own troops. Consequently he was completely ignorant as to where the French were and what they were doing. They, on the other hand, had no such inhibitions and through vigorous patrolling had built up a good picture of Cumberland's dispositions.

Early next morning, although his main body was still not up, d'Estrées sent his light troops around both flanks of the Hanoverian army and had them penetrate deeply enough to threaten Cumberland's supply route back through Herford towards Minden. Astonishingly, without waiting to verify the strength of these French thrusts, far less establish what was behind them, Cumberland decided to fall back as soon as night fell. No preparation for a retreat had been made and his staff barely had time to alert the troops let alone plan the movement properly. Some units failed to receive orders at all, while those who did were left in ignorance of any timetable or the routes they were to take. Confusion quickly descended into chaos and the French, realising what was happening, pitched in.

Soon nervous Hanoverians were blazing away in the darkness at anyone they encountered – without troubling to discover whether they were friend or foe. Only the Prussian regiments serving as the rearguard held together until they reached Bielefeld. There the streets were choked, not only by stragglers but with abandoned supplies, baggage wagons and other transport. Naturally enough the temptation proved too much and the French pursuit suddenly evaporated in an orgy of plundering. Saved by this uncovenanted respite, Cumberland broke contact and passed the bulk of his men safely across the Weser by the night of 16 June.

For the moment he was reasonably secure, but although he had left some light troops behind on the left bank of the river, Cumberland was more blind than ever and had no effective means of divining where and when the French would cross. The Prussians were detached to serve as a garrison for Minden until Frederick, scenting disaster, recalled them in early July. Cumberland thereupon replaced them with a mixed force of three squadrons and three battalions, posted on both sides of the river, and then sent a further two squadrons and two battalions several miles downstream to cover his supply base at Nienburg. Otherwise everyone else sat tight at Hameln to await events.

On the other side of the river it was a whole month before d'Estrées, once again under pressure from Versailles, eventually moved forward and crossed the Weser just above the town of Holzminden. The operation was necessarily a protracted affair, but Cumberland's reaction was slow and confused. A series of increasingly strong detachments was sent south to observe the French, but at the last moment he decided against a proper counter-attack and instead took up a position just to the east of Hameln. There his army was carefully deployed on the lower slopes of the 286 metre-high Obensberg. This was the highest point of a heavily wooded ridge running more or less parallel to the Weser and about two to three miles back from it. His main fighting position ran in a line from the village of Voremberg on his left, through Hastenbeck and then out on to more open ground in the direction of Hameln. It was a strong position, rendered more so by three large artillery batteries properly dug in behind substantial earthworks. But Cumberland was badly outnumbered and d'Estrées anticipated that he would not stand. However, having the steep-sided Obensburg at his back meant that Cumberland would have to withdraw laterally and so d'Estrées saw an opportunity to trap him against the ridge and destroy him.

At daybreak on the morning of 25 July Lieutenant Général Chevert was ordered to move with three brigades on the village of Voremberg. His task was to pin down Cumberland's left long enough for another corps under the Duc de Broglie, still operating of the left bank of the Weser, to cross the river further downstream near Tündern and pitch into Cumberland's right. Once both were engaged, d'Estrées would then bring up his main body for the decisive blow in the centre.

Alas for his hopes, morning raised a thick mist in the Weser Valley and when it eventually cleared at about 05.30 hours it was clear Cumberland had no intention of going anywhere, but remained dug in on the high ground. Contrary to his expectations, d'Estrées found himself committed to a frontal assault and that meant waiting until all his troops were up and properly deployed. Predictably, perhaps, that also took rather longer than he had anticipated and although they were eventually in position by about 17.00 hours, with a long summer evening still ahead of him, he decided to postpone the attack until the following morning.

Notwithstanding the odds, Cumberland awaited him with a reasonable degree of confidence. His right wing was very comfortably secure behind a stream called the Haste. This meandered north-westward in the direction of Hameln through some boggy meadows and any attempt to circumvent it would meet the guns of the fortress of Hameln itself. His left he considered equally secured by the village of Voremberg. His army was therefore deployed accordingly. Seniority entitled Zastrow to command of the right wing, which no doubt suited Cumberland as it gave him little opportunity to commit any blunders. It comprised two red-coated Hanoverian infantry brigades in the front line under Generals Spörcken and von Block, with a total of nine battalions, backed up by another brigade in the second line comprising four more battalions under von Zeppelin. A large proportion of Cumberland's cavalry, comprising ten Hanoverian squadrons under Colonel von Dachenhausen, was also assigned to the right wing, but the fact they too stood in the second line suggests that they were initially parked there simply because there was nowhere else to put them.

The centre, commanded by the Hessian General-leutnant von Wutginau, was comprised of three blue-coated Hessian infantry brigades totalling eleven battalions in the front line. They were backed up by two Hessian cavalry brigades in the second which also totalled eleven squadrons.

The left, under the Brunswick general Imhoff, was deployed with two brigades of blue-coated Brunswickers totalling eight battalions in the front line, and three red-coated Hanoverian brigades in the second; amounting to two battalions of the *Garde* and four line battalions under Keilmannseg and Hodenberg respectively.

In addition, there were a number of smaller detachments scattered on and around the battlefield. The dominating height of the Obensburg was occupied by three companies of Hanoverian *Jäger* under Major von Freytag. They were good troops and ideally suited to defending its wooded slopes, but they were far too few in number. Below them three grenadier battalions under von Schulenburg were assigned to protect a ten-gun battery close by Voremberg. Similarly a brigade under von Hardenberg, consisting of four battalions of grenadier companies, was posted forward of the main battle-line to protect an artillery battery of twelve heavy guns sited just east of Hastenbeck. There were various other smaller detachments scattered in the direction of Hameln, covering the gap between the fortress and

Cumberland's right wing. One of them, as we shall learn, was going to play a crucial role in the battle.

For their part, the French had a comfortable superiority in numbers. Chevert had started off the day before with a substantial force comprising the infantry brigades of *Picardie*, *Navarre* and *La Marine*, totalling twelve battalions together with an additional one formed from their respective grenadier companies. There were also three battalions of light troops.[4] Now, though, the plan had changed. Since Cumberland was going to stand and fight, d'Estrées reinforced Chevert with another brigade[5] and tasked him with turning Cumberland's left rather than assaulting it directly. That meant getting up on to the ridge and taking the Obensberg.

In the meantime it was now the Marquis d'Armentières who was tasked with engaging the Voremberg position head on. For that purpose he had three brigades of French infantry and a small Austrian brigade, totalling fourteen battalions deployed in the front line. These were, in turn, backed up by a further four battalions of the *Champagne* brigade, and the promise of four more battalions of red-coated Swiss who were still coming up from Holzminden. He also had a reserve of twelve squadrons of dragoons, dismounted to serve as an additional infantry brigade.

The centre, under the Marquis de Contades, whom we shall meet again at Minden, comprised sixteen French battalions in four brigades and was backed up by almost all of d'Estrées' heavy cavalry, mustering thirty-three squadrons in all.

The left wing, under the Duc de Broglie, was necessarily the strongest in terms of infantry; there were three ordinary brigades of French infantry, each of four battalions, and an elite brigade comprising four battalions of *Grenadiers de France* and two of *Grenadiers Royaux*. In addition there were a further ten battalions of Imperial troops from the Palatinate and four French cavalry brigades totalling twenty-four squadrons.

Finally, in reserve d'Estrées had six squadrons of *Royal-Carabiniers* under the Marquis de Poyanne and eight squadrons of hussars.

In all he had something in the region of 10,000 cavalry and 50,000 infantry, supported by sixty-eight guns, while Cumberland mustered little more than half that number, with about 5,000 cavalry, 30,000 infantry and only twenty-eight artillery pieces.

Cumberland's Last Battle, 26 July 1757

Notwithstanding his numerical advantage, d'Estrées was suddenly wary of tackling Cumberland head on. As an anonymous French officer recalled:

As the marshal [d'Estrées] had inspected the position of the Duke of Cumberland, as much as possible, he decided to advance around the heights, and attack the enemy on his left flank. And all staff officers were of his opinion. To this intent, he detached Mr de Chevert at midnight with the brigades of *Picardie*, of *Navarre*, of *la Marine*, the *Volontaires de Flandres* and *Hainaut*, and those of the army. These three brigades sustained by the brigade *d'Eau* were to attack the enemy's left wing. The success of the day depended on this attack, because it was thought impossible to debouch into the plain, as long the enemy were masters of the heights in front of the woods.[6]

Accordingly, d'Estrées sat tight, waiting for news of Chevert, who as it happens was taking his time. The Comte de Lorge, who was bringing up the Brigade *d'Eau*, had contrived to get lost in the wooded approaches and it was not until 09.00 hours that he was up and Chevert at last was ready to go. Preceded by his grenadiers, he started up the slopes with his men deployed in battalion columns and the sound of his musketry provided the signal for the rest of the army to go forward. Naturally enough it also alerted Cumberland that his left was about to be turned and he reacted swiftly. There was a mixed detachment of Hanoverians, comprising two cavalry squadrons under Colonel Dachenhausen, and two infantry battalions, under a Colonel Breidenbach, posted nearly a mile behind the right wing at Afferde covering the road earmarked for a possible withdrawal. Instead, Cumberland now ordered them to march around the north of the Obensberg to Freytag's assistance. Knowing full well they would take some time to arrive, he also ordered Hodenberg to go directly up there with his own two battalions and three of Hardenberg's grenadier battalions, while Schulenberg on his own initiative added another.

Up on the top, meanwhile, events were moving quickly. Freytag, aware that he was very badly outnumbered, made no attempt to hold the forward slopes, but instead waited until Chevert's leading brigade (*Navarre*) reached the summit and then ambushed it. Unable to see what lay in front amongst the rocks and fallen trees, and with Schulenberg's grenadier battalion coming up on their left, the French halted and waited for support. It did not, however, take long for them to realise they were largely opposed by skirmishers. A bayonet charge was ordered and cleared the summit in short order, tumbling Schulenburg's men back too. Well satisfied, Chevert then dragged up some light artillery to advertise his presence, only for Hodenburg to arrive with his own little brigade and Hardenberg's grenadier battalions. This stabilised the position – but the Hanoverians were not strong enough to retake the summit and so it all bogged down into a static firefight.

Down in the valley below, the rest of d'Estrées' men had moved off on cue, but d'Armentières ran into trouble at once:

> The marquis d'Armentières, who had under his orders the brigades of Imperial troops [and], *de Belzunce, de la Couronne* and *d'Alsace*, supported by the dragoons on foot, had to direct his advance on the heights along the edge of the wood. The brigade of *Champagne* at the orders of Mr d'Anlezy, supported by the brigade of *Reding,*[Swiss] was to attack outside the wood …
>
> With the first musket-shots of Mr de Chevert's attack, the army started to move foward, the field artillery and the regimental guns taking the lead, which gave the enemy a terrible defeat. The marquis d'Armentières found but little resistance, the regiment of *Champagne* encountered a fierce resistance, having to pass a ditch in order to get on a battery of 8 pieces which was blocking its advance. With the first salvos it fell into disorder, which however, lasted only for a moment. It opened fire, and captured the battery in an instant.[7]

In reality, d'Armentières' advance got bogged down in the broken ground almost at once and when his reserve brigade (*Champagne*) came up it was accidentally counterattacked by Schulenberg's grenadier battalion – which was in fact retreating down the hill! As on the Obensberg, the attack stalled while d'Armentières awaited the arrival of Reding's Swiss. Contades, on the other hand, did well, storming forward and quickly capturing a projecting spur known as the Schmiede Brink and establishing his own artillery there. Suitably encouraged, d'Armentières resumed his attack, capturing the battery in front of Voremberg, while Contades likewise overran the Hanoverian guns to his front. This was then the cue for d'Estrées to order Broglie to lead the left wing against Hastenbeck itself:

> Mr de Guerchy and Mr de St. Pern, who were to attack Hastenbeck, formed 3 columns of the regiments of *du Roi*, the corps of *Grenadiers de France* and the regiment of *Solar* [the *Grenadiers Royaux*]. They advanced at the same time the army started moving. They had hardly approached the village to half a cannon-shot, when one saw it in flames; one does not know whether it was the enemy or our howitzers. It is certain that they

were willing to defend it, as they had started to dig trenches, partly for their retreat, and partly for the counter-attack. The fire did not prevent the *Grenadiers de France* from advancing into the village, while the regiments of *du Roi* and *de Solar* advanced to the left and to the right of it. As the corps of *Grenadiers de France* debouched, it was hit by cannister from a distance of hardly half a musket-shot from the enemy, which however, did little damage. The commanding officer, not hesitating a moment, ordered a half turn to the right, and rushed against the wood, still occupied by the enemy, which had to abandon a gun, many knapsacks, entrenching tools, and the like.[8]

So far things were going well, and d'Estrées decided the time was right to order forward his cavalry to complete his victory. No doubt he was already mentally rehearsing his despatch to Versailles, but quite abruptly the battle degenerated into a comedy of errors.

First the young Erbprinz[9] of Brunswick counter-attacked at the head of 2/Behr and sent the *Grenadiers de France* tumbling back into Hastenbeck. However, so impromptu was the counter-attack that most of his brigade remained standing where it was, leaving him unsupported. Nevertheless, in the confusion, and much to their bewilderment, the rest of the French infantry was ordered back over the Haste. It was now about 13.00 hours and Cumberland thereupon gratefully seized upon this fortuitous disengagement to order a general retreat by way of Afferde. 'I ordered the Army to retreat,' he wrote, 'which was done in the greatest Order and with the greatest Reluctancy, the common Soldiers despising all Superiority and Danger desiring to be led on in revenge'.[10] And well they might, for they had scarcely been engaged and his timing, alas, was to say the least unfortunate. While undoubtedly hastened by the Erbprinz's counter-attack, the French disengagement was actually in response to a quite different and altogether much more dangerous threat which had suddenly developed by Voremberg, as an anonymous French officer recalled, albeit a little confusedly:

By the account [above], I have given of the different attacks, one is aware, that we had now seized the hills and the village of Hastenbeck, and that the cavalry could debouch in order to attack the enemies in the plain. How great was the astonishment of the whole army, as the corps of *Grenadiers de France* were ordered to withdraw into the village of Hastenbeck. Also, the artillery was to retire past the ravines again, that lay between the wood and the village. The occasion of this movement was as follows: The rather close woods did not allow Mr de Chevert to follow the enemies and reconnoitre their movements. They withdrew and took the brigade *d'Eau*, which supported the brigade of *la Marine*, in flank. On this very unexpected attack, and after a persistent fight, this brigade was forced to give way to the superior enemy.

Right at the beginning of this attack, a general staff officer made off, claiming that he wanted to search for help, but did not return to the battlefield. He went to the marshal and announced having observed an enemy column of more than 9 or 10,000 men turning our right wing. To this news, the marshal sent all light troops to the camp, because he feared it would be plundered by the enemy; and almost the whole cavalry was moved to the right wing. At the same time he ordered the army to halt, and gave orders to the artillery to move back.[11]

At the outset of the battle, it will be recalled, Cumberland had responded to news of Chevert's assault by ordering Dachenhausen and Briedenbach to march against him around the north side the Obensburg. This obviously took some time, but by midday Briedenbach's two battalions were in position to commence an assault straight up the hill. There they surprised the Brigade *d'Eau* and promptly put in a bayonet charge. The French immediately gave way and tumbled straight down the hill towards Voremberg. There, in a curious repeat of Schulenberg's accidental action earlier that morning, they mistook Reding's red-coated Swiss for Hanoverians and fired into them very successfully. They too ran and then, just to complete the French discomfiture, Dachenhausen turned up with his cavalry and rode into the tumbled mass of fugitives. Little wonder then, with his right wing seemingly collapsing and a panicking staff officer reporting a massive attack coming in, that d'Estrées should fear the worst and commence a general withdrawal. Astonishingly, both armies were in effect each running away from the other.

Over on the French left, however, de Guerchy could see that the rest of the Hanoverian army was actually withdrawing and so disregarding his orders he led the *Grenadiers de France* forward again and was quickly joined by d'Estrées, who countermanded the orders to retire. Some of the French officers, like our anonymous writer, were of the opinion he should have mounted an immediate pursuit, but after all the excitement d'Estrées, like Lord Wilmot at Edgehill over a century earlier, was understandably of the opinion that 'we have got the day, and let us live to enjoy the fruit thereof'.

For Cumberland that fruit was bitter. His troops had fought well, inflicting 1,054 dead and 1,277 wounded on the French for a loss of 311 killed, 886 wounded and 207 missing.[12] Nor, as his own report recounts, did they consider themselves beaten, but Cumberland himself evidently was.

Having abandoned Hanover and Brunswick to the French, he retreated northwards. On 11 August, King George, embittered by his son's abandonment of a battle which his soldiers had won, instructed him to seek terms with the object of at least saving the army. Hemmed in at Stade, on the river Elbe just below neutral Hamburg, Cumberland surrendered on 8 September. Neither he nor his troops passed into formal captivity but the Convention of Kloster Zeven required the Hanoverians to remain where they were, while the allied Hessian and Brunswick contingents were to return home. So too did Cumberland, whose father seemingly never forgave him.

For a time it seemed that Frederick was also finished. Indeed, for a time Berlin itself was occupied by the Austrians. Then, on 5 November, he won a stunning victory over a combined French and Imperial army at Rossbach in Saxony. Although Georg, Duke of Brunswick-Lüneburg, had ordered Cumberland to surrender in order to save Hanover, King George now repudiated that surrender. Britain was still at war with France and that war must go on. The army was to fight again and a new commander for it was sought in the shape of a Prussian general – Prince Ferdinand of Brunswick.

Chapter 2

Ferdinand of Brunswick and the King's Enemies

Aged about thirty-eight, Prince Ferdinand was both the younger brother of the reigning Duke of Brunswick and the brother-in-law of King Frederick of Prussia. He was an experienced soldier and if, unlike Cumberland, he had not commanded armies before, he had been trained in the Prussian service under Frederick. Indeed, only days before heading west he had taken part in the latter's crushing victory over the French at Rossbach. He therefore possessed all the right personal and political connections and no-one could doubt his suitability for his new role.

Mindful of his predecessor's political difficulties, Ferdinand laid down certain conditions before accepting command. He required full authority to conduct his operations and run the army as he saw fit, and was to be given the necessary financial support – and powers to use it. Above all, however, he was not to be 'the plaything of the Hanoverian ministry' and wanted to have direct access to King George, rather than work through Münchhausen. Ultimately he was answerable to the British government and his correspondence was with the King and with his Secretary of State, the Earl of Holderness.[1]

In the meantime, such was the urgency of the situation that without waiting for formal confirmation of these terms Ferdinand arrived in Hamburg on 23 November to take up his command. The French were already reported to be on the move and, despite the lateness of the season, he resolved on an immediate offensive with the aim of imposing his authority on a demoralised army before the French could destroy it. Three days after his arrival Ferdinand marched. The going was painfully slow. The roads were appalling, the men out of condition and the draught horses and oxen weak and underfed. It was 13 December before he got his men as

18

far south as the Aller, a major tributary of the Weser running from east to west. There he could go no further for the French held the crossings. Embarking on a winter campaign was asking for trouble at the best of times. Predictably enough this one literally bogged down amidst foul weather with neither side finding either the opportunity or the enthusiasm for any serious fighting. The French sat tight behind the Aller, and on Christmas Eve Ferdinand reluctantly ordered a retreat. Yet the operation achieved three things. It frustrated the French advance, the army broke out of the constricted area in which it had been penned, and, most important of all, it started to regain its confidence and with it a degree of faith in its new commander. It also provided a breathing space in which to rebuild, clothe and re-equip the army itself – and this provides an appropriate point at which to join Prince Ferdinand in taking stock of exactly what he had inherited.

To some modern historians, the Seven Years War and the other European conflicts of the eighteenth century are the 'Lace Wars'. They were, it is popularly thought, fought by armies of ferociously disciplined peasant soldiers led by bewigged aristocratic officers; and all of them fantastically garbed in uncomfortably tight-fitting uniforms designed for display rather than utility. The reality, on active service at least, presented a rather more complex picture.

While officers, for example, were drawn in large part from the aristocracy and landed gentry, that was in itself a reflection of contemporary society rather than a reactionary aberration. Wealth and patronage elevated princes and aristocrats to the highest levels of command commensurate with their ambitions just as it did in civil life. Otherwise, for the most part the ordinary regimental officers, particularly in the infantry, were found from among the poorer landed gentry and the middling sort of people. They often belonged to 'Army' families with a tradition of service, but little wealth. Nevertheless, it was always possible for 'commoners' to rise if they had the ability and there were probably rather more of them around than might at first appear to be the case.

The rank and file were equally diverse in origin. Countrymen naturally accounted for a high proportion, especially in the cavalry, which tended to be recruited from farmers' sons, but otherwise they might come from anywhere. Whilst there were no doubt some criminals in the ranks, wished by magistrates on a frequently ungrateful army, it is a mistake to regard eighteenth century armies as some kind of ambulant penal institution. Then, as now, most soldiers were far more self-reliant and resourceful with the relationship between officers and men a good deal more balanced than popular legend allows.

Infantry

On all sides the infantry were, as always, the most numerous element, and in terms of military accountancy were numbered by battalions rather than by individuals or by regiments. The reason was simple enough. While it was not uncommon to find regiments with two or occasionally more battalions, most regiments just had one. Consequently, both the generals marshalling their own resources and the intelligence officers measuring those of the enemy counted them in the common currency of battalions.

All in all, at the outset Ferdinand found himself mustering fifty-five infantry battalions. There were twenty-nine red-coated Hanoverian battalions, fourteen Hessian battalions and ten of Brunswickers, both in dark blue, and one each from Sachsen-Gotha and Buckeburg, in white coats and blue coats respectively.[2]

Those battalions, commanded by a lieutenant colonel or in his absence a major, were themselves comprised of several individual companies, each commanded by captains. The number of companies varied somewhat from army to army, but the total number of personnel in the battalion remained broadly constant. In theory a battalion *might* number anything up to about 700 men, but it was very rare indeed to encounter one of that strength and the optimum size was generally regarded as being more like 500, although as a general rule of thumb about 300 men was sometimes more realistic once operations were underway.

This was in part a simple matter of attrition. There were battle casualties of course, but these were far outweighed by sickness, exhaustion, straggling and desertion. Even without those variables the process of decay was hastened by the designation of a certain number of men as grenadiers and drawing them off into discrete companies. On active service these elite grenadier companies were in turn brigaded together in quite separate ad hoc battalions. Not only were they then used to spearhead attacks, but frequently they would be sent off on detached operations and were expected to get themselves killed while performing all manner of wonders. As Maurice de Saxe acerbically complained: 'Grenadiers are wanted everywhere. If there are four cats to chase, it is the grenadiers who are demanded, and usually they are killed without any necessity.'[3] This in turn imposed a considerable drain on their parent units, which constantly had to give up more men to replace those casualties. In the longer term, too, the loss of so many of the best soldiers in a battalion also weakened the pool of potential NCOs.

In all, three out of the twenty-nine Hanoverian battalions were formed of grenadiers, as well as two each of the Hessians and Brunswickers. Their tall mitre-shaped caps and other petty sartorial distinctions aside, there was no difference by this period in the equipment of grenadiers or those of the ordinary *musketiers* and fusiliers. Swords were carried by all, but more as a matter of tradition and as the mark of a soldier than for any practical purpose beyond splitting wood and poking camp-fires. Hand grenades had also fallen out of use and, so for all practical purposes, all infantrymen irrespective of their designation were identically equipped with *flinte,* or flintlock, muskets and bayonets.

The maximum useful range of the musket was generally held to be no more than about 300 metres, but in reality it was a good deal less. There were some dramatic exceptions, such as the 'perfect volley' delivered by General Wolfe's men at Quebec in 1759, but detailed studies suggest that at ranges of 100 metres or less casualties were inflicted by just five-and-a-half percent of the bullets ordered to be fired.[4] Anticipating such statistical analyses, Saxe acidly commented: 'Powder is not as terrible as it is believed. Few men in these affairs are killed from in front or while fighting. I have seen whole salvoes fail to kill four men.'[5]

Consequently, whilst some troops are known to have opened fire at ranges up to 300 metres, and occasionally at even longer distances, for all practical purposes the maximum *effective* range of the flintlock musket was at best only 100 metres. Even then experienced officers recommended closing the distance even further before opening fire. In 1746, for example, Lieutenant General Henry Hawley referred to a 'large Musket shot' as being three score yards, or just fifty metres, and anticipated subsequent volleys being fired at closer range.[6] Injunctions to wait until you could see the whites of your opponents' eyes before shooting were no mere hyperbole, and conducting firefights at twenty-five to thirty metres distance was not unknown.

There was, therefore, no need for concealment in the modern manner. Quite the opposite, for it was far more important to see and be seen since one of the principal characteristics of black powder weapons is the quantity of white smoke generated by each discharge. Once the infantry engaged they were to all intents and purposes operating within a massive smoke screen. It was therefore vital that they could at once see that the battalion appearing through the murk in front was wearing British or Hanoverian red, French or Saxon white, or for that matter the dark blue worn by Hessians, Brunswickers and Prussians, rather than the slightly lighter blue preferred by German regiments in the French service. When soldiers were fighting at such close range there was simply no time for mistakes. It was far from fool-proof of course, and, as we have seen, some red-coated Swiss were shot up at Hastenbeck by French soldiers mistaking them for Hanoverians. Conversely, hostile units might be allowed to approach unmolested in the mistaken belief that they were friendly. Easy recognition was essential. Even then units might simply appear as a darker shadow in the smoke and traditionally French units tied a white cravatte in at the top of the pole on which their regimental colours were mounted. This, at least, was usually visible above the smoke of battle and so too were the oak leaves with which Hanoverian colours were festooned.

As to how they actually fought amidst that smoke, traditionally the British and most German armies practised a form of fire control known as Platooning. Originally this saw the battalion's firing line arbitrarily divided up into equal sized platoons before going into action. These were, in turn, allocated to one of three or four 'Firings', which then delivered their volleys in a predetermined sequence. It no doubt looked very pretty at a review, but in reality it was cumbersome and ineffective. Consequently, by the 1750s it was being replaced by the much simpler Prussian-style 'Alternate Firing', by which platoons (or rather companies) were paired off and each loaded and fired alternately. What was more, there was also a growing willingness to fire by whole ranks or even for the whole battalion to deliver a single massive volley and then follow it up with a bayonet charge through its own smoke.

The French had always preferred to deliver their volleys by ranks rather than platoons, and it seems to have been generally agreed by most contemporaries that the initial volley or series of volleys delivered by French troops was therefore heavy and frequently effective. The problem, however, lay in sustaining it. More often than not, if the firefight was prolonged any meaningful form of fire control was cast to the winds as the troops gradually engaged in what was termed a *feu de billebaude* – a rapid but disorderly fire, delivered by every man with a musket in his own time.

Instead of focussing on winning the firefight, French officers therefore preached instead the twin virtues of mobility and decisive shock, delivered by columns, six deep, charging with the bayonet. The upshot was that while the popular stereotype of thin battle-lines of British redcoats being attacked by French columns is popularly associated with the Napoleonic Wars, manoeuvring and rapidly attacking in column was in fact at the centre of French infantry tactics throughout the eighteenth century.

Nevertheless, it ought to be emphasised that both doctrines preached flexibility and that although there was a decided preference for the bayonet, French infantry would fight in line, or in a combination of line and column, just as British and German ones employed Alternate Fire or volley and bayonet tactics according to circumstances.

Cavalry

Just as the basic building block of the infantry was the battalion, comprising 300-500 men a piece, so the cavalry were reckoned by squadrons, each comprising two or three troops or companies and mustering a total of about 100 men, rather than by regiments. Seemingly as a general rule of thumb, a ratio of about one squadron of cavalry for each battalion of infantry was widely reckoned to constitute a balanced force.

For his part, Ferdinand inherited fifty-two squadrons to match his fifty-five infantry battalions, of which there were thirty-four Hanoverian squadrons and eighteen Hessian ones, although he had not at this stage any Brunswick cavalry.

Those cavalry notionally fell into two principal types; horse and dragoons. The first were often armoured and were regarded as heavy battle cavalry, whilst the latter were supposedly lighter and so cast in a supporting role. Dragoons were in fact originally raised as mounted infantry, but by the 1750s only the French persisted in employing them as such. Generally speaking they were regarded simply as a cheaper alternative to Horse, and in terms of their mounted role there was actually no real difference between dragoons and their supposedly heavier (and still socially superior) counterparts except that their horses tended to be cheaper and their organisation was different. Two of the Hanoverian squadrons were guard units, but of the remaining thirty-two squadrons half belonged to eight regiments of *Kurassiere* (without armour), each with two squadrons and the remainder to four regiments of dragoons each with four squadrons. Similarly, the Hessians designated their heavy cavalry as *Reiters* and fielded five regiments each with two squadrons, while once again the two dragoon regiments had four squadrons apiece.

So far as basic tactical doctrine was concerned there was no great difference in theory between the armies. It should be emphasised that even the French were not accustomed to dismounting their dragoons *during* a battle. If they went into battle on horseback, they fought on horseback.

Squadrons were generally deployed in three ranks and the troopers were to ride closed up, boot to boot. The intention was to provide as solid a front as possible, for it was reckoned that a looser formation, or one mounted on lighter horses, would burst apart on contact. Conversely, if both parties were in all other respects equal they would each, quite literally, try to push the other back, using the second and third ranks to add weight. However, although there was a common doctrine, the actual practice was a different matter.

Since success was reckoned to depend in the first instance on maintaining a solid formation and in particular a level front rank, doing so was regarded as absolutely paramount. Unfortunately, in peacetime most armies lacked any meaningful opportunity to conduct proper cavalry manoeuvres. Consequently, when they were called upon to do so in wartime there was an understandable tendency towards caution, or rather to march and manoeuvre slowly, almost timidly, in order to carefully preserve the integrity of that all-important tightly closed formation.

In the Prussian service, on the other hand, it was a rather different story. On his accession to the throne in 1741 the young King Frederick had inherited just such a cavalry. Afterwards it was claimed that even basic horsemanship was lacking and that the troopers were afraid of their big horses. Regarding his cavalry as all but useless he had revitalised its training. Exactly the same tactical principles were maintained but the training was intensified first to improve horsemanship and then, above all, to practice movement and manoeuvres at a much faster pace in order to restore the cavalry's proper speed and mobility. The results were everything that could be asked for, and under officers such as General von Seydlitz the Prussian cavalry became an elite force.

Naturally enough Prince Ferdinand, as a Prussian general himself, was dismayed at the comparatively lacklustre performance of the cavalry belonging to his new command. His very pragmatic solution was to immediately beg from Frederick the loan of a Prussian cavalry brigade, comprising two dragoon regiments each of five squadrons, and another five squadrons of hussars besides. This was not simply a reinforcement but was also intended to serve as an exemplar of how cavalry should move and make proper use of shock action. In this he was strikingly successful so far as his German cavalry was concerned, but the British cavalry contingent, when it arrived, was slower to learn. In time they too would understand the trick, but the French would require another fifty years to do so, and in the meantime they were to pay a heavy price.

Artillery

Broadly speaking, apart from siege work, artillery support took two forms. Most infantry battalions included an organic light artillery detachment, usually comprising two rather small cannon, sometimes completely crewed by regular gunners but more usually by just a cadre assisted by the infantry themselves. These guns were doubtless of some comfort to the infantry, but their practical effect appears to have been negligible.

Like that of the cavalry, the performance of the Allied artillery proper, at first left much to be desired. As we saw at Hastenbeck, the Duke of Cumberland simply deployed his available heavy guns in a series of fixed batteries dug in behind earthworks and then very largely left them to their own devices. Co-ordination with his infantry was limited to the allocation of a number of battalions to provide local protection for the guns rather than the other way around. To be fair, Cumberland intended from the outset to fight defensively and his guns were neither particularly modern nor mobile. Nevertheless, there was no denying the quantitative and qualitative superiority of the French artillery and its gunners. At first there was little which Ferdinand could do to improve matters and his artillery would let him down in the 1758 campaigns just as it had failed Cumberland. Paradoxically, part of the problem was that while the artillery commander, the Graf zu Schaumburg-Lippe, had a considerable reputation as an artillery expert, this was founded on his interest in the science of gunnery. His talents as a practical artillerist and administrator never lived up to his reputation and it was not until the arrival of the British contingent that the artillery improved in effectiveness. To anticipate matters, not only did the British contingent include a very good artillery train of its own, but Ferdinand was able to procure an additional twenty-eight modern guns through the good offices of Lord George Sackville in his capacity as Lieutenant General of the Ordnance. Additional gunners were relatively easier to find. At this period artillery personnel comprised two different groups; the trained artillerists and the *handlager* who helped haul or push the guns into position and carry the ammunition. In the ordinary way of things the *handlager* naturally picked up a working knowledge of gunnery and therefore when new companies were raised they were easily absorbed alongside the gunners proper and replaced in their turn by drafting infantry or militia.

At this stage that expansion still lay in the future. Otherwise, in general terms, once Ferdinand had the opportunity to take his men in hand, to restore discipline and morale and to see them properly clothed, fed and shod, he found himself in possession of a good well-trained and properly equipped professional army. Nevertheless, it was a still a relatively small one for the magnitude of the task it faced. Ferdinand not unreasonably estimated that quite exclusive of ordinary replacements he was going to need at least an additional 10,000 men – and even that assessment would soon prove totally inadequate. Yet the means of finding them were severely limited.

In a sense a large part of the problem was the very professionalism of the army. The successful application of its tactical precepts demanded well trained and highly disciplined regiments. Replacement drafts could be absorbed into the ranks of existing units relatively easily, but to recruit and train entirely new regiments to stand alongside them was reckoned a different matter entirely. Over the course of the war only two rather weak battalions were added to the Hanoverian line and two to the Brunswick army, and even then they seem to have been employed for local defence rather than serve as part of the field army. Similarly, no new cavalry regiments at all were raised, although an existing Brunswick dragoon regiment was converted to a heavy *Karabinier* regiment and added to the army in 1759.

In large part the answer was the raising of an astonishing number and variety of what were termed light troops. All armies had already possessed them, to a lesser or greater degree, from the very beginning. It is important, however, to distinguish between the small units of *Jäger* and hussars which existed at the outset, and the private armies which followed.

Notwithstanding the vicarious employment of spies and other forms of intelligence gathering, the quickest and most straightforward way of finding where the enemy was, and in what strength, was simply to go out and look for him. Conversely, it was only sensible to make every effort to prevent the enemy doing the same. It was, in short, one of the classic roles of cavalrymen, but there was a problem. Generally speaking the large horses required by heavy cavalry were strong but not robust enough for the rigours of constant employment on outpost and scouting work, especially in bad weather. Experience on all sides showed that they very quickly broke down and this was a major reason for the widespread reluctance to use cavalry aggressively in a scouting role but rather to preserve it for 'a better occasion'.

Instead, these outpost duties were normally assigned to a third type of cavalry; the outlandishly dressed hussars. Originally Hungarian, they were mounted on small horses and ponies whose natural hardiness had not been bred out of them in pursuit of greater physical size. The men who rode them were seemingly similar in character, and one bemused British officer described them thus: 'A nasty looking set of rascals, the picture you have in the shops in London is very like them though it does not represent their rags and dirt – they make no use of tents; at night or when they rest they run their heads into some straw or any stubble and the rest of their persons lies soaking in the rain. It's said that some private hussars have this campaign got about 2,000 German crowns, nay some advance it to pounds. They drink more brandy than water and eat I believe more tobacco than bread.'[7]

Those in question were actually some of the famous Prussian Black Hussars and entirely typical of their kind. They did not sit easily on the peacetime establishments and only the French, Prussian and Austrian armies had retained any great number of them after the previous war. Once hostilities began, however, there was a desperate scramble to recruit as many as possible. Hussars were most popular, but there were also *jäger zu Pferde* or mounted *jäger*.

The latter, together with their dismounted colleagues, the *jäger zu füss*, provided a semi-organic infantry support for the hussars. Largely recruited from foresters they were traditionally dressed in hunting green and armed with rifles rather than smooth-bored muskets. As specialists there were never very many of them; hence just the three companies defending the wooded Obensberg at Hastenbeck. Like the regular infantry it was very difficult to expand their numbers effectively and so in time of war it had been found necessary to supplement them with cheap and cheerful mercenary units, armed with ordinary muskets.

These were supposedly recruited in neutral states such as Hamburg or Denmark, but in reality were raised by military contractors who, on both sides, filled the ranks with deserters, former prisoners of war and any other mercenaries who came to hand from every corner of Europe. From just four companies of *jägers* in 1756 they expanded to no fewer than fourteen infantry battalions and twelve companies of mounted *jägers* by July of 1760, and a further five battalions were added by the war's end. Thus by that time they formed nearly a quarter of the Allied infantry.

Like the hussars, they were often dressed in an even more exotic fashion than their regular counterparts. Ostensibly this was to aid recognition but, in large part, it also reflected the Emperor Maximilian's famous remark that his *landsknechts* were allowed to dress as colourfully as they pleased, because their lives were so brutish and short that they deserved such indulgence.

Frederick the Great was famously disdainful of such troops, despite employing them in great numbers. Initially these mercenary corps lacked the discipline, training and equipment of regular units and were intended on all sides to be employed in *kleinkrieg* (literally small war or petty skirmishing) operations.

In reality, such was the spiralling need for ever more men that they found themselves called upon for other duties, including serving in garrisons and in conducting ever larger detached operations. Eventually, towards the end of the war, much of the distinction between them and the regular troops blurred.

Ferdinand Rides Out

At the beginning of 1758 all the above lay in the future, and even while embarking upon the expedient of sanctioning the recruitment of light troops, Ferdinand was still only too conscious of the impossibility of expanding his regular forces to any significant degree in the short term. Whilst the French Army was sufficiently large enough to be able to allocate additional troops for the German war, and even to rotate units home, Ferdinand found it difficult to rebuild and maintain the regiments he had, let alone raise more. Frederick had once promised help and whilst there was no doubting the value of the loaned cavalry brigade, no Prussian infantry could be spared. Realistically, any additional regular infantry units could only be found in Britain. The question was whether Britain was prepared to supply them.

Britain was at war with France, yet frustratingly impotent. The war had begun in America and was still being fought there and in India and almost everywhere between – except in Europe. The Channel, which had prevented a French invasion of England at the beginning, impartially prevented a direct assault on France.

In September 1757 a major expedition had been launched against the port of Rochefort, only to founder in a welter of indecision and return without even landing the troops. It was only a Court of Inquiry.

A far more direct approach was needed and the German war offered it. British gold was already being provided to pay for His Britannic Majesty's army there. To some, providing actual British troops as well potentially offered a far more effective means of prosecuting the war against France than the coastal raids, but first Ferdinand had to demonstrate that it was realistic.

The opportunity soon presented itself. By mid-February of 1758

Ferdinand felt confident enough, despite the weather, to resume his break-out. The French, by contrast, were anything but confident. Their supply lines were overstretched leaving them cold, wet, hungry, sick and demoralised. Their officers were just as unhappy, and the Duc d'Richelieu, who had succeeded d'Estrées, soon departed to be replaced by the Prince de Clermont. He, at least, was nothing if not realistic and, according to a near contemporary history of the campaign, advised Versailles that: 'I found your Majesty's Army divided into three parts. The part which is above ground is composed of pillagers and marauders; the second part is underground; and the third is in hospital. Should I retire with the first; or wait until I join one of the others?'[8] The story is almost certainly apocryphal, but accurate.

Ferdinand's plan was nothing if ambitious. Moving forward on 18 February a demonstration pinned the French on the Aller while the main body marched west to Verden, just short of the confluence of the Aller and the Weser. The bridge there was seized and Ferdinand's forces then pushed upstream to secure a crossing over the Weser itself at Hoya. Of itself this was significant, but when some Hanoverian hussars started raiding on the other side of the river the French garrison of Bremen was incontinently evacuated. With equally little cause the French commander in the area, Saint-Germain, far from menacing Ferdinand's flank took it into his head to withdraw as well, all the way back to Münster. This had far-reaching consequences for it allowed Ferdinand to establish a secure supply line from Bremen up the Weser to Neinburg, which in turn served as a base for further operations towards Minden. Clermont, justifiably alarmed, fell back, hoping to make a stand near Hameln, but Minden surrendered on 15 March after a siege of just two days. By now Clermont was in no doubt that his army was in no condition to fight anyone and determined on a retreat all the way back to the Rhine. Ferdinand, whose own men were by now exhausted, was content to let him go. In just six weeks, and without fighting anything approaching a major battle, he had liberated Hanover and cleared the rest of Westphalia. His headquarters was now established at Münster and he could give his men a rest with some confidence. Not only had they proved themselves, but he now had hopes of reinforcement.

The French evacuation of Bremen considerably eased the supplying of his army, but yet more important during the campaign two British warships had forced the abandonment of Emden too. It was promptly occupied by British seamen and British marines, a token force but sufficient to lay a claim to the place until the arrival of a proper garrison in the shape of

Brudenell's 51st Foot. A single newly-raised battalion was obviously little more than a token, but Britain was now, for good or ill, fully committed to the German War.

Encouraged, and materially strengthened by the opening of his river-borne supply lines, Ferdinand essayed another and yet more ambitious campaign in May. This time, it was to be carried out in conjunction with a British expedition against Ste. Malo, in Brittany. He intended to cross to the left, or west, bank of the Rhine hard by the Dutch frontier and then push southwards to get between the French and the Meuse and so trap and destroy them. Ferdinand was still, notionally at least, heavily outnumbered by the French, but it was anticipated that the concurrent Ste. Malo operation would draw off French troops who would otherwise be sent against Ferdinand. Whether the two operations were also intended to test the merits of coastal expeditions against the continental option is not completely clear, but the British government was inevitably going to look upon them in that light.

In the event Ferdinand's essay did not quite come off. It started off well when he boldly violated Dutch neutrality by throwing a pontoon bridge across the Rhine just inside their border and by 3 June his whole army was across and heading south.[9] Clermont feared that he was making for the Meuse and ordered his army to concentrate at Rheinberg, south of Wesel, in preparation to fall back across the Meuse if necessary. Fortunately, common sense soon prevailed with the happy realisation that Ferdinand was in effect on the wrong side of the river and that he had very little chance of getting back across it if anything went wrong. A comedy of miscommunication then followed as *Marechal* Belle-Isle, the French Minister of War, attempted to co-ordinate operations between Clermont and another French army under Prince Soubise, with letters constantly crossing and being misinterpreted. The upshot of it all was that Clermont found himself fighting a defensive battle against Ferdinand at Krefeld on 23 June.

Krefeld

The French position at Krefeld was very well chosen and to defend it Clermont had no fewer than 47,000 men mustered in 111 squadrons and seventy-four battalions. His right wing was effectively anchored on some woods and marshes extending towards the Rhine, and the main battle line strongly posted behind a substantial ditch known as the Landwehr, which had only a few crossing points. The ground in front of this ditch was flat, but cluttered with farmsteads, hedges and ditches, with the town of Krefeld forward of his right and the village of Sankt-Tönis covering the left wing which itself rested on Anrath.

A frontal attack offered little chance of success, particularly since Ferdinand was outnumbered and had only 33,000 men in fifty-five squadrons and thirty-seven battalions. On the other hand, the Allied troops were in far better condition and, above all, far more confident. Calculating that the French would sit tight behind the Landwehr, Ferdinand planned to outflank the enemy's left wing. He would hook around Anrath to roll up Clermont's line and drive the French into the Rhine. First Spörcken, with thirteen battalions and twenty-three squadrons, was to drive in the French forward pickets and hover menacingly about Krefeld as if to threaten their right, while Oberg, with six battalions and six squadrons, demonstrated against the Landwehr crossing points. The remainder of the army, under Ferdinand himself and his nephew, the Erbprinz of Brunswick, advanced to Sankt-Tönis. At about 04.00 hours on the morning of 23 June a final reconnaissance was carried out from the church tower in the village and Ferdinand confidently gave the order for the flanking attack to begin.

This was to be launched against Clermont's left rear, which was itself covered by a large drainage channel known as the Great Ditch. Although Ferdinand was aware of it he does not appear to have appreciated just what a formidable obstacle it posed. The Erbprinz, with nineteen battalions and a couple of squadrons, was to assault across it by the small village of Holterhöfe, less than a mile south of the Landwehr crossing at Am Stock. Meanwhile, the Herzog von Holstein-Gottorp, with his Prussian cavalry brigade and three Hanoverian regiments besides, was to move a mile or so further on to Votzhöfe, the idea being to pitch into the French as they reeled back from the Erbprinz' assault.

Unfortunately, visibility, as well as movement, was considerably hampered by the various hedgerows, farm buildings and thickets and it was some time before Clermont finally realised that Ferdinand's offensive was developing. As anticipated, he had responded to the threatening moves made by Spörcken and Oberg by deploying his army in front of his camp. The main fighting line formed behind the Landwehr from Fischeln on the right to Am Stock on the left. In the centre, behind the infantry, Clermont deployed two lines of cavalry. A reserve of *Carabiniers* and dragoons was formed *en potence* on the open left wing and prudently he also posted four battalions towards Anrath which was itself occupied by 200 infantry and 200 cavalry of the *Légion Royale*.[10] As intended, however, Clermont anticipated that the Allied assault would be coming in on his right wing and so threw some 800 light troops forward to occupy Krefeld and posted the *Grenadiers de France* and the *Grenadiers Royaux* in reserve behind his right wing and the *Navarre* Brigade in reserve behind the centre.

So far so good it seemed, but about noon Clermont's equanimity was abruptly upset when the *Légion Royale* and the other four battalions supposedly defending Anrath fell back on the camp. Realising that Ferdinand was actually trying to outflank him on the left, he reacted swiftly. Sending Saint-Germain against him with the brigades of *La Marine, Touraine, Brancas* and *Lochmann*,[11] he also re-deployed a number of squadrons in support.

Consequently, the Erbprinz found himself with a much tougher fight on his hands than he anticipated. Saint-Germain and his men grimly held on along the ditch, repulsing three full scale assaults in as many hours. Details of these assaults are lacking, but given the nature of the ground, broken up as it was by farm buildings and houses, hedges, ditches, and manure heaps, the fight must have soon degenerated into an equally shambolic *feu a billebaud*. At last, at about 17.00 hours, the Erbprinz launched his grenadiers in a last attack which finally prised the French off the ditch and pushed them back towards their camp. There then followed an equally difficult struggle to sort out the scattered and jumbled regiments and companies and put the Hanoverians back into some sort of order, for the inevitable counter attack was developing.

It was at precisely this point that Holstein-Gottorp ought to have intervened with his Prussian and Hessian cavalry. Instead, to his frustration he was unable to locate a way over the ditch, which was much more of an obstacle than had been anticipated. It increasingly looked as if he might be reduced to being a helpless spectator of the unfolding crisis. Fortunately, just at the last moment, an unguarded crossing was discovered at Engerhöfe, a few hundred metres east of his position. Three Prussian squadrons and a Hessian one were promptly sent across, only to be just as promptly charged by the *Carabiniers* and *Royal Roussillon Cavallerie* and tumbled back again. Undaunted, Major-General von Urff had also got across at the head of the Hessian *Leib-Regiment* and the *Leib-Dragoner* in time to counter-charge the pursuing *Carabiniers*, and allow Holstein-Gottorp to pump more units into the fight.

In the meantime, the Erbprinz managed to rally about four battalions, or at least their equivalent, resupply them with ammunition and send them forward under Major General von Gilsa. He, in turn, was charged by the Comte de Gisors at the head of four squadrons of *Carabiniers*, who were shot down by the advancing battalions at about twenty paces range. That was cutting it a little fine and some of the cavalrymen briefly broke through before being driven back. In any case, the cavalry fight had by now grown general with all twenty Allied squadrons opposing just fourteen French ones. Having at last formed a proper front, Holstein-Gottorp swept the field. The Erbprinz too had sorted out the rest of his command and he and Gilsa now moved forward again to link up with Oberg, who had finally crossed over the Landwehr and into the fight.

By now it was about 18.30 hours, but Clermont's last reserve was coming up. The *Navarre* Brigade and the *Grenadiers de France* and *Grenadiers Royaux*, totalling eighteen battalions, were hurrying across from the right wing. Unfortunately their advance was impeded by the great mass of infantry and cavalry falling back from what had been the left wing. The Comte de Lusace, however, rallied the grenadiers and proposed to lead an immediate counter-attack. They were elite troops and above all fresh, while Ferdinand's army was tired and probably short of ammunition. Clermont must have been tempted, but he was also aware that Spörcken's equally substantial command had not yet intervened. Prudently the grenadiers were halted and fell back to Fischeln, where they formed up to cover the retreat of the rest of the army.

At this point Spörcken should have intervened. The French could hardly hold off Ferdinand's men coming at them from the west and at the same time defend the main Landwehr crossing north of Fischeln. Yet he sat tight. His problem was that he had no idea what was happening. As elsewhere on the flat battlefield, visibility was restricted. He was aware of course that the battle was underway and the severity of the fighting was only too clear both from the noise and what will have been a steadily increasing cumulus of powder smoke. That in itself was cause for concern for it suggested, correctly enough, that Ferdinand was not rolling up Clermont's flank as easily as he had anticipated and might even have been in trouble. He could, of course, have pitched in regardless, but would then have been unable to respond to any request for assistance or even in a worst case scenario cover Ferdinand's retreat. Yet he received neither orders from Ferdinand nor even an update as to the situation. It was Hastenbeck all over again. Ferdinand was a better general than Cumberland had been, but the battle was still fumbled by a basic failure in communication. By the time Ferdinand found Spörcken himself it was too late. Clermont had broken contact and was withdrawing southwards. In all, it would appear that Ferdinand inflicted some 5,200 casualties on the French and took another 3,000 prisoners, all for the loss of about 1,800 men.

Eventually Clermont withdrew as far as Köln, where he resigned and was replaced by the Marquis de Contades. A somewhat confused campaign then followed which almost saw Ferdinand trapped, before re-crossing the Rhine to deal with a dangerous threat which had developed in Hesse. Strategically Ferdinand had failed in his aim of destroying the main French field army, but his twin feats of crossing the Rhine and then safely escaping back on to the right bank excited the imagination. Above all, however, he had fought the French in a major battle, the first since Hastenbeck nearly a year earlier, and he had triumphed.

But what of the corresponding operation at Ste. Malo?

Chapter 3

The British Army Goes Buccaneering

The British contribution to the summer campaign was a series of amphibious operations against the French coast. The government at the time was an uneasy wartime coalition between the Duke of Newcastle and the formidable William Pitt, together with their respective supporters. Newcastle, although largely seen as a comparatively ineffective Prime Minister, was a supporter of the King and consequently favoured intervention in Germany. However, the Hanoverian dimension was a problem in that there were voices questioning whether the heavy subsidies to Prussia and other German states were really being spent in Britain's interest – or in Hanover's.

Pitt, as Secretary of State for the Southern Department and therefore directly responsible for prosecuting the war against France, was opposed to such continental entanglements. Instead he was firmly convinced that a direct assault on France and its overseas possessions was going to be more effective and far more popular with a sceptical public. Consequently, he favoured sending British troops not to Germany but to the French coast. There they would be seen to be striking at France, but yet avoiding any conflict of interest in regards to Hanover.

Notwithstanding the failure of a similar expedition to Rochefort the year before, there was also justification for a raid on Ste. Malo in that the port served as a base for the numerous privateers preying on British merchant shipping. In the wider strategic sense Brittany was a long way from Flanders, let alone from Germany, and a descent there would therefore stretch the French coastal defences. At the simplest level every French battalion kicking its heels by the seaside from Calais to Brest, or even beyond, was one battalion less available for the German war.

Politically Pitt was on very sound ground. The practicalities, though, were another matter.

In April 1758 the officers of no fewer than sixteen regiments received warning orders to prepare for service and by the middle of May some 13,000 men were encamped on the Isle of Wight. In the event, one of the regiments, Talbot's 74th Foot[1], was held back for service on Jamaica, but the others, including three battalions of Footguards, were formed into five brigades, each commanded by a major general. In addition, there were three companies of the Royal Artillery under Lieutenant Colonel Thomas Desaguliers, mainly intended to service a substantial train of siege guns, and there were also nine troops of light dragoons or light horse mustering 540 troopers in total.[2]

The latter were an innovation, or rather an experiment, and, as such, rather than convert an existing unit or raise an entirely new one, a single troop was provided by each of the regiments of dragoon guards and dragoons then serving on the British establishment. Distinguished by leather jockey caps and light boots, and with accoutrements altered to permit them to fire their carbines on horseback, they were trained up as hussars and were intended to serve as scouts and pickets during the intended operations.[3]

Command of the expedition was confided to Charles Spencer, 3rd Duke of Marlborough. Other than as the inheritor of his famous great-uncle's title, and more importantly his formidable political and social connections, he had no obvious military qualifications for the job and had seen no service since commanding a brigade at Dettingen all of fifteen years before. His second-in-command, Lieutenant General Lord George Sackville, although junior to Marlborough was a more experienced and more intelligent officer. While his protégé, James Wolfe, is generally credited with the introduction of the Alternate system of fire control to the British Army, Sackville certainly accelerated the process and may actually have been its original begetter. As it would eventually turn out he was no great captain but he was, nevertheless, a thoroughly competent officer, well qualified to prevent his superior from making any great blunders. As Horace Walpole gleefully informed one of his correspondents: 'The Duke of Marlborough commands, and is, in reality commanded by Lord George Sackville.'[4]

By 27 May the whole lot had embarked and, just three days later, as Ferdinand crossed the Rhine, set sail accompanied by two squadrons of the Royal Navy. The larger one, commanded by Lord Anson and Sir Edward

Hawke, was to cruise off the French naval base at Brest in order to ensure that there was no interference with the other squadron and the transports under Richard Howe. He, for his part, was to land the troops in France, directed by the Army officers and generally provide any and all assistance as necessary.

Ste. Malo

The destination was still secret, but those involved shrewdly guessed 'from our being so cruelly crowded on board of the transports' that the voyage would be a short one one, and that meant France.[5] Sailing straight across the Channel, Howe's squadron struck Cap La Hougue by about 08.00 hours on 2 June 1758. However, bad weather during the Channel crossing and then an extraordinary succession of mishaps and delays meant that the transports following slowly after him did not actually arrive off their projected landing place of Cancale Bay until seventy-two hours later. By then, of course, the French were thoroughly forewarned.

Shortly before noon, Commodore Howe, with the Duke of Marlborough and Colonel Watson, the Quartermaster General, went in with an armed cutter to reconnoitre the beach. There they had the excitement of being fired upon by a small battery and, finding themselves satisfied as to the practicality of a landing, soon returned to the fleet. Four frigates sufficed to silence the battery and that evening the British advance guard went ashore, as laid down in orders: 'Ten companies of grenadiers, completed to a hundred men, rank and file each ... The grenadiers of the Guards and Bentinck's, [5th Foot] remain with their regiments; so that the grenadiers of every other battalion, except the Duke of Richmond's [72nd Foot] as the youngest, were to prepare for this service. The grenadiers to be divided into two battalions. Major General Mostyn to command Bentinck's and the grenadiers.'[6]

To all intents and purposes the landing, just before sunset, was unopposed. There were some musket shots fired at long range by a few of the local militia but a detachment of the regular *Boulonnois* Regiment and a couple of companies of the *Marboef* Dragoons, posted in Cancale itself, departed with what their opponents derided as indecent haste:

> No sooner were the grenadiers drawn up on the beach, than Lord Down, with twenty of Kingsley's [20th Foot], marched thro' a very narrow pass, up into the village, where they were met by a Colonel of the militia, and his servant. Lord Down called to him, and told him if he would surrender

himself, he had nothing to fear; but he foolishly refused quarter, and, together with his servant and their two horses, was shot dead upon the spot.[7]

And that, seemingly, was the extent of the initial resistance. The grenadiers took up a covering position on the low hills overlooking the beach, where the first of the infantry brigades was brought ashore. That night some 'scenes of horror, and many of inhumanity' in the village were supposedly checked by summary executions, although Corporal William Todd of the 30th Foot reckoned it to be exaggerated and blamed the zeal of the Captain of the Provost Guard, Sergeant Lloyd of the 1st Footguards, who was paid £5 for each man hanged and no questions asked.[8]

The following day Marlborough and Sackville established their headquarters in Cancale, while the rest of the army was brought ashore and promptly stuffed themselves silly on the oysters covering the beach. It was not until Wednesday, 7 June, at daybreak, that it all got properly underway. Major General George Boscawen was assigned with the two 'youngest' regiments to remain behind to await the arrival of the heavy artillery, which had been delayed by the dismasting of its transport. In the meantime, his raw recruits were to be set to digging entrenchments to protect the bridgehead.

The rest of the expedition moved out, heading due west in two columns. The first column under Sackville, consisting of the two grenadier battalions and the Guards and Mostyn's Brigades, 'fell into the great road to St. Maloes'. The other, and less fortunate, column led by the Earl of Ancrum had a rather harder time. Notwithstanding the efforts of an advance party comprised of 200 pioneers, the infamous bocage (thick hedgerows bordering a patchwork of small fields) compelled Waldegrave's and Elliot's brigades to sometimes move across country in single file.

Eventually, and despite a continual harassing fire from local militia concealed in the hedgerows, the army arrived near Ste. Malo. The town itself was relatively small but lay at the mouth of a long bay forming a natural harbour where the River Rance met the sea. It occupied a very strong position and could only be approached along a narrow spit of land extending a mile westward from the village of Paramé.

Most of the army was ordered to encamp at the east end of the bay, to the south of Paramé, but the Guards brigade was posted out to the left (south) as a flank guard, covering the road from Dol and Granville. While the main body was occupied in pitching its tents, the light horse and the pickets of the day were ordered to advance up the road from Paramé towards the walls of Ste. Malo. The demonstration cost them a couple of horses, but as events proved it was successful in masking what was to come next.

That night, at 23.00 hours, and under cover of darkness, Major General John Waldegrave swung south-west to the walled village of Ste. Servan with the pickets and light horse and his own infantry brigade. As it lay directly across the harbour mouth, possession of the village would seal off the entrance and allow the British to directly attack the shipping trapped there. Corporal Todd of the 30th Foot takes up the tale:

> When we came up to the Gates they were strongly Barricaded up & 5 Regiments of the Enemy's troops with, so that our General Order'd 4 pieces of Cannon to play upon the Gate-way we were at & they soon Demolish'd the Gates & Shattered several Houses, so that we March'd in and took possession of the town. The Enemy's troops retreated out at the other end into the Garrison of St. Malloes & we begun Immediately to set fire to the ships that lay in the Harbour betwixt St. Mallows and St. De Van [St. Servan]. The tide being out it was quite dry where they lay, the Enemy had run them uphither to Escape us taking them. However we set them all on fire, which was Upwards of 170 Vessels, with the Dock Yard, Rope Yard & all the Store House etc. Here was a 74 Gun ship & several others a Building & very near finished which was all distroy'd & quite Burnt down.[9]

It was quite a fire, and still burning when the British withdrew a couple of days later. Ste. Malo itself was summoned to surrender in due form but the governor, the Marquis de Chatre, predictably declined the invitation. The weather, which had been constantly bad from the very beginning, culminated in a gale and thunderstorm on the night of 8 June, causing havoc in the camp as an unknown officer or volunteer relates: 'Many of our canvas hovels were overturned by the violence of the wind: and even those whose habitations withstood the storm, were little to be envied; for, by the incredible impetuosity of the rain, they were almost drowned within their tents.'[10] The French, snug in the town, doubtless regarded the weather as divine intervention.

Next day the light horse spread itself about the countryside hussar-fashion, bringing back much needed provisions: 'Great plenty of Sheep, Hogs, Fowls, Butter, Bread, Wine, Brandy which we those days past had so greatly wanted. However we fell to Cooking, some Killing sheep, Others pulling Fowles etc, whereby in a short time our Scarceity was turned into great plenty & we Now Live Exceedingly well.'

Less well received was the news that a French army, supposedly between 10,000 and 40,000 strong, was advancing to the relief of the town. It had already been realised that the fortifications were too strong for a direct assault, and with an army approaching, however large it might be, there was no time either for Marlborough to use his artillery to batter the place into submission. That night the army struck camp and once again marched in two columns back to Cancale. In the end it took nearly three days before the last rearguard – the Guards brigade and the grenadiers – was re-embarked, but all were safely aboard long before the French very cautiously appeared.

Safely embarked, Marlborough and Sackville immediately began looking for alternative landing sites, or at least went through the motions. Next day, the grenadier companies and the Guards were ordered to prepare for another landing. Granville, a small town to the northeast of Ste. Malo, was reconnoitred, but, although pilots were obtained from Guernsey, it was in the end decided not to be worth the effort.

Even during the withdrawal, foul weather continued to dog the expedition and it was 24 June before it was back on the British side of the Channel. Then, seeming contrarily, it bore off again to France, first essaying a landing at Le Havre and then at Cherbourg. In both cases, although they went through the motions and hoisted out the flat-bottomed boats, the weather was considered unsuitable and the landings aborted. Finally, with sickness rife and the horses starving for want of forage, they called it a day and returned in overcrowded transports to the Isle of Wight on 30 June.

All in all it had been a pretty sorry business, plagued from start to finish by that bad weather. At least, however, they had displayed a good deal more determination than Mordaunt had done the year before. Called to account in a personal interview by the King, the two generals adroitly managed to placate him. Exaggerated claims were presented as to the numbers of French troops (supposedly as many as 60,000) diverted from Germany, and of the immense damage undoubtedly done to French shipping and naval stores in the harbour of Ste. Malo. Whether it justified the considerable effort expended was a different matter and when the radical politician Charles Fox declared that the whole business amounted to breaking windows with guineas he was not so very far wrong.[11]

The contrast with the events in Germany during exactly the same period could not have been clearer. Ferdinand had crossed the Rhine, unequivocally won major battle at Krefeld, and notwithstanding the fact he would shortly be chased back across the river, there could be no doubt of his success and the prospect which it raised of more such victories to come. Pitt personally remained unmoved, but on 20 June 1758 he was forced to concede to the cabinet that once Marlborough's operations had shut down it might then be possible to 'spare 6,000 men to be employed where they could be of most service'. Nevertheless, he remained obdurate and three days later suddenly had the happy inspiration that the pledge might be fulfilled by sending across some of the numerous cavalry who were otherwise idly kicking their heels at enormous expense.[12]

Grumbling that their assignment would compromise Britain's defences, the commander-in-chief, Lord Ligonier, grudgingly identified six regiments and warned them off for service. By any standard, a substantial reinforcement of fourteen squadrons was going to be very welcome to Ferdinand (and indeed to Frederick of Prussia), but if Pitt hoped thereby to satisfy those demanding large scale intervention in Germany, he was disappointed. This cavalry needed to be properly supported, and that meant sending infantry as well.

One battalion, the 51st Foot, was already out in Germany still forming that opportunistic garrison of Emden. Two more battalions were found to make up a brigade for John Waldegrave, who accepted the posting to Germany with no expressions of regret. That, for the moment, saw the barrel scraped clear to the bottom, but even Pitt was forced to recognise that a single infantry brigade was wholly inadequate, and so three additional battalions were pared from the expeditionary force and formed into a second brigade under Kingsley of the 20th. As one battalion was taken from each of the first three brigades this obviously entailed a re-organisation, but the greatest change occurred within the higher echelons for both Marlborough and Sackville followed Waldegrave in literally jumping ship.

The King, who obviously had a close personal interest in the matter, actually nominated the 74-year-old Lieutenant General Thomas Bligh to the command of the contingent destined for service in Germany. This dismayed both the Duke, and his second-in-command, Sackville. Notwithstanding the relatively small size of the expeditionary force, Germany promised to be a proper war and in any case both of them, as Sackville put it, were 'sick of coasting' and 'buccaneering'.[13] Some particularly shameless intrigue effected an exchange which saw Bligh reluctantly placed in command of the next phase of the coastal operations, while Marlborough and Sackville went off to Germany instead.

Cherbourg

If Bligh was bitterly disappointed at being robbed of a last chance of glory, he still knew his duty and set about demonstrating how he thought it ought to be done. On 4 August, the day after Marlborough disembarked at Emden with his little army, Bligh set sail with the Guards brigade, three other infantry brigades, four troops of light dragoons and the same three companies of the Royal Artillery which had been at Ste. Malo, although this time they left their heavy guns behind.[14]

Three days later they were off Cherbourg. Since the last British expedition had menaced the place at the end of June, the French had entrenched a line running from Equeurdreville, about two miles to the west of Cherbourg, along the coast for about four or five miles, with several batteries, including one with no fewer than ten brass 24-pounders. Defending the town and standing ready to man these fortifications were total of some 9,000 men under the Comte de Raymond, including at least four regular battalions.[15]

Much good it did them, for the Commodore and the General resolved to outflank the defences by landing on the beach at Ste. Marais about five miles west of the town. At about 15.00 hours on the afternoon of 7 August the signal was hoisted for all the frigates, bomb ketches[16] and cutters to run inshore and begin bombarding the enemy troops seen drawn up in readiness behind the beach. This 'seemed greatly to disconcert the French cavalry', as Corporal Todd related:

> A very Heavy Cannonading Ensued from our ships that made the Enemy soon quit the shore & fly up the rising ground. We could see them run in the greatest Consternation & we begun to Disembark with the utmost Expedition. And as we got ashore we Lay down Close upon the Beach, near the water edge, that our ships might fire Over us in case the Enemy Advance to make any Attack upon us, before all out troops could be Landed.[17]

This unusual technique was successful, and was aided by the fact of there being a noticeable drop from the land on to the beach which acted as a natural breastwork. Rather to the astonishment of all concerned, 'never did an enemy behave in a more dastardly manner; they retired with only a few shots, and left the English to finish their landing in the utmost security.' There was an expectation that an immediate advance on the French fort at Querqueville might have followed, but Bligh, perhaps displaying an old man's caution, elected to remain on the beach that night 'in a very irregular manner, on a spot of ground, not more in extent than 400 paces; so that had the enemy attacked them in the front and on the left, they would have been obliged to fight with infinite disadvantage'. Those on the beach were certainly unhappy at the situation and strong pickets were pushed out and the village of Urville occupied. All night long there was a continual harassing fire from the hedgerows and Corporal Todd complained of numerous alarms which compelled everyone to stand to arms.

Not that it made any difference. The next morning the rest of the army, including the cavalry and artillery, disembarked without hindrance. The light horse, along with the grenadiers and two guns, were ordered to advance on Equeurdreville, followed by most of the British army – with the exception of a column which acted as a flank guard – following a road along the rising grounds. To their surprise, the fort had been abandoned. As the day wore on another party of light horse was then sent to reconnoitre the high road by Hanneville while the vanguard marched by the low road directly to the rear of the other forts. The latter found the lines along the coast and the batteries likewise empty all the way to Cherbourg itself, which was unfortified to landward. No regular troops were seen, and according to Corporal Todd the only hindrance to the advance came from:

> The Malitia, Coast Guarders, Pandours etc that constantly keeps firing at us on the March out of Woods & behind Hedges etc, but as they won't stand to face any party of men, but runs in the Utmost Confution when they see us Advance towards them, we Kept marching slowly on in a line with the other Collumn. And we have strong scowering partys upon the flanks through the Woods & Hedges that is very thick & troblesom for us to get through.[18]

However, at about 11.00 hours there steady advance was halted when they were met by a deputation from the town, seemingly made up of civic officials, offering to surrender the place. The military commander, the Comte de Raymond, was obviously in an unenviable position. With only four regular battalions, he was hopelessly outnumbered and the town itself defenceless. He might still fight, and indeed arguably it was his duty to fight. In doing so, Cherbourg itself would be turned into a battleground. Understandably enough the civilian leaders refused to see it destroyed in a pointless battle they could not win.

The proposal was therefore straightforward. Raymond and his men were to be allowed to retire unmolested with two cannon, to a camp near Valognes about fifteen miles to the south-east, while the town itself was to be ransomed. Accordingly, the grenadiers marched in at 16.00 hours and took over the barracks just vacated by the Irish Regiment *Clare*. The rest of the army camped outside and next day working parties were ordered into the town to assist the gunners and engineers with the task of first re-opening the harbour entrance, which had been blocked by the sinking of a number of vessels in the channel, and then destroying it. By 15 August, the mole, docks, works, magazines, forts and the defences of the harbour had been destroyed. Rather economically, the rubble was then tipped into the basins and channels rendering them useless. Four ships were also carried off along with a considerable quantity of other trophies. This comprised no fewer than twenty-one cannon, including all ten of those brass 24 pounders, together with the town's bells, claimed as a traditional artilleryman's perk by Colonel Desaguliers. Rather less creditably, these 'public' prizes were augmented by the decision to send out foraging parties, who drove in vast quantities of cattle, hogs, sheep and poultry to be consumed in place of the inevitable bread and cheese available from the fleet. Of itself this was sensible enough, but of course the foragers soon extended their activities to:

> Wine, Brandy, Cyder, salt Butter, Large pots full, & some flower & Bread … Every man had Orders, that was off Duty, to dress and Cook what they pleas'd, both for themselves & there Comerades that was upon Duty, so that everyone is very Bussy now, Either upon Duty of Else Cooking, & we scarce have a tent but all there Canteens is full of Wine, Brandy or Cyder. And here is several Large Houses with great Cellars full that we can go & get what we please, but Orders is given that if any man be found Intoxicated he will be severely punished.[19]

It was not just a continued bacchanal as various minor expeditions were mounted into the countryside, partly to pick up intelligence and generally to intimidate the local militia, who continued their sniping from the hedgerows.

Generally speaking the French remained quiescent and only one of the forays appears to have gone wrong, as bitterly recounted by Colonel Elliot of the light horse:

> The general, attended by some of the commanding officers, going out to reconnoitre with a detachment of grenadiers, and a party of light horse,

some of the French cavalry appeared at a distance. Captain Lindsey, of the light horse was immediately ordered to attack them; at the request [as is said] of some young gentlemen, who were desirous of seeing the horse engage: he accordingly advanced at a brisk pace, without detaching from his front and flanks; and falling in with a body of infantry, posted behind a hedge, received a severe fire, which obliged the light horse to wheel about, and retire. Captain Linsey was mortally wounded by a musket shot, and died, universally regretted, as a worthy young man, and one of the most intelligent, active, and industrious officers in the service. What pity that such merit should have been unnecessarily thrown away, to gratify the rash impertinent curiosity of those, who had no right to dictate on such an occasion.[20]

In the end, their work done, the British troops marched down to the beach at 17.00 hours on 16 August and began re-embarking. In all they had lost about twenty killed and thirty wounded during the entire affair, but although a fine parade was made in London of those captured guns, there was a feeling of disquiet that the 'victory' had not actually achieved anything. The French had not been met and defeated in the open field as they had been in Germany, and Ferdinand was now under considerable pressure again and another expedition was deemed necessary.

Disaster at Ste. Cast

Oddly enough, when choosing another objective, Bligh and Howe decided to have another go at Ste. Malo. They were probably correct enough in thinking that another attack on the place so soon after the last would come as a surprise, but what they actually hoped to achieve there was a different matter. What was more, having decided to make another attempt they hatched the eccentric notion of avoiding Cancale Bay and instead approaching the town from the west, which meant that they would be on the wrong side of the River Rance.

Accordingly they came ashore near Ste. Lunaire on the evening of 3 September. For the time-being, at least, they moved rapidly away from the shore. Having established his headquarters in the village, Bligh immediately sent five companies of grenadiers to neighbouring Ste. Briac, to burn the shipping there, and a detachment of 100 men to reconnoitre the area up towards Dinard which lay at the mouth of the river directly over by Ste. Malo.

All this was achieved easily, but there then followed several days of fruitless reconnoitring and what seems to have been fairly indiscriminate plundering and burning. At one point Corporal Todd reckoned he 'could discover plainly 22 Towns or Villages all on fire this night, in different parts'.

The problem of course was the River Rance. It did not take the commanders long to realise their mistake. The fortifications of Ste. Malo were designed to defend the mouth of the river and the harbour behind. Any attack across the river would therefore face upwards of fifty heavy guns and Howe, whose sailors would be required to carry the soldiers across, flatly refused to contemplate it. Bligh then considered finding another crossing point further upstream and coming at Ste. Malo from the east, as his predecessors had done. Without the navy's boats, however, this could only be achieved by marching twelve miles upstream to the bridge at Dinan. Not surprisingly everyone very quickly shied away from that particular idea. Unpalatable as it seemed, it appeared that there was no alternative but re-embark and if necessary try again somewhere else. Unfortunately there was a problem.

During the initial landing two of the flat-bottomed boats capsized in the surf with the loss of some seventy men. Since then the weather had been growing steadily worse and, with a strong north-westerly blowing, Commodore Howe advised it was unsafe to bring the troops off. Nor for that matter, given the exposed position and the rocky bottom, could he afford to remain off Ste. Lunaire in hope of an improvement. It was simply too dangerous. Even from the start the army officers had complained uneasily that if they were not bold enough they faced criticism from an impatient Navy, yet at one and the same time they feared the consequences of the Navy's uncertain support. Now their worst fears were realised.

All Howe could offer was that if the army was to march some fifteen miles further west, he ought to be able to pick them up off the beach at Ste. Cast instead. There was no alternative, and so on 7 September Bligh ordered out a vanguard of 200 grenadiers to secure the road, but delayed marching with the main body until next day. This was unfortunate because this time the French were not going to sit on their hands waiting for the British to go away.

The governor of Brittany, Armand Vignerot-Duplessis-Richelieu, the Duc d'Aiguillon, was assembling every man he could lay his hands on and was determined to intercept the British. Eventually he managed to muster twelve regular battalions, besides two formed militia battalions, the usual coast-guard militia, some dragoons and artillery.[21] He was probably outnumbered but, as events would prove, he had more than enough men for the job that needed to be done.

On Friday, 8 September 1758, Bligh's men commenced their march, much harassed by the inevitable skirmishers and the equally inevitable dirty weather. Passing through deserted communities, and sometimes burning villages, they got as far as the River Arguenon without any real problem. Next day, as they proceeded slowly along the narrow, muddy roads, plundering and burning everything in sight, there was a growing realisation that more and more enemy troops were appearing. As these invariably faded away when approached it was at first assumed they were just militia. The following night, while encamped at Matignon, they were disabused of this notion when a deserter came in to warn that 30,000 troops were encamped not four miles away.[22] Bligh was, by rumour, supposedly dismissive of the warning and still rather inclined to believe that they were only militia. In a meeting of the senior officers, however, Major General Elliot forcefully advocated that if they did not intend to fight then they should retreat immediately and 'be as expeditious as possible in the reimbarkment'. Seemingly, there was some grumbling at this but the doubters were soon disabused of their complacency at 02.00 hours next morning when French drums were heard beating the *générale*.

Bligh did likewise and at 04.00 hours on 11 September, as soon as it was light enough to see the way, he got the army moving northwards towards Ste. Cast. Most of the army was now formed in two columns, with the Guards Brigade under Major General Drury and the grenadiers under Colonel Griffin forming the rearguard. After a difficult march through narrow lanes enclosed with the usual thick hedgerows and orchards they successfully reached an open field, dominated by a windmill overlooking the beach at Ste. Cast. It was there that things began to go wrong.

> The embarkation was immediately begun; but by a kind of obstinacy in some officers, the boats were rowed too far in quest of their respective ships, when at such a critical time, they should have been embarked in those nearest at hand. The transport boats did not return with that regularity or punctuality which was requisite, and when they came, some were employed in carrying off horses and cows instead of men, notwithstanding all the attention and authority of the sea officers, who behaved with great conduct and moderation.[23]

In the meantime, aided by local guides, the French were coming on fast. D'Aguillon himself was first on the scene, arriving with some of his dragoons at the gallop only to promptly dismount them as the ground was unsuitable for mounted action. Next was the Marquis de Broc with a strong detachment of eight companies of grenadiers, twelve picquets and another 200 dragoons. This was at about 09.00 hours.

> The enemy's infantry soon followed their dragoons, and shewed themselves from the hills, the duke D'Aiguillon having reconnoitred the different passages, by which his troops could descend to the attack, made his dispositions. M. le Comte de Balleroy, with the regiments of Bourbon, Brissac, Bresse, and Quercy, was to make his entrance (looking from the shore to the sea) by the right: M. D'Aubigny with the regiments of Boulonnois, Brie and the battalions of Fontenai-le-Comte, of Marmande, and the first of des Volontaires Etrangers by the left. M. de Broc had orders to march with his detachment straight to the centre of the English army. The chevalier de S. Pern was kept in reserve with the second battalion of Penthievre, and the third des Volontaires Etrangers ... While these dispositions were making, which were done with as much expedition as possible, M. de Villepatour brought up the artillery from Brest, and M. de Urtuby that from St. Malo: they were planted in battery below a mill, between the right and center of their army.[24]

The French artillery proved dramatically effective: 'Three boats full of their soldiers were sunk, many more killed in boats on their way to the fleet.'[25]

At about 11.30 hours, once all were in position, the French started to advance with the column on their left coming down the slope by a hollow way, headed first by the grenadiers of 1/*Volontaires Etrangers*, and then the grenadier companies of *Boulonnois* and *Brie*. The intention was to take possession of a wood in which to form a battle line and then move forward under cover of the sand-hills at the rear of the beach.

At first they came under heavy fire from the bomb ketches and cutters, which allowed the grenadier companies and the 1st Footguards to take up a defensive position behind a sandbank. It was not an ideal position since the reverse slope meant that the rear ranks could not fire, but no doubt they got by through passing loaded muskets forward to the front. The real danger came on the right where the French were attempting to debouch from the lane:

> The grenadiers of the guards upon the right, commanded by lieutenant colonel Clavering, faced this lane, and beat them off as fast as they attempted to come on ... The enemy made several efforts of this sort, in

which they suffered extremely from the musketry of the grenadiers. At last one of their officers, quicker sighted than the rest, perceiving these fruitless and bloody attempts, pulled off his hat and waved it to his comrades; and instead of troubling himself with the sand bank turned short to the right, and run along the shore behind it; the enemy followed him immediately, which gave liberty to the crowds that came down the hill to extricate themselves from the defile, and form an extended line along the beach, opposite our army; this officer was killed, who thus led this first column, which was followed by two others with great spirit and valor. This small remnant of the British army was drawn up on uneven ground, and began now with an irregular fire from right to left: this was returned by the enemy, and the engagement continued for some time with doubtful success. The French having such a great superiority in number, the English troops were in danger of being surrounded and cut in pieces ... No prospect of victory, or even escape remained, except by boats. Sir John Armitage was shot through the head at the beginning of the action; many of the officers fell, and a great number of men were slain. At length their ammunition, which was far from being compleat, began to fail; they were seized with a panic, they faltered, they broke, and fled in the utmost confusion: some ran to the sea, and endeavoured to save their lives by swimming towards the boats, which were ordered to give them all possible assistance. General Dury being wounded, took to the sea, where he perished, and this was the fate of a great number. The enemy no sooner perceived our troops give way, than they pursued them, though in an irregular manner, and a considerable slaughter ensued.[26]

A stand was made for a time by a prominent rock at the south end of the beach, but once their ammunition was exhausted the last of the rearguard surrendered and thereafter it became a matter of pulling survivors from the water. In all it appears that some 1,400 men were lost, of whom one French account enumerates exactly as 732 prisoners, plus about thirty officers (including five naval ones), with the balance killed or drowned. The French, by contrast, admitted to 160 dead and 350 wounded.[27]

King George II never forgave Bligh for the fact that so many of the British casualties were his Footguards, and after such a disaster Pitt's coastal raiding was at an end. Colonial adventures aside, the war was now to be prosecuted in Germany.

Chapter 4

Highe Germanie

In Germany, meanwhile, the British contingent arrived to find the war now wearing a somewhat grimmer aspect and that the bright promise of that victory at Krefeld had faded all too quickly.

Thanks to the communication problems which plagued Ferdinand's handling of the battle, Clermont had succeeded in extricating his army from the debacle, rather battered but still more or less intact. Nevertheless, there was no doubting that the French were badly defeated and he lost no time in falling back to Köln. That retreat in turn exposed the Austrian Netherlands. The opportunity was far too tempting to be ignored. The Erbprinz promptly occupied Roermond, whilst Hanoverian light troops even penetrated deeply as far as Tirlemont, Charleroi and Louvain, inspiring panic in Brussels and Liege. Dusseldorf also fell without a fight and that in turn inspired preparations by the French to evacuate Köln itself. However, while Clermont was a beaten man and had requested to be relieved of his command, other French officers were made of sterner stuff. A cooler appraisal of the situation by *Marechal* Belle-Isle, the French Minister of War, concluded that Ferdinand's position was actually shaky in the extreme. He had badly over-extended himself and, as he still only had a single bridge over the Rhine at his back, he was very vulnerable indeed to an intelligent counter-stroke.

It was principally to be led by Lieutenant General Louis George Êrasme, Marquis de Contades. Born in 1705, Contades was a well experienced and competent soldier who had previously served with some distinction in Italy and Flanders. His orders were to relieve Clermont and if he found that Köln had been evacuated by the time he arrived he was to immediately re-occupy it as his base for an offensive intended to force Ferdinand back across the river.

Contades, displaying some energy, wasted no time in getting the French army moving again. Ferdinand, uneasily aware of the precariousness of his situation, decided to mount a spoiling attack. The plan was to seize some high ground at Allrath, some sixteen miles north-east of Köln and there invite a battle. In such an encounter he was confident of inflicting sufficient damage on the French to be able break contact and withdraw northwards at his own pace. Unfortunately his plan miscarried. First Contades moved faster than expected and therefore got to Allrath before him. Worse, a bottleneck on a vital bridge at one point left Ferdinand's army cut in two. Fortunately, Contades, although alive to the opportunity so unexpectedly offered to him, was too cautious to seize it. In spite of Lieutenant General Chevert's urging, he decided to wait and ensure that all his own men were up and properly in position before moving into the attack. Predictably, by the time they were formed up to his satisfaction night was drawing on and it was too late to begin the battle.

Next morning the Allies were gone. Nevertheless, Ferdinand then tried again and this time he proved to be rather too clever by half. On the night of 24 July 1758, he abruptly broke contact and instead of withdrawing northwards as expected, he marched west towards Roermond. The intention was to threaten, or at least appear to threaten, Contades' line of communications and so compel the French to fall back. Ironically, the operation was carried out so efficiently that the intended diversion completely miscarried. So silently did Ferdinand and his men move off that far from hurrying in anxious pursuit, Contades did not even learn what was going on until two days later! Then, far from panicking at the chimerical prospect of having his communications cut, he at once realised that Ferdinand had blundered. All that he needed to do was ignore him and march north. Once he was positioned between Ferdinand and the bridge the Allied army would be completely trapped with no line of retreat except into internment in neutral Holland, and no alternative but to fight on French terms.

Worse, in concert with Contades' offensive, the Prince de Soubise was ordered by Belle-Isle to march into Hesse at the same time and threaten Hanover. Where Contades was solidly competent but overly cautious, Soubise was personally brave, but as a commander timid and utterly devoid of any obvious military talent. Rather, he was a courtier and the very epitome of the popular caricature of the sybaritic but incompetent general of the *ancien regime*. Fortunately for him, however, he had a very able second in Lieutenant Général the Duc de Broglie – or 'Broglio', as contemporary British writers insisted on calling him.

By 10 July a total of thirty-two squadrons and thirty-nine battalions was concentrated at Friedberg, of which Broglie commanded the advance guard comprising twelve squadrons, fourteen battalions and the obligatory complement of light troops.[1] Soubise retained personal command of the rest and also had a 7,000 strong Imperial contingent from Wurtemburg under his command, although they were reckoned unreliable and persistently trailed some days behind him. Even without the Wurtemburgers, the two generals had more than enough men for the job. Facing them was Lieutenant General Johannes Casimir Prinz zu Isenburg-Budingen with just two squadrons and two battalions of regulars, to which the Landgraf of Hesse had added another five squadrons of cavalry and three battalions of militia, besides various other small detachments.[2]

Heavily outnumbered as he was, Isenburg made no attempt to hold Kassel, but decided to withdraw northwards on 23 July. He had, however, left it a little late and the French were closing in fast so he decided to fight a delaying action near the village of Sandershausen to the north-east of the city. It was a challenge Broglie accepted with relish and, after a surprisingly stiff little engagement, the battle ended in near disaster for Isenburg as the militia battalions in his centre collapsed. He was lucky to get his regulars away, but the wretched militia surrendered in droves after having already been demoralised by rumours that they were to be sold into the British service.

After the battle, Soubise made himself comfortable in Kassel for the next three weeks. Hanover was completely exposed but he did surprisingly little to exploit his victory beyond sending some raiding parties forward to Göttingen, Münden and Warburg. Perhaps that was all he interpreted his orders to require of him. As it was, with Ferdinand still on the wrong side of the Rhine, the results were impressive enough. The government in Hanover promptly abandoned the place and fled, with its papers and files to Stade, at the mouth of the Elbe. Even Ferdinand, still at Roermond, was moved to demand the immediate evacuation of the 7,000-odd French prisoners detained at Stade and beg in their place two British battalions to serve as a garrison. In the event, with the arrival of the British contingent at Emden on 3 August, this would be unnecessary, but for Ferdinand it did indeed mean it was high time he was back across the Rhine.

That, however, might be easier said than done. On 30 July, Contades sent Lieutenant General Chevert up the right bank of the river to capture Ferdinand's pontoon bridge.[3] This had earlier been moved upstream from the Dutch border and now spanned the Rhine at Rees, about eleven miles from Wesel. This was much more convenient both from a diplomatic and a practical point of view, but with a French garrison in Wesel it was already living dangerously. Simultaneously, Contades tried again to intercept Ferdinand, this time at Dülken, about twelve miles south east of Krefeld. It was a well-chosen position, for in order to march from Roermond to the crossings over the river Niers, Ferdinand was going to have to pass his army through a three mile-wide gap in a string of lakes running parallel to the Meuse – and that gap was about to be blocked by Contades. Ferdinand resigned himself to what was probably going to be a brutally difficult assault on 3 August, but instead Contades once again bottled it, drew back and took up a quite different defensive position at Rheindahlen. Having done so he congratulated himself on having avoided the trap set him by Ferdinand!

With the road to the Rhine thus unexpectedly opened to him, Ferdinand assigned Holstein-Gottorp and his Prussian cavalry to 'amuse' Contades while he marched hard for Rees and what he hoped was safety. Instead the intermittently bad weather took a turn for the worse and, in driving rain, the roads flooded or at best turned to near bottomless mud.

Consequently Chevert got to Rees first.

With word of his coming, the Brunswicker, *Generalleutnant* Philip Ernst von Imhoff, left a detachment of 500 men to guard the bridge itself and with all the other troops at his disposal moved out to fight. With six battalions and five squadrons totalling about 3,500 men, he took up a defensive position to the east on some nearby high ground at Mehr, on 5 August.[4] With a little over 5,000 men Chevert outnumbered him, but had a very scratch force indeed. Initially he had set off with two brigades of regular infantry, four squadrons of the *Du Roi* Dragoons and some light troops, but the constituent units were very weak. Chevert's two brigades were fielding five battalions apiece rather than the usual four.[5] If not quite so decrepit as Clermont had claimed a couple of months earlier, those battalions must therefore have been averaging rather less than 300 men apiece. Consequently, passing through Wesel he picked up an additional 2,000 men from its garrison. Unfortunately they were all militia. There were nine companies of *Grenadiers Royaux*, who were supposedly more or less reliable, but otherwise most of the militiamen were used to fill out the ranks of his weak regular battalions.[6] It proved to be a fatal mistake.

That afternoon Chevert attacked. His initial plan was simply to engage Imhoff head-on with the *Brancas* Brigade on this right and the *Reding* Brigade on his left, both deployed in two lines with three battalions up and two behind. As the ground was bad, being cut up with hedgerows and

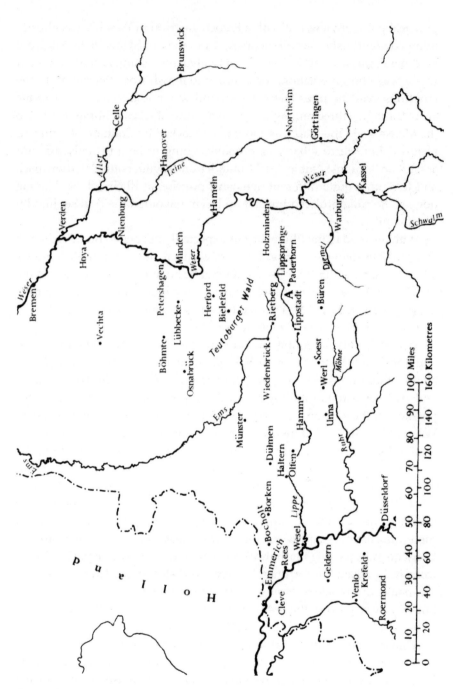

General map of Western Germany – the seat of the campaigns.

coppices, the dragoons formed his reserve. While Imhoff was thus engaged, Chevert's light troops, strengthened by the *Grenadiers Royaux*, were intended to hook around the Allied left and seize the bridge by a coup de main. Instead, as often happens, de Chavigny, commanding the light troops, managed to get drawn into a fight for one of Imhoff's outposts covering the road into the village. Initially this was successful, but Imhoff was determined to fight aggressively and while the fighting raged on his left, he began assembling a counter-attack on his right. This build-up in turn caused Chevert to draw the *Brancas* brigade and *Du Roi* Dragoons closer to his centre. Prudent as it was, this move meant that de Chavigny and his light troops were left out on a limb.

Realising they were unsupported they initially halted and refused to go on. Worse, the *Grenadiers Royaux* actually fell back in some confusion. Appalled, Chevert galloped across to rally them, only for Imhoff to choose that very moment to launch his assault on the open flank of the *Reding* Brigade, with the regiments *Stolzenberg* and *Imhoff*. The Swiss, for their part, replied with a shaky volley and promptly bolted. There were simply too many militiamen in their ranks and no sooner was the brigade rallied than it fell apart again. On Chevert's right, meanwhile, de Chavigny's light troops, no longer backed up by the *Grenadiers Royaux*, similarly crumpled under a Hanoverian counter-attack. Unsurprisingly, at that point Chevert's remaining infantry brigade also followed suit. Only the all-regular *Du Roi* Dragoons stood firm to cover the flight as the French infantry tumbled back to Wesel, having lost 517 killed, wounded and captured as well as ten guns and a field hospital. Imhoff and his men, who had fought very creditably indeed, suffered only about 200 casualties.[7]

The bridge was saved and although it proved necessary to move it further downstream, owing to the water-level in the Rhine rising due to the rains, Ferdinand and his army and all its guns, baggage and camp followers, were safely back across on the right bank by the evening of 10 August.

The British Arrive

It took a few more days for everyone to sort themselves out, safely dispose of the pontoon bridge (once again stowed away across the Dutch border) and recover all the supplies accumulated at Rees, before moving east to a rendezvous with the newly arrived British contingent at Coesfeld.

As noted in the previous chapter, Lord Ligonier, who succeeded Cumberland as commander-in-chief, had reluctantly rousted out no fewer than six regiments of otherwise idle cavalry in response to demands for some troops to be sent to Germany. Commanded by the young Marquis of Granby[8] and Sir John Whitefoord, these comprised: The Royal Horse Guards (otherwise better known simply as the Blues) and Bland's 1st King's Dragoon Guards, both with three squadrons, and Howard's 3rd Dragoon Guards; Campbell's 2nd Royal North British Dragoons (the Greys); Cholmondley's 6th Inniskilling Dragoons; and Mordaunt's 10th Dragoons, all with two squadrons apiece.

According to best practice of the period, those fourteen squadrons of cavalry[9] ought to have been mirrored by a similar number of infantry battalions. In fact, of course, there were just six of them – together with four companies of Invalids under Colonel John Parker.[10] Napier's 12th Foot and Stewart's 37th Foot were sent out to join with Brudenell's 51st Foot and form a brigade under John Waldegrave, while Kingsley's 20th Foot, Huske's 23rd Royal Welch Fusiliers and Home's 25th (Edinburgh) Regiment were filleted from the coastal expeditionary force to make up a second brigade under Major General William Kingsley.

The Royal Artillery contribution initially comprised just six lieutenants and 120 non-commissioned officers and men under Captain William Phillips, but in the following March a further one-and-a-half companies was sent out so that by the time they found themselves at Minden the gunners would amount to three companies under Captains Samuel Cleaveland, Forbes MacBean and Griffith Williams, with the whole commanded by Phillips. It should be noted, however, that the Royal Artillery's company organisation was purely intended for administrative purposes. At a tactical level all three simply formed a pool from which sufficient personnel were drawn to man 'brigades' of guns, or for whatever other duties might be required of them. At Minden the British artillery would be deployed in the form of a heavy brigade and two light brigades. The first, under Forbes MacBean, comprised ten medium 12-pounders. One of the light brigades, commanded by Captain-Lieutenant Duncan Drummond, had two light 12-pounders, three light 6-pounders and four howitzers. The second, under Captain-Lieutenant Edward Foy, had four light 12-pounders, three light 6-pounders and two howitzers. In addition to these brigades there were a pair of light 6-pounders allocated to each of the six British infantry battalions, and largely crewed by infantrymen under the supervision of trained gunners.[11]

Their arrival in Germany was a touch shambolic, due to a combination of shoals in the Ems estuary, a shortage of pilots to navigate them and insufficient wharfage on which to land them. This saw the various units and parts of units put ashore up and down the river. Not until 5 August were they concentrated with their headquarters at a village called Heyde, just inside the Bishoprick of Münster. Ahead lay a long and tedious march across a sandy heath which became even more tedious when it began to rain, as Lieutenant Colonel Oughton of the 37th eloquently recorded in his diary for 11 August:

> The General beat at ½ past 2. March beginning from the left it was near 5 before our Regt. began to Move, there being a defile to pass closs by the left of the Camp. a great deal of small rain had fallen in the Night, & it continued driveing 'till between 5 & 6 when it began to rain hard, & a violent Cold Wind riseing drove the rain with so much impetuosity that nothing cou'd resist it. The ground at first, was greasy & Slippery from the trampling of so many Men & Horses before us, but that was Soon succeeded by Slop, & Slop by deep puddle that in the Lanes the Men March'd almost up to the Knees in thick Mire, Crossing some plow'd Lands it was difficult to drag out ones Legs, and when we came again to the Moors, the Wind & rain Continueing with great Vehemence the whole Country was inundated and dry land (like pictures of the Deluge) appeared only here & there; all Track was lost, & no Man knew whether his next Step would take him to his knees, his Waste or his Neck. Captain [Anthony] Blunt & several Men who fell were over head & Ears. To add to our Misery, the difficulty of Marching occasioned frequent halts which left whole Regiments standing in the Water; this with the Coldness of the Wind & Rain not only numb'd our Limbs, but Chill'd our very Vitals. How many perished dureing the March is not yet known, I saw but one Myself, but either immediatly or Consequentially it must be the Fate of Many. We pitch'd our Tents about 4 o'clock in the plow'd Lands & Cornfields round the Town of Aahus, the Moor first Mark't out for Encampment being all under Water. Officers & Men Crouded into the Town as fast as they could Self preservation & relief from our present urgent distresses being the Sole Motive of Action Subsisting Among us.[12]

There they halted for two days, 'the Rain still Continuing with the same Violence'. The artillery and the baggage was stranded at Cumberland's old depot at Nienburg and Lieutenant Colonel George Scott of the 25th Foot was ordered to collect the sick and other stragglers there, while another temporary hospital was established in Aahaus itself. Both bread and ammunition were ruined and with little or no food to be found in the town 'the Gardens about it were Maurauded without Mercy'.

On 14 August the rain at last stopped and the men marched to the rendezvous at Coesfeld, still wading through deep water and over a boggy moor. There they met the Hessian *Generalmajor* Burkhardt Wilhelm von Fürstenberg with two squadrons, two battalions and a detachment of hussars.[13] On hearing of the difficulties which the British had encountered, the Germans assured the newcomers that *they* had marched eleven days without halting to reach the camp. At any rate there they all waited while both their own baggage and the rest of Ferdinand's army came up. Marlborough paid his respects to Prince Ferdinand on 19 August and he, for his part, reviewed his new British troops three days later '& expressed much Satisfaction at their appearance'.[14]

Notwithstanding the damage done by that dreadful march down from Emden, their equipment was new and their horses large and healthy. Ferdinand's own army by contrast presented a much more rough-and-ready appearance with 'nothing new, nothing clean, except its weapons'.[15] Far from looking like the product of a Potsdam parade ground, Ferdinand's men looked like the veterans they were, and as was their privilege as old soldiers, they no doubt looked down on the new arrivals with a fair degree of condescension.

As far as the British infantry was concerned, it did not take long to reciprocate and demonstrate that they too were old soldiers. Half of them, after all, had been to Ste. Malo. There, notwithstanding the efforts of that enterprising hangman, Sergeant Lloyd, they quickly accustomed themselves to supplementing the flinty ration bread and cheese by plundering the countryside, and dignifying their robberies by the name of foraging. If they did not behave quite as shamelessly as those who sailed on the later expeditions, that was only through lack of opportunity. Now they were once again in a foreign country and not much inclined to distinguish between Frenchmen and Germans. Strong measures were required by way of example and their predilection for foraging probably accounts for the decision that winter to partly break up the Ste. Malo brigade, by taking out the 23rd Fusiliers and replacing it with the 51st Foot, who had been in-country long enough to recognise the boundaries of acceptable behaviour. Nor were the 'irregularities' confined to marauding. The rivalries soon turned nasty, especially when it came to territorial disputes over quarters and foraging areas. On 1 September *Oberstleutnant* von Ahlefeldt of the Hanoverian *Füss-garde* Regiment and Lieutenant Colonel Oughton of the

37th Foot were appointed commissioners 'to hear & determine any dispute that might arise between the different [Allied] nations; and all Soldiers were forbid under the Severest penalties to draw their Swords on each other'.[16]

Three days later Oughton recorded that 'Orders given to the Patroles to fire on the Marauders, and an Officer of each Nation to go along with the Provost who has orders to hang Without Mercy all whom he shall discover Marauding'. Not that it seemingly made much difference. On 6 September the troops were forbidden to take any more forage out of houses and next day 'Orders repeated against Marauding'.[17] And so it continued over the weeks and months to come and indeed was often encouraged, tacitly or otherwise, by quite senior officers who ought to have known better. Sir John Whitefoord, for example, not only formed his own forage depot at the town of Rheine to prevent it being carried off in the night by 'Jews and Hanoverians, both damned pilferers', but evicted a Hanoverian unit from what he regarded as his area, with a threat to arrest its commander and send him to Münster.[18]

Even without such frictions and the inevitable outbreaks of insubordination and criminal behaviour as the boundaries were being pushed, Ferdinand's men found their new allies' behaviour unsettling. Colonel Mauvillon of Ferdinand's staff wrote afterwards that 'Braver troops there cannot indeed be found in the world when on the battlefield and under arms before the enemy; but here their military virtue ends'.[19] The officers in particular were viewed as unprofessional and lacking the devotion to duty reckoned characteristic of German officers. In reality, this impression was just as deceptive then as it would be in two world wars. The outward style might be different but the studied casualness of British officers frequently disguised a thorough knowledge of what they were doing. It was just considered bad form to appear too keen and warlike.

Glad though he was to see the British troops, Ferdinand might therefore be forgiven for being a little wary of them, and especially of their commanders – the Duke of Marlborough and his *eminence gris*, Lord Sackville – for right from the beginning there lay trouble. Both of them were personally in bad odour at court and their appointments had very much been forced by the government on an unwilling King, who grumbled he had nothing to do but sign the papers. Unsurprisingly, as the Duke of Newcastle rather delicately put it, the King 'was a little out of humour'.

Born in 1706, Marlborough was the second son of Charles Spencer, 3rd Earl of Sunderland and Lady Anne Churchill, herself the younger daughter of the 1st Duke.[20] While at least one contemporary spoke glowingly of his good sense, modesty and generosity, Horace Walpole, on the other hand, cattily, but probably more accurately, commented on his ignorance, carelessness and profuseness. This was all too evident in his career, in which he also displayed an alarming lack of tact.

Marlborough supposedly performed creditably enough in command of a brigade at Dettingen in 1743, but as neither side there did anything much more complicated than bludgeon each other, it may be doubted whether he was actually called upon to do much more than sit on his horse bravely. Afterwards, however, he threw up his command and joined with the Earl of Stair and others in condemning the partiality displayed by the King towards his Hanoverian troops. This was hardly calculated to endear him to his Hanoverian monarch. It might, arguably, have been explained by political opportunism, for there was then a widespread feeling in the country that British foreign policy in Europe was being driven by Hanover, but on arriving once more in Germany in 1758 he again displayed the same xenophobia demonstrated by Whitefoord. There he quickly discovered that the Hanoverian von Spörcken, who had formerly been junior to him, now outranked him as a *General der Infantrie*. In an extremely petulant letter to Pitt, written the day before he 'waited upon' Ferdinand for the first time, he threatened to resign if he were not immediately made senior to Spörcken with an ante-dated promotion of his own.[21]

There is no doubting that Marlborough was entirely the wrong man to command the British contingent in what was to all intents and purposes a Hanoverian army, and that, left to himself, King George would probably have been only too happy to accept his resignation. However, his government thought otherwise and Marlborough's splenetic prejudice was rewarded with promotion to the rank of full general! Whatever Ferdinand's feelings, he had no alternative but to acquiesce since the British were his paymasters and the only hope of further reinforcements. Nevertheless, allied to the growing misgivings about their apparent lack of discipline and even the need to provide interpreters for non-German speakers serving in a German army, the cordial feelings expressed in public must have been counterbalanced by serious misgivings in private.

Minor Operations
Fortunately a few weeks of inactivity followed, allowing things to settle down a little. Contades by this time deployed no fewer 117 squadrons and 104 battalions mustering about 12,000 cavalry and 48,000 infantry, including a newly arrived contingent of some 9,000 Saxon troops.[22] However, he was

content to anchor his left wing on the fortress of Wesel and stretch the rest along the Lippe, eastwards as far as Lünen. Now with two French armies to contend with, Ferdinand had moved east to cover his base at Münster and preserve his freedom of movement. Otherwise, he too stayed pretty much as he was. His side of the Lippe was covered by the Erbprinz of Brunswick and Holstein-Gottorp with a total of twenty-eight squadrons and fourteen battalions. This was effectively no more than an outpost line, but from 3 September the Erbprinz's force included four British squadrons under the Marquis of Granby, comprising the Greys and the Inniskillings. This no doubt provided invaluable experience for them – and for their commander – but early in October things started moving again.

Although Contades and Soubise were both in a position to place pressure on Ferdinand, neither of them was willing go forward until each knew what the other was doing. Eventually it was Soubise, probably a little to his own surprise, who made the first move by advancing on Göttingen with the belated intention of threatening Hanover. Isenburg, still battered by his defeat at Sandershausen, could only fall back on Hameln and by 12 September the French light troops under Fischer were quite literally at the gates of Hanover itself. Much to Belle-Isle's dismay, however, far from co-operating vigorously with this promising offensive, Contades determinedly remained sitting safely behind the Lippe and at first his support amounted to little more than making encouraging noises. Soubise, having penetrated as far as Northeim, then reverted to form and, deciding he was too badly exposed, began falling back again.

Ferdinand, discovering what was happening, riposted with an opportunistic attempt to recapture Kassel before Soubise could return there. *Generalleutnant* Christoph Ludwig von Oberg was sent off with 14,000 men and came dangerously close to doing just that. Arriving outside the city on 26 September, he found the French rear echelon already preparing to evacuate the place. *Oberst* Lückner characteristically proposed to go straight in with his light troops and had he done so would likely have found very little or nothing to stop him seizing it. Oberg hesitated, however, and decided to play safe and wait for Isenburg, who was only a day behind. Given that Soubise was by now only ten miles away, this was a mistake. There was little question that Kassel could be stormed out of hand and while it was doubtful he could hold the place afterwards if the French determined to take it back, he could certainly do a very great deal of damage to the French magazines and transport before withdrawing. As it was, once again displaying some unwonted energy, Soubise marched his men through the night and, in his own estimation, arrived just in time to dash Oberg's hopes.

At that point the Hanoverian general should probably have called it a day, but instead he stubbornly hung around in the vicinity until 9 October. By that time Contades had reluctantly been stirred into action; fixing Ferdinand's attention by undertaking a threatening advance to Hamm on the River Lippe, more or less due south of Münster. The real object of this move, however, was to cover the sending of a substantial detachment under Chevert and the Duc de Fitz-James to reinforce Soubise. The immediate result was that when Oberg did finally withdraw he was attacked, heavily outnumbered and badly beaten, in a well conducted battle at Lutterberg on 10 October.

Ferdinand for his part initially conformed to Contades' advance by concentrating the bulk of his forces at Münster to await developments, but then on 12 October he learned of Oberg's defeat at Lutterberg and resolved on another bold counter-stroke. Three days later he moved out, intending to swing around to the east, interpose his army between Soubise and Contades, and then attack the latter whilst he was still weakened by the absence of the detachments under Chevert and Fitz-James. By 17 October Ferdinand was at Lippstadt, while the French, kept guessing by a variety of demonstrations along the river, were still largely scattered in detachments stretching along a front of twenty miles.

During the night of 17/18 October, Ferdinand's advance-guard, led by Holstein-Gottorp and the Erbprinz, and comprising all ten of the Prussian dragoon squadrons, fourteen other squadrons, and fourteen battalions including the six British ones, threw bridges over the Lippe at Benninghausen. They were followed next day by the main body.

Once across the river, the mounted elements of the advance guard had pushed on towards Soest, some twelve miles to the south-west. Warned of their coming, the local French commander, the Duc de Chevreuse, called up reinforcements from nearby Werl and stood-to in readiness with some tweny-four squadrons and five battalions. After a time, he formed the unlucky view that he had been imposed upon and without troubling to send out scouts or vedettes to verify that all was clear, he ordered his men to stand down. With a certain inevitability, no sooner had they relaxed than Holstein-Gottorp and the Erbprinz burst in upon them, took some 260 prisoners and pursued the rest another ten miles further on to Werl. The French garrison there promptly decamped along with the fugitives, without making any attempt to hold the place. Having then chased them all halfway to Unna, the two leaders decided that they were getting a bit carried away and that it would be prudent to regain contact with their long lost infantry support. They, for their part, had only just arrived at Soest and, having been marching all night, were too exhausted to go further. Suddenly the situation was becoming dangerous. Contades was marching down from Hamm, just ten miles to the north. Chevert, returning from Hesse, was a similar distance to the south, and a third French column under Armentiéres was closing in from the east. Very sensibly Ferdinand called the operation off and re-crossed the Lippe.

Contades for his part quickly came to the happy realisation that, just as at Roermond, Ferdinand had inadvertently uncovered his base, and hastily sent off Armentiéres with seventeen battalions and twenty-two squadrons to try and seize Münster, which was barely defended by only four battalions. In this he almost succeeded.

Armentiéres arrived in front of Münster on 25 October and began his preparations for an assault, but Ferdinand had reacted quickly and three days later Holstein-Gottorp reached the town with his advance guard to find the French gone. Armentiéres was pursued, but it was a half-hearted business and he got clean away. Both sides were exhausted and it was time to go into winter quarters.

Soubise was rewarded for his victory at Lutterberg by being promoted to *Marechal de France*. On the other side of the Lippe, meanwhile, there had been another and rather more significant change of command.

Although the British contingent had played a full and active part in these latter operations on the Lippe, the Duke of Marlborough did not. It is clear from army orders that dysentery had broken out some time ago and was becoming serious, if not endemic. A saturated landscape is not conducive to proper drainage at the best of times and as early as 23 August the eating of green fruit was being prohibited.

On 6 September a more strongly worded order declared that 'fresh Pork [was] forbid to be sold in Camp to prevent Fluxes which began to rage much among the Men'. More ominous was another order a week later declaring that, 'No bread Waggons to be sent with the Sick to the Hospital, especially Men in Fluxes'.[23] Now one of those so afflicted was the Duke of Marlborough. While his soldiers were spreading fear doubt and despondency across the Lippe, he had been left behind sick and died at Münster on 20 October.

Chapter 5

Spring 1759

Sackville's succession to the command of the British contingent ought to have represented a fresh start after Marlborough's prickly debut. Indeed, when the Duke of Newcastle congratulated him on his promotion, he rather naively began by anxiously urging the continuance of 'that good understanding between the British and Electoral troops which the late Duke of Marlborough so successfully maintained'. Unfortunately, he also rather sheepishly added 'his Majesty was pleased to declare his intentions that your lordship should be appointed General and Commander-in-Chief of the British forces in Germany in the same manner that the Duke of Marlborough was, except as to the posting officers upon vacancies'. Hitherto convention had allowed commanders in the field to promote officers to fill regimental vacancies or staff appointments on the spot. Sackville, seemingly, was not to enjoy this privilege.[1]

Newcastle had reason enough to be nervous about this codicil. By the same post, Lord Ligonier was also anxiously reassuring Sackville that: 'I am extreamly [sic] *and* sincerely concerned for the death of the Duke of Marlborough, and would have felt it more of a publick [sic] loss if you had not been there to supply his place. The King has appointed your Lordship Commander-in-Chief in his place, and I wish it had been with all circumstances that might have made it entirely agreeable to you. But some incidents that arose from commissions filled up by Mr. Bligh has made his Majesty take the resolution never to give powers, even of posting officers in Europe, nor could all the ministers, and after them your humble servant, move him.

'He said you might recommend those you thought worthy, and he would then confirm or not your recommendations. Now, my dear lord, you will judge wrong if you think this is done to Lord George Sackville, for that is not the case.'[2]

That, alas, was exactly what Lord George Sackville did think. 'It is certainly a very mortifying circumstance to me,' he responded with understandable hauteur, 'to see the powers given to commanders in chief taken away from me in the first instance ... the alteration must be looked upon by the officers of the army as a mark of His Majesty's disapprobation'.[3] In all fairness Sackville had good reason for his mortification.

Notwithstanding the apparent importance of purchase in the Georgian army, the judicious application of patronage and influence was vital to secure the desired vacancy or lucrative staff appointment. Denying a commander those customary powers of patronage was a serious matter indeed, both in itself and in its inevitable implication that Sackville lacked the full confidence of his King.[4]

Lord George Sackville

It has been strongly argued by Piers Mackesy, in his revisionist defence of Sackville's role at Minden, that this was indeed the case and that the King was actuated throughout by a strong dislike of him. Born in 1716, Sackville's ambition and early rise to prominence was a direct reflection of his being the third and favourite son of the first Duke of Dorset. He received his early political education by acting as his father's private secretary when the latter was serving as Lord Lieutenant or viceroy of Ireland – and his military one by directly entering the army on 11 July 1737 as a captain in Lord Cathcart's Horse otherwise known as the 1st Carabiniers.[5] On 19 July 1740 he next became lieutenant colonel of Bragge's 28th Foot (without troubling to occupy the intervening rank of major) and then attracted sufficient attention during the Dettingen campaign of 1743 to earn a brevet commission as colonel.[6] This was an unambiguous mark of royal favour and reinforced when next he succeeded to the substantive colonelcy of Thomas Bligh's 20th Foot on 9 April 1746 before moving on in quick succession to the colonelcies of the 12th Dragoons and then the 3rd Horse[7], and finally the 2nd Dragoon Guards on 5 April 1757. His smooth upward progression was facilitated not by purchase, but by exactly the benevolent exercise of 'interest' which he himself was now to be denied.

While his father's influence and the friendship of Philip Bragge gave him his initial start, his subsequent advancement owed everything to the warm patronage both of the Duke of Cumberland, and more importantly to the King himself. And this despite the fact he had, seemingly, blundered politically on his return from Ireland in 1754 by attaching himself to the Leicester House Set; a shadow court centred around the Prince of Wales.[8]

With an eye to the future it might have seemed only sensible for Sackville to associate himself with the young Prince rather than the aging King. However, although George II was not yet dead, he was notoriously vindictive and Sackville's apparent defection certainly caused him to complain of having been 'most ungratefully abandoned'.[9] Nevertheless, it is important not to read too much into this comment in retrospect, for there was evidently more spleen than substance to the outburst. Although now aligned with the political opposition, Sackville's military career did not visibly suffer thereby. His politics were no impediment to his becoming a major general in 1755. Less than three years later Lord Ligonier warmly wrote to him in January 1758 confirming his appointment to the staff, declaring 'I only say in addition that his Majesty struck off with his own hand Mordaunt, Conway and Cornwallis. I have no more to say but that Lord George Sackville will be declared Lieutenant General next Monday, and that I have laughed more in two hours at Cobham this day than in two months in London.'[10]

The three generals in question were peremptorily dismissed for their dismal failings in the abortive expedition against Rochefort in 1757. This was the first of the coastal raids. The intention had been to storm the fortress which was correctly reported to be ill-fortified and weakly defended, yet after a week of dithering, James Wolfe, the future conqueror of Quebec, disgustedly told his uncle: 'Admirals and Generals consult together, and resolve upon nothing between them but to hold a council of war ... this famous council sat from morning till late at night, and the result of the debates was unanimously not to attack the place they were ordered to attack, and for reasons that no soldier will allow to be sufficient.'

King George was not much impressed either. There was a committee of inquiry (in which Sackville participated) but there was no court martial and no need for one when all that was required for the King to draw a pencil through their names.

By contrast, and perhaps pointedly so, Sackville's perceived ingratitude as a politician appears to have been pragmatically redeemed in the King's eyes by what the Duke of Cumberland earlier described as 'a disposition to his trade which I do not always find in those of higher rank'. In short he might deplore Sackville's politics but yet still approve his soldier-like behaviour.[11] Lord George was patently not yet in the King's black book, wherein the iniquities of bad officers were recorded, and so he still received his promotions in due season.[12]

Certainly this supposed royal displeasure was no impediment to Sackville going off buccaneering and afterwards presenting the meagre success at Ste. Malo in a sufficiently favourable light to be 'permitted to come with the troops to Germany'.[13] There is no real reason, therefore, to believe that Ligonier was being disingenuous in reassuring Sackville that the withholding of patronage was a matter of policy rather than a reflection of Royal prejudice. Whether, as Sackville feared, Prince Ferdinand truly appreciated this is a different matter. Notwithstanding the courtly tone of their subsequent correspondence, the Prince was aware of the influence reputedly wielded by Sackville over the unfortunate Marlborough and may well have considered him equally culpable in the difficult early relations between British and German troops. The question now was whether he was seen to be capable of the whole-hearted commitment demanded by Ferdinand.

Winter Quarters

Personalities aside, the problem remained that His Britannic Majesty's Army in Germany, to which the British contingent now belonged, was not a coalition army in the conventional meaning of the term but was actually the Hanoverian Army and its auxiliaries. The British contingent at first stood apart in that whilst it was unquestionably under Ferdinand's command, it was not yet fully integrated in the way that the Hessians and Brunswickers were. That had been made very clear by Marlborough's petulant insistence that he should not be subordinate to Spörcken. It, therefore, now behoved Sackville not only to demonstrate his effectiveness as an ally, but also his acquiescence in a happy assimilation of his own forces with the Hanoverian ones.

With no immediate prospect of action, the various regiments of the British contingent were settled into winter quarters; most of the infantry in Münster and the cavalry in the bishoprics of Paderborn and Osnabrück. Once they were all settled in their cantonments, Sackville then turned over command to Granby and took himself home.[14] There, having briefed all concerned, both in and out of government, as to the present situation and future prospects – and received repeated admonitions from the government as to curbing expenditure – he applied himself to three pressing matters on Ferdinand's behalf.

The most urgent need after the 1758 campaign was for more men and perhaps even more importantly the not inconsiderable sums of money to pay for them. In terms of regular infantry there were simply no more to be had in Germany. Hanover itself was already stretched to the limit maintaining the existing regiments and Hesse and Brunswick scarcely less so. By various shifts and expedients a couple of additional battalions were scraped together here and there, but nothing substantial could be hoped for then or in the future.

Light troops, both cavalry and infantry, were a different matter, if they could be hired from neutral Denmark, Holland, Switzerland or anywhere else that offered them. Constantly being swamped by the far more numerous French light troops, Ferdinand was keen to recruit more of his own, but that required money. He was already in direct communication with London on this and urged Sackville to press the matter in person. As early as 31 December 1758 he was anxious enough to write to Sackville expressing his fears that time which should be spent on preparations was instead being wasted in discussions. He urged immediate action and in particular urged early authorisation of the proposed increase of the light horse, which Ferdinand considered of such importance that he was prepared to decrease the infantry in order to augment the cavalry – and he closed by declaring that he knew of no-one so capable as Sackville of accomplishing it.[15]

This was shortly followed up with another letter in which Ferdinand commented that he did not yet know whether Britain was prepared to take any more German troops into pay but rather intriguingly hinted that it might be difficult to find good ones. Clearly his plans to increase the numbers of light troops were not going to be reliant on laboriously enlisting individual volunteers, but were to be accomplished by engaging with military contractors – at a price. Unspoken was the implication that if British gold was not immediately forthcoming to obtain their services, French gold might hire them for the other side instead. Happily this crossed with a letter from Lord George on 19 January, professing himself overcome by Prince Ferdinand's kind remarks and assuring him that the augmentation of the light troops, both Hessian and Hanoverian, had already been agreed, in spite of the great difficulties raised by the Treasury in regard to the increased expense.[16]

Unfortunately, Sackville had rather less success in obtaining British reinforcements to augment Ferdinand's regular infantry. The abandonment of the ill-fated policy of coastal expeditions ought to have released at least a brigade or two of infantry for service in Germany, not to mention the so-badly needed light troops of cavalry. Yet, incredibly, the government was instead fretting once again at the renewed threat of a French invasion. The militia as far north as Yorkshire was being mobilised and not a single battalion or troop of regulars could be spared. In fact it would not be until after Admiral Hawke's dramatic victory in Quiberon Bay in late November 1759 that the fear of a French invasion finally disappeared. In the meantime, even replacement drafts to bring the units already out in Germany back up to strength were hard to procure. Thus, at one point Sackville even warned Ferdinand that the King had held out the prospect of drafting 300 men from Ireland but then cautioned that the viceroy (then the Duke of Bedford) 'may upset this project'.[17]

Nevertheless, the men were eventually found, and on 23 February he was able to tell Ferdinand: 'Our recruits for the cavalry are partly embarked, and also some for the infantry. I wish I could tell you that some battalions will follow them, but I see less chance of this than ever, for the alarms for the kingdom are increasing ... I repeated the need of augmenting the army in Germany. He [Pitt] replied that if it could be done, he would be the first to put a hand to it, but that it would be dangerous in a country such as this to stretch the cord too much; the public must be humoured, and before all else sufficient forces must be kept here to put us beyond all reach of danger; that we did not yet know what part Denmark and Holland would take; and that in short, we must not think of any reinforcements from here whatever; but that if your Highness should suggest adding some troops from Brunswick (Hesse and Hanover having already done their utmost) he would willingly be the first to urge their payment (although he would be going outside his own department, as he had nothing to do with that of finance) even if the number should amount to two thousand. Then I spoke to him concerning the Artillery. He answered without hesitation, "you know the state of it better than I do. If we can spare some without risking too much, I see no difficulty about it."'[18]

In that last matter at least, Sackville, in his other capacity as Lieutenant General of the Ordnance, was happily able to oblige. Ferdinand had impressed upon him that not only was he out-gunned by the French but the Hanoverian guns in particular were obsolete and far too weighty – requiring far too many horses to haul them on to the battlefield and then being quite immovable without them. Not only did Lord George succeed in having two additional companies of the Royal Artillery sent out, but he also obtained no fewer than twenty-four new and much more mobile cannon for the Hanoverian and Hessian armies and sufficient money to find the men to handle them by retraining some of Ferdinand's infantry, and conscripting militia.[19]

While the lack of additional cavalry and infantry was disappointing, Sackville could therefore be reasonably satisfied with his accomplishments when he returned to Germany in late March, and began to make preparations for the coming campaign.

The immediate concern was to shake everyone down and ensure that they were battle-ready, which, for the British infantry at least, meant re-iterated orders to practice the Alternate Firing method rather than the old-fashioned Platooning. An equally important step was a partial re-organisation of the British contingent. Granby came back out with him, now as a lieutenant general, and, as second in command, was confirmed as having overall charge of the British cavalry. Whitefoord, however, went home and in his place came two of Sackville's colleagues from Ste. Malo; Jack Mostyn and Granville Elliot, each destined to get a cavalry brigade.[20] Both of the infantry brigadiers, Waldgrave and Kingsley, remained in place, but there was a reshuffle amongst their battalions. At the outset of the winter four of the six battalions were quartered in Münster itself, but as the town also served as Ferdinand's headquarters he insisted on having both battalions of the Hanoverian *Füssgarde* there too. This meant that the other two British battalions had to be quartered elsewhere; one in the village of Reinen and another in Steinhorst.[21] Now the opportunity was taken to post them to different brigades, perhaps to level the size of each but also, as suggested earlier, to break up the Ste. Malo brigade. Ironically, at Minden both brigades, together with the *Füssgarde*, would then form a division under the direct command of *General der Infantrie* August Friedrich von Spörcken!

The Debacle at Bergen

Ferdinand himself had an altogether more difficult problem to master. Essentially it boiled down to the fact that by the end of April 1759 he could muster only 71,798 men all told. Against that the French army of the Lower Rhine under *Marechal* de Contades had been reinforced over the winter to something in the region of 66,000 men formed in ninety-one squadrons and 100 battalions. Were he only facing Contades, Ferdinand might have had considerable grounds for optimism, for not only did he outnumber the French but there was no doubting the superior quality of his own men. Unfortunately, he also had to take into consideration the Army of the Main, now under Broglie, which had forty-five squadrons and another fifty battalions totalling an additional 31,000 men, based on Frankfurt.[22]

Essentially the French plans remained as before. Contades was to take the field in June and push Ferdinand across the Weser while Broglie came up from the south by way of Hesse. Unlike Soubise, he could be relied upon to do so with some determination. Ferdinand, for his part, recognised that despite the disparity in numbers, standing on the defensive was not a realistic option. Nor, for that matter, was taking the field against Contades likely to ease his difficulties. The *Marechal* was simply too cautious to co-operate, especially as he was slightly outnumbered. If threatened he would most likely remain safely behind the Lippe, drawing Ferdinand forward to no good effect, while Broglie came up through Hesse to get into his rear. Realistically, as the Prince explained to Holdernesse, the only sensible option was to leave a substantial covering force in front of Münster while he himself marched rapidly to join with Isenburg and launch a spoiling attack against Broglie, whom he recognised as the real threat.

Secrecy was vitally important in order to avoid tempting Contades into doing something exciting in his absence. Therefore, leaving Spörcken in command at Münster, he set out almost alone on the morning of 22 March, ostensibly to inspect those troops still cantoned around Paderborn and Lippstadt. Instead he drew most of them out of their quarters and 'marched directly to the country of Hesse, through roads no army had ever passed before, and encamped, on the 26th, at Rotenberg on the Fulde'. By this rapid and unexpected march he had outflanked the French outposts along the Lippe and for the moment at least cut Contades' communications with the Austrians. So far so good, but the roads ahead were infested with French and Imperial troops making a nuisance of themselves in Thuringia and menacing the Prussians. His aim, therefore, as he had explained to Holdernesse, was that 'My advance-guard will march from Fulda on the 29th towards Franconia, so as to drive the Imperial troops back as far as Bamberg, if possible. If we succeed, then I shall march against the French, using the route from Fulda, via Budingen, direct to Frankfurt, so as to oblige the French to abandon their great supply-depot at Friedberg and thus delay the start of their operations.'[23]

Ferdinand's offensive began well. Isenburg's existing corps of nine battalions at Kassel was reinforced by eleven squadrons drawn down from Paderborn, including a British cavalry brigade comprising the three squadrons of the Blues, and two each of the Scots Greys and the Inniskillings.[24] Holstein-Gottorp, with thirteen Prussian squadrons[25], five infantry battalions and some light troops, was to screen the right flank, while the Erbprinz was given the largest column with nineteen squadrons, fifteen battalions and some light troops. He was also given the task of clearing the Imperial troops out of Thuringia which he proceeded to do in dashing style:

March 31st, the Hereditary Prince, with only two squadrons of black hussars, defeated, near Molrickstadt, the regiment of Hohenzollern cuirassiers, and entirely dispersed them; numbers were killed, and 55 made prisoners. The regiment of Wurtzburg infantry, which was along with them, being thus deserted by their cavalry became a sacrifice to the hussars, who took 130 of them prisoners, and cut the rest to pieces. The next day he marched to Meinungen, with two battalions of grenadiers and some light troops, where he made the garrison prisoners, consisting of two battalions of the Elector of Cologne's troops, and found a considerable magazine. He thence proceeded to Wasungen, and made prisoners the regiment of Naget. General d'Arberg, who was on his march with one battalion and some grenadiers to support that place, came up after the affair was over. A brisk cannonading however ensued, but he was soon obliged to retire with such precipitation that the light horse could not come up with him in their pursuit. The same time the Duke of Holstein dislodged a party of French from Fryenstenau, [Freiensteinau] making two officers and fifty-six men prisoners. Colonel Stockhausen also with a detachment of some Hessian hussars and light troops, attacked the regiment of Savoy dragoons with such vigour that they cut the major part of them to pieces, and took two rich standards from them, which they brought to the head-quarters.[26]

So far so good. Ferdinand was taking a risk in stirring up the enemy in an area which he needed to move through swiftly but the Erbprinz had also been co-operating with the Prussians under Prince Henry. It was hoped this would convince everyone that Ferdinand's ambitions lay in that direction – and thanks to his customary secrecy even the Erbprinz thought that to be his intention. Unfortunately, he failed to convince Broglie and the French general recognised that he himself was the real target. Accordingly he begged substantial reinforcements from Contades. Unaware of this, Ferdinand now concentrated his own forces at Fulda. The Erbprinz's column, reinforced by the British cavalry brigade, now formed the centre, with Holstein-Gottorp still on the right and Isenburg on the left. After a brisk march, he found himself confronting Broglie at the small town of Bergen, some three miles north-east of Frankfurt, on the morning of 13 April 1759. This was not entirely unexpected, but unfortunately Ferdinand turned out to be dangerously ignorant of how strong the French really were and what they were doing.

In fact, in anticipation of his coming Broglie was occupying an uncommonly strong position which had been identified as ideal for the purpose as far back as January. Bergen lay astride the road to Hanau in the middle of a natural defile just over three miles wide, bounded on the north by the river Nidda and on the south by the Main. Fully a third of that distance was taken up by a square mile of woodland spreading southwards from the village of Vilbel, where Broglie had a pontoon bridge accessing the depot at Friedberg. This natural obstacle was increased by the fact the wood itself was also cut across by a number of streams feeding into the Nidda, perpendicular to any advance. On the south side of Bergen, on the other hand, there was a fairly steep escarpment and then a mile of deceptively open ground stretching out towards the Main. Unfortunately, it was a marshy flood plain obstructed by streams and ponds and no place for troops. To all intents and purposes the only practical fighting ground was the bare 1,000 metre-wide gap between Bergen and the Vilbel woods. The town was also a formidable obstacle in itself, surrounded by a substantial wall and ditch and further enclosed within a number of thickly-hedged orchards and their attendant agricultural buildings, but yet it was in effect no more than an outwork covering Broglie's main position.

Running due north to Vilbel from the town's west gate was a sunken road. This road presented Broglie with a conveniently situated main fighting line, which he had ample time to strengthen with an abatis – a thick obstacle belt of interlaced apple trees hewn from the orchards and arranged with their sharpened limbs projecting towards an attacker. To defend this already formidable position, Broglie had forty-four squadrons and forty-six battalions, besides some 700 light troops for a total of some 30,000 men in position by 08.00 hours on 13 April – with even more under Saint-Germain expected the next day. Just as importantly he also had no less than forty-five heavy guns.

Ferdinand, with less than 24,000 men, had no hesitation in deciding on an immediate assault – a decision all the more reckless in that nearly a third of his men were cavalry, who were going to be of little use. Light troops aside he had in fact no more than twenty-nine infantry battalions, and they would have very little artillery support. Furthermore, the decision to attack was based on a faulty appreciation of the situation, one which placed undue reliance on a report that Broglie was still somewhere between Frankfurt and Bergen. Consequently, Ferdinand all too readily leapt to the conclusion that the French general had not yet fully occupied the position. Time was already running short before he must return to Westphalia and any reports that Saint-Germain was approaching must have leant added urgency. If he was to accomplish anything he had to move immediately, but even then the offensive was compromised by poor staff work.

On the night of 12 April 1759 the three Allied columns were still separated and Ferdinand took the risky decision to unite them on the battlefield. However, his orders were not actually issued until between 23.00 hours and midnight and this allowed insufficient time for the commanders to be alerted and to bring their men up in time.

The assault was intended to go in at 06.00 hours but only Freytag and his light troops were in position at that hour. The Erbprinz was up, but only just, and was still deploying his men, while Imhoff, although close, had not yet arrived. Worse, Holstein-Gottorp was still three hours away. Impatient, Ferdinand rode on to a low hill, the Am Hohen Stein, to survey the French position – and probably due to a mixture of anxiety and wishful thinking, he completely misconceived the situation. Freytag had already reported the Vilbel woods to be held by light troops and although he had captured the village itself, the woods were no place to fight a battle. No matter, Ferdinand was content for Freytag and his *jäger* to contain them for knew he was going to have to drive straight through the centre and that meant first taking Bergen. He could see that the denuded orchards and hedgerows around the town were full of troops, but he was unable to ascertain just how many. In fact two brigades of Swiss and German troops totalling eight battalions were already ensconced there.[27]

Of itself that might not have mattered, but the abatis lining the sunken road behind the town not only protected Broglie's main fighting position, but effectively screened it from view. To Ferdinand, the fact he was unable to see any French troops in that direction confirmed his erroneous intelligence that the bulk of them were not yet up. Strictly speaking that was true in so far as they were not lining the sunken road, but were being held back a little. Broglie placed the five-battalion-strong *Piédmont* Brigade[28] behind Bergen itself, supported by two battalions of *Alsace Infanterie*. Then, formed in battalion column, came two more brigades, one of them Swiss and the other French. On the left were twelve Saxon battalions supported by another eleven French ones, again deployed in battalion columns in order to be able to manoeuvre rapidly when called upon to intervene. Finally the cavalry, with little space to deploy forward, were divided between the two wings in three lines, with the dragoons in reserve.

Ignorant of what was really facing him, Ferdinand decided to seize the moment and attack at once. The Erbprinz was accordingly ordered to slant across and come down on Bergen from the north, while Isenburg, as soon as he arrived, was intended to attack straight up the Hanau road. At the first gallant rush, *Generalmajor* von Gilsa, heading the Erbprinz' advance guard, comprising two Brunswick grenadier battalions and 100 more Hessian grenadiers[29] quickly got into the orchards, despite heavy artillery fire from the flank and musketry from the defenders. That artillery fire from Broglie's hitherto unseen main position must have been a surprise and understandably as soon as he got entangled in the hedgerows his attack stalled. Trying to find out exactly what was happening, Ferdinand himself rushed forward with the headquarters grenadier companies[30] only to be ignomiously caught up in the debacle as Gilsa's men came tumbling back. It was hardly an auspicious beginning to the battle – and things were about to get very much worse.

Unsympathetically, the Erbprinz immediately ordered Gilsa to go straight back in with two fresh battalions. Rallying the first wave and carrying them forward with him, he once again stormed into the orchards but then for the first time came up against the abatis. At this point Broglie reckoned it was time to counterattack. Four battalions in column formation[31] were sent around the south side of Bergen, while eleven more rapidly advanced through the town and along its northern side[32]. With both flanks beaten in, Gilsa went back again, and this time abandoning two of his three cannon.

Ferdinand still kept the battle going by flinging in battalions piecemeal as they came up, but Broglie launched another counter-attack, throwing in another eight battalions and personally leading some of them straight down Bergen's main street.

Gilsa was wounded and his men finally forced back. Just then Isenburg came up with the four squadrons of the *Dachenhausen* Dragoons and the single battalion of grenadiers which formed his advance guard and was promptly ordered into the assault. Surprisingly enough, with the aid of some of Gilsa's men his cavalry actually reached the east gate of the town before falling back. Ferdinand ordered them forward but by now most of the French artillery had been moved up to line the sunken road. Once again the Hessians and Brunswickers fought their way into the orchards – and once again Broglie counter-attacked. This time the gallant Isenburg was killed and at that the heart went out of his men and they fled, pursued by some of the French cavalry. A timely intervention by General Urff, at the head of four Hessian squadrons, stopped the pursuit but now Ferdinand went on to the defensive and braced himself for a general attack. Broglie, however, saw no reason to oblige him and sat tight.

The belated arrival of Holstein-Gottorp's column towards mid-day tempted Ferdinand to essay another assault, which for the first time was to be properly co-ordinated and directed. Perhaps the most striking indictment of Ferdinand's handling of the battle thus far was that not only was he badly outnumbered to begin with but he failed to get most of his men into the fight. To all intents and purposes the battle had been fought by part of the Erbprinz' column, only one of Isenberg's battalions and none at all of Holstein-Gottorp's. In short, it would appear that half of Ferdinand's infantry never fired a shot, while the bulk of his artillery, eleven 12-pounders, only arrived after the repulse of Isenburg's ill-fated attack.

That was now intended to change, but Broglie for his part also took advantage of the lull to reinforce his main fighting line by bringing up some of the Saxon troops who had hitherto been sheltered behind the Vilbel Woods. Seeing these additional units and artillery moving into position, Ferdinand decided that the French were about to go over to the offensive and so cancelled his own attack. The battle then settled down to a desultory exchange of artillery fire. As the afternoon wore on it became clear that in fact Broglie was not going to be tempted out of his near impregnable position. By about 18.00 hours with the light beginning to fade, Ferdinand decided to call it a day and withdraw. The dead were buried, the wounded collected and by 22.00 hours that night they were all on their way back, covered by a rearguard under the Erbprinz. In all, Ferdinand had lost some 2,671 men killed and wounded against the French 1,800 or so, and to no purpose. There was, however, one minor but significant footnote. Listed amongst the casualties were an officer and four troopers of the Blues, the first British combat losses since their arrival in Germany.[33]

The fact of the matter was that despite Granby's praise for his pre-battle briefing, Ferdinand had completely mismanaged the battle from start to finish. Even allowing for his readiness to believe that the French position was not yet fully manned, he had failed to concentrate his own forces before launching his first attack. Just two battalions of grenadiers were hardly adequate to capture Bergen all by themselves. Afterwards there was a rumour picked up by Sir Joseph Yorke, the British minister at The Hague, that the battle was lost because the Erbprinz had attacked prematurely. He certainly had, but it was Ferdinand who sent him in and that was no doubt why the rumour never gained any traction. Instead, His Serene Highness sought a scapegoat in his artillery commander, who had belatedly come up with Isenburg. Even then, given the degree to which the Allied guns were outmatched in number and effectiveness, it is hard to see that they would have made much difference. The reality was that Ferdinand only had himself to blame for the debacle – and the mismanaged battle presented an ugly foretaste of what was to come at Minden.[34]

As it was, Ferdinand was lucky to get away almost unmolested. It is hard to avoid the impression that Broglie found it difficult to believe his luck in having been handed such an easy victory. At any rate his first priority once he found Ferdinand gone was to ensure the safety of the supply depot at Friedberg, ignored by Ferdinand in his anxiousness to close with Broglie.

Before the battle, Fischer and his corps were sent up there with orders to set fire to it if it appeared to be in danger of capture. Now Broglie sent another twelve squadrons and an infantry battalion to reinforce Fischer, while he remained on the battlefield expecting a renewed attack. At first only a few light troops followed Ferdinand, more with a view to keeping in touch with the Allied forces rather than with any serious attempt to harass their retreat. That came later.

Ferdinand's withdrawal was slow. His men, unsurprisingly, were exhausted and as usual the weather turned bad. That, in turn, persuaded Ferdinand to allow them to move independently in small detachments under their own officers, rather than see them dissolve into a cloud of stragglers. As it was, it meant they were reverting into the style of the marauding armies of the Thirty Years War, and they immediately paid the price.

On 18 April one of Ferdinand's staff officers, carrying the dispersal order, was picked up by a French patrol. This was too good an opportunity to miss and over the next couple of days the French light troops raided at will, cutting off detachments and spreading fear and despondency in all directions. As it was, by 21 April the pursuit was called off. Broglie had remained at Bergen, and even his light troops, feeling a little exposed and short of supplies, turned back.

Ferdinand halted at last to give his men some badly needed rest and pull them together again. He knew only too well that the war was about to resume in Westphalia.

Chapter 6

Approach March

Ironically, while Broglie was fighting and winning his handsome defensive victory at Bergen, Contades was back in Paris, thrashing out a complete change of strategy. Until now it had been assumed by all concerned that in the coming year the main French effort was once again to be made in Westphalia by the Army of the Lower Rhine. However, with only 66,000 men, Contades was understandably reluctant to do anything so rash as to hurl them straight against Ferdinand's 72,000. Consequently, Broglie was expected to even up the odds by pushing north through Hesse and threatening the Allied rear. Notwithstanding his eventual timidity, Soubise had already demonstrated the feasibility of the strategy the year before and there was every expectation that it would succeed under Broglie's leadership. Hence Ferdinand's ill-fated spoiling attack to try and disrupt this dangerous combination.

Instead, Contades turned up at Frankfurt like the Devil at prayers – with a completely new plan. The diversionary role was now to be assumed by Armentiéres with a rump Army of the Lower Rhine comprising just twenty squadrons and eighteen battalions, and amounting to less than 20,000 men. The greater part of the French forces in Westphalia were to be switched from the Rhine to the Main and, by the end of May, Contades was able to concentrate no fewer than 106 squadrons, 102 battalions and 168 guns, besides the usual array of light troops. He did not, for a time, have the services of Broglie for this was not an equal partnership and when Broglie's contribution to the enterprise was reduced to a mere thirty-one squadrons and eighteen battalions, he promptly disappeared on sick leave to cool down! Contades viewed the departure of his rival with no obvious signs of regret. The Chevalier de Muy was temporarily appointed to command in his place and preparations went on apace for the advance north.

Ferdinand, for his part, decided that in the circumstances he too needed to concentrate his forces in readiness to counter this dangerous threat. Kassel was once again to be evacuated and its magazines back-loaded to Minden and Hameln. By 5 June 1759, he had opened his headquarters at Werl, some twenty miles west of Lippstadt, and the greater part of the army, including Imhoff's corps of observation, which had hitherto been keeping an eye on Broglie, was ordered to concentrate there and at Soest. This was to be the forward point of a salient, anchored on his right flank by Münster and on the left by Lippstadt. From there Ferdinand hoped to be able to cover both threats – a thrust eastwards by the Army of the Lower Rhine under Armentiéres aimed at his Münster base, and the inevitable advance through Hesse by Contades. Hopefully, he might thereby be able to fend off one while dealing with the other. For added security substantial outposts were established at Haltern, under Wangenheim, covering the approaches from Wesel, and under Wutginau at Marsberg and Büren, forward of Lippstadt.

The latter detachment, at Büren, comprised six squadrons and all seven British infantry battalions, who were ordered up for the purpose from Münster on 7 June; that is the two existing brigades, plus a seventh battalion formed by combining the six grenadier companies under Major John Maxwell of the 20th Foot.[1]

In the meantime, having been reluctantly rejoined by Broglie, Contades commenced his advance covered by the usual thick cloud of light troops. By 10 June they had reached the line of the Diemel, forcing Wutginau to fall back from there and concentrate at Büren. Thus far Ferdinand had been somewhat in the dark as to Contades' intentions, and was still somewhat apprehensive of a thrust down the Weser directly threatening Hameln. Now it appeared that the French proposed to tackle him head on and accordingly he marched to take up a strong position on the high ground at Büren, from where Lord George Sackville wrote a fairly encouraging letter to Lord Holdernesse on 16 June, assuring him that:

> The night before last, we came into this camp, after a most fatiguing and distressing march ... We are now in sight of the enemy's camp; it seems to be posted not far from Wunnenberg. Prince Ferdinand's and Marshal Contades' reconnoitring parties met this morning between the two camps, and the Duke of Richmond and Col. Fitzroy saw at a distance some of their old acquaintances, who by degrees approached and entered

into conversation, till Marshal Contades sent to the French officers to return to him. Our position is extremely strong…indeed this whole country is so cut up by ravines, and the hills rise so quick upon each other, that whoever is to act offensively must take his measures with the greatest ability to secure success.[2]

Alas, as a fighting position it suffered from the fatal defect that it was so strong that no general in his right mind would obligingly fling his men against it. Contades was not only in his right mind, but after a day's skirmishing soon came to the happy realisation that Ferdinand could not only be turned out of the Büren position with relative ease, but that a thrust northwards beyond his left flank would interdict his lines of communication towards Minden and Hanover, as a British officer related:

Here the two armies remained inactive for some time in sight of each other, their advanced posts not being above a mile and a half asunder, without making any attempt, as the position of each was equally strong, and inaccessible, both by art and nature. M. de Contades did not think it advisable to quit his advantageous camp to attack the Allies, although he was greatly superior in numbers after the junction of M. de Broglio; but in order to take advantage of this superiority, he formed a design of turning their left. For this purpose M. de Broglio was ordered to proceed from Lichtenau to Ettelen [Atteln]. On the 18th a large detachment under the command of M. de Xavier was advanced to Nordbrecken, and their light troops seized on the town of Paderborn. This party was ordered to proceed by forced marches round the left of the Allies, with an intent to cut off their communication from the Weser, and that part of the bishopric of Munster situate along the river Ems. This manoeuvre of the enemy determined his Serene Highness (who could not spare a detachment to observe Prince Xavier) to change his position and march to Rhittberg. [Reitberg] The Allied Army accordingly on the 19th struck their tents, and marched to Lipstadt, in the neighbourhood of which place they encamped; and on the 20th, they passed the river Lippe above and below the town, and retired towards Rhittberg, pitching their camp near to that town in an advantageous situation, having the river Ems in their front, with their right extending to the village of Windenbrue, and their left to that of Newkirchen. They were not in the least molested in this march, nor was there any attempt made on their baggage, which was covered by all the grenadiers of the army and the light troops.[3]

Ferdinand had broken contact successfully, but in doing so he was for a time blind as to what the French were up to. In fact his situation was becoming ever more dangerous. Lippstadt remained in his hands with a small garrison under General Hardenberg, but significantly Colonel Boyd, the British commissary, was also left there with a secret commission to supersede Hardenberg if he entered into a premature capitulation. Münster was also potentially threatened, for Armentiéres was now on the march masked by the usual screen of light troops but almost certainly heading for the city.

Outnumbered as he was, Ferdinand was only too keenly aware that should either fortress, or God forbid both, be laid under siege he might have great difficulty in relieving them in the face of Contades' superior forces, yet the loss of them would almost certainly compel a retreat across the Weser. That would in itself open up even more unpalatable decisions. He might choose to cover Hanover and preserve his communications with Prussia, but in that case he would almost certainly lose contact with the base at Stade and with it his British lifeline. The advice he received in his extremity was largely confined to encouragement, but not otherwise particulary helpful. His old master, Frederick, enjoined him to fight. Significantly, King George stipulated that whilst he was not qualified to say more without a fuller picture of the situation, Ferdinand should ensure that Stade was properly garrisoned and provisioned. Otherwise, wrote Holdernesse soothingly, 'Your Serene Highness is entirely free to follow your own judgement and wishes, and whatever the event His Majesty will always be persuaded that your decision will have been the best and most suitable. Nothing could equal the limitless confidence which His Majesty places in the consummate capacity of which Your Serene Highness has given so many striking proofs.'[4] In other words, Ferdinand was on his own.

Remembering the fate of His Majesty's once favourite son after Hastenbeck, 'limitless confidence' was not as comforting as it might have been. Towards the end of June, Contades, with his forces well closed up again, forced Ferdinand's hand by marching north along the western edge of the Teutoburgerwald. By the 29th he was at Lippespringe and 3 July saw him at Bielefeld. Ferdinand was forced to conform by falling back towards Gütersloh. He had little choice at this point, but it meant Contades was moving inexorably towards the point where he might be able to cut Ferdinand off from the Weser.

Ferdinand's principal adviser now and throughout the war was his private secretary, Christian Heinrich Philip, Edler [Squire] von Westphalen.

Oddly enough he was not a military man, but he was a clear thinker and at this critical juncture presented Ferdinand with a well-reasoned appreciation of the situation.

As he saw it, Contades was probably considering two options: either to move north-eastwards to besiege Hameln, thereby opening the Weser as a supply route and exposing Hanover itself to attack, or he might head further north, by-passing Hameln in favour of Minden. Neither option contemplated that Contades might first to seek out and destroy the Allied army. Instead Westphalen recognised that the French strategy was to outmanoeuvre and strangle it. He therefore recommended that in either event Ferdinand must attack, which, since Bergen, he had been singularly reluctant to do. If Contades opted to besiege Hameln he should be attacked there and if he was beaten the campaign was as good as over. Granted, if the battle was lost the fortress would fall, but it would do that anyway if Ferdinand made no attempt to relieve it. As to Minden, Westphalen foresaw both risks and opportunity. There, if the Allies attacked and were beaten, they would lose the great magazines at Osnabrück and Münster, but on the other hand the French would still need to besiege those places and Lippstadt and Hameln as well, which ought to at least offer a breathing space to recover. Indeed, he also recommended that in either event Ferdinand should begin by recalling Wangenheim's detachment which was marking Armentiéres. Münster was capable of looking after itself in the short term and Wangenheim's men were going to be of far more use in strengthening the main field army against the crisis to come.[5]

Suitably bucked up, Ferdinand duly decided to attack, but then Contades once again moved first, passing through the Bielefeld gap to reach Herford on 8 July. Ferdinand, still avoiding battle, had by then fallen back to Osnabrück where he hoped to rendezvous with Wangenheim. He was not yet cut off from Minden, but now he rather belatedly realised that Contades was closer to there than he was. Next day the Erbprinz was hastily sent off with twelve squadrons and fifteen battalions to throw himself into the place before it was too late. Then, leaving just two squadrons and four battalions to look after the back-loading of the magazines at Osnabrück, Ferdinand anxiously hurried after him with the rest of his army.

If any one man could be said to be responsible for the Battle of Minden being fought, it was Johann Christian Fischer. Born in Stuttgart in 1713, he was, for a time, employed as a groom in the service of Armentiéres, but during the siege of Prague in 1742 he made a name for himself by organising some of his fellow grooms into a small partisan corps. Under the patronage of senior officers such as the legendary *Marechal* de Saxe it grew rapidly in size and reputation, serving as the prototype for a host of other irregular corps. By July 1759 Fischer held the rank of *general-de-brigade* and was possessed of a well-deserved reputation as a leader of light troops. He was just about to increase that reputation dramatically.[6]

Minden was important both as a supply depot and as the key to a strategic choke point, the Porta Westfalica, where the Weser passed through a gap in the Wiehen Gebirge into the North German Plain. It was in effect the western door to Hanover. Not surprisingly it was a fairly strong fortress in its own right. Situated on the left or west bank of the Weser it was protected on the south side by a marshy stream called the Bastau and on the east by the river itself. The only approach on that side was across a stone-arched bridge. On the right bank the bridge was in turn protected by a hornwork and ditch, itself spanned by a drawbridge.[7]

Yet this apparent strength, and the fact that initially it lay a comfortable distance behind the Allied lines, was its undoing, for Ferdinand had contented himself with sparing a single battalion and various detachments and rear area details to serve as a garrison under Georg Ludwig von Zastrow[8]. Unfortunately although the French were not yet interposed between Ferdinand and the fortress, they were now a good deal closer to it than he was. Quite inevitably in the ordinary way of intelligence gathering, Fischer quickly learned how weakly garrisoned the town was and lost no time in acquainting Broglie. He, in turn, was more than ready to seize what might be a fleeting opportunity and on the evening of 9 July he sent off his younger brother, the Comte de Broglie, with 1,500 cavalry, 1,200 infantry, and Fischer's corps, as an anonymous British officer related:

> They arrived before Minden at break of day, and summoned it to surrender. Major General Zastrow, who commanded in that place, refused to comply with the summons, and the town was immediately invested. The French general determined to attempt the taking of it by assault; but the weakest part was on the other side of the Weser, and they had neither boats not pontoons to effect the passage of that river. A reconnoitring party, however, found by chance a float of timber, by the help whereof Fischer's corps with 300 volunteers immediately crossed over, and attacked the head of the bridge, while M. de Broglio favoured the attack by a brisk cannonade on this side. They at last forced that post, and entered the town about 9 o'clock in the evening. General Zastrow with the

garrison, consisting of a Hessian battalion and some piquets of different corps, amounting in the whole to 1500 men, were made prisoners of war.[9]

Actually the action appears to have been brisker than even this sparse account suggests. Once Fischer was across the river he opened up with a couple of light Rostaing guns, partly to alert young Broglie that he was in position and partly for effect as he launched his own assault. That effect was pretty dramatic for the garrison of the horn-work immediately bolted for the imagined safety of the town, leaving the drawbridge down! Fischer and his chasseurs charged straight after them, got in by the gates before they could be closed and then careered through the streets to seize the west gate from behind. Once it was opened, in came Broglie's men and almost as soon as the shooting ended Fischer's irregulars fell to plundering the town and its stockpiled stores. They certainly felt they had earned that right, but this was the Age of Reason and Broglie's regulars stepped in to restore order by force. Unkindly, it might be observed that Fischer's men seem to have put up more of a fight for the booty than the garrison did. At any rate, by midday it was all over; Zastrow, his garrison and his stores were secured, and Ferdinand's uneasy position had become critical.

He had already realised that Osnabrück and Münster were too exposed to serve as his magazines and that he needed to switch his main supply route from the Ems to the Weser. Nienburg was once again to serve as the army's principal magazine, and so all the flour that could be loaded was being sent up there from Osnabrück, together with the field bakeries. At the same time, as we have seen, Ferdinand marched the army east towards Minden, sending the Erbprinz ahead to secure the place. Alas, for all his energy the latter was still twenty miles away when he learned the town had fallen. To make matters worse, having taken Minden the French were then themselves only a day's march from an unprotected Nienburg, while at the same time d'Armentiéres had closed up on Münster and opened his siege lines. To reach either town required a two-day march by the Allied forces, and choosing one would inevitably result in the loss of the other.

Ordinarily Ferdinand was a firm believer in some of the dictums laid down for Generals in Francis Grose' *Advice to Officers of the British Army*, that:

You must be as absolute in your command, and as inaccessible to your troops, as the Eastern sultans, who call themselves the lord's vice-regents upon earth. In fact, a commander in chief is greater than a sultan; for if he is not the Lord's vice-regent, he is the King's, which in the idea of a military man, is much better.

As no other person in your army is allowed to be possessed of a single idea, it would be ridiculous, on any occasion, to assemble a council of war, or, at least, to be guided by their opinion: for, in opposition to yours, they must not trust to the most evident perception of their senses. It would be equally absurd and unmilitary to consult their convenience; even when it may be done without any detriment to the service: that would be taking away the most effectual method of exercising their obedience, and of perfecting them in a very considerable branch of military discipline.

You have heard that secrecy is one of the first requisites in a commander. In order, therefore, to get a name for this great military virtue, you must always be silent and sullen, particularly at your own table; and I would advise you to secure your secrets the more effectually, by depositing them in the safest place you can think of; as, for instance, in the breast of your wife or mistress.[10]

In Ferdinand's case that was Westphalen. Otherwise he was at once admired and notorious for his secrecy and for a reluctance to take others into his confidence. On 14 April Sackville had written privately to Holdernesse that 'he [Prince Ferdinand] is too wise to trust his secret intentions to anybody further than is absolutely necessary for the carrying them into execution'.[11] Now, in his extremity, as Sackville recounted, he surprised his generals by asking for their opinions, with reasons, in writing:[12]

The news [of the fall of Minden] found us at Bomte in the most disagreeable and critical condition possible. It was necessary however to come to an immediate decision; the Prince, who seldom asks opinions, was pleased upon that occasion to call upon General Sporcken, General Imhoff and myself to give our thoughts on the party he was to take. It is not very easy to form opinions without hearing all that the person knows who puts the questions to you … however, I never will make difficultys, and I instantly returned my answer …

If it was absolutely in your Serene Highness's power to secure Munster, I should strongly advise your abandoning the Weser, and confining yourself to keeping those countries which would best enable us to carry on the war, as I do not conceive that the enemy would venture to establish their winter quarters in

Hanover, whereas if they were once in possession of Munster, &c. it would be most difficult to dispossess them. But as your Highness doubts whether Munster is yet in your power to save, I do not hesitate to declare it as my opinion that it is most for the King's service and the good of the common cause first to attempt the saving of our magazines at Nienburgh, &c., as by that means a battle may ensue, and, if le bon Dieu nous aide,… I should hope your Serene Highness, in consequence of a victory, would remain master of Westphalia likewise. But if, from further intelligence, your Serene Highness sees it impracticable with any degree of probability to succeed in securing the Weser, and in bringing the enemy to a decisive engagement, what I have said in regard to Munster must weigh down all other considerations, especially as we shall by that means preserve our communication with England and Holland.[13]

… General Sporcken was absolutely for coming hither, Imhoff for returning to Munster, upon a supposition that the enemy must have taken Nienburgh, as we had three marches and they only one forced march to get thither. We were afterwards called upon to talk the affair over … and I joined entirely with General Imhoff and was for returning instantly to secure Munster, but however the other part was taken, and by it we have given up immense magazines, lost winter quarters in a country that would have supply'd us with forrage &c. without expense to the publick [*sic*], and our nearest communications with England and Holland cut off.

Ferdinand's mind was made up, but while Imhoff's contrary advice was taken at face value and had no obvious effect on his future career, Sackville evidently upset the Prince badly. 'What I have heard gave most offence,' wrote Sackville afterwards, 'was my having said I should not be surprised if the British troops were recalled immediately since their country was in danger, as the nearest communication with England was readily given up'.[14]

As it happens, the British government was indeed expressing similar concerns, especially when communications were abruptly cut as French patrols fanned out across the countryside in the wake of the Allied evacuation of Westphalia.

Here, again, there was room for misunderstanding. Whilst the heads of the British government were by convention ministers of the Crown, they were not as subservient to the throne as their German counterparts. Even Ferdinand's master, Frederick of Prussia, had been constrained to warn him that the English constitution made it necessary to cultivate the confidence of the ministers as well as the King, since they in turn had to explain themselves to a sceptical public. This, as we have seen, was especially true when it came to balancing British and Hanoverian interests. A part of the British Army was presently serving in Germany, only because the British government had calculated that aiding the Hanoverian war effort was the most effective way of engaging the French and keeping them at arms-length from England's shores. Therefore the government was bound to get nervous if by retreating eastwards the British contingent put itself beyond immediate recall in the event of a serious threat or actual invasion. This was evidently Sackville's honest advice as to the likely reaction of a British government which he knew was decidedly jittery about the prospect of a French invasion. It was certainly not a personal threat to withdraw the British contingent if Münster was not succoured and the line of retreat to Emden secured. Yet, somehow, it appears that Ferdinand saw it as such and Frederick's letter of warning was interpreted to mean that Sackville was inspiring or at least encouraging the ministry's concerns rather than merely reflecting them.[15] For Ferdinand, and probably Westphalen, it was not simply that to quote Grose again, 'it would be ridiculous … to be guided by their opinion: for, in opposition to yours, they must not trust to the most evident perception of their senses'. Sackville, they suspected, was guilty of deliberate disloyalty.

It certainly did not help that Sackville had written to Ferdinand at the end of April, praying 'that if possible the whole of the British corps may be together'.[16] To the Prince this was a complete anathema. During the last war the various Allied contingents – the British, the Hanoverians, and the Dutch – had marched uneasily alongside each other, each in their own national formations, each under their own generals and acting according to their own national policies and priorities. Command and control had been a nightmare, even on the battlefield itself. After Fontenoy in 1745, the British blamed their defeat on the Dutch failure to properly engage, while the Dutch complained of the British precipitation. Mutual trust was totally absent and outright hostility never far away.

By contrast, from the very outset of his command Ferdinand had striven, very successfully, to create a fully integrated army in which Hessian officers could be assigned to command Hanoverian troops, and Brunswick officers to command both. At Minden the British infantry would be commanded by a Hanoverian general. It was sometimes a difficult balancing act, but it worked. Unfortunately, as we have seen, from the day of their arrival the British had strongly resisted such integration. It did not help of course that whilst the Hanoverians, Hessians and Brunswickers shared a common language, religion and culture, the British did not. Few, if any, except perhaps the men of the 51st, spoke German, but there was no question of the late and unlamented Duke of Marlborough's tantrums being lost in translation. Consequently, Sackville's request in April, although politely expressed and outwardly reasonable, must have reinforced Ferdinand's belief that the British and in particular their commander, were not wholly committed to the enterprise.

Yet Sackville gave no hint of disagreement in his subsequent correspondence both public and private, and indeed expressed confidence in Ferdinand and his leadership. Nevertheless, the Prince appears to have harboured a resentment of him which would in time burst forth on the plain of Minden.

That lay in the future and for the moment Nienburg had quite literally been saved in the very nick of time. Its garrison comprised only two companies of militia, but on 11 July *Generalmajor* Emmerich Otto August von Estorff was sent off on a forced march with 400 cavalry and the same number of infantry mounted behind. Next day, just five miles from the town, he intercepted and scattered the French. For the moment Ferdinand still had magazines to sustain him and still had a conduit for more supplies through Stade and Bremen, but he remained in in an awkward situation. Münster and Lippstadt were still holding out, but could not be relieved and were as good as lost. At least they were still useful in tying down a significant number of French troops who would otherwise reinforce Contades, but not for much longer.

In the meantime, in order to cover Nienburg, Ferdinand immediately sent the Erbprinz to take up a position at Petershagen, on the Weser just seven miles due north of Minden. This was on 14 July 1759, and finding the French had vacated the Minden Plain in favour of a more secure camping ground on the south side of the Bastau, Ferdinand soon joined him and pushed Wangenheim further south to prepare a fortified line only a little over two miles north of Minden itself. Its right was to be anchored on the village of Stemmer; its centre lay in front of a long, narrow village called Kutenhausen; and its left rested on the Weser a little to the front of a third village called Todtenhausen, which for a time would lend its name to the coming battle. Undisturbed by the French, the fortifications were complete within the week and with Nienburg reasonably secure, Ferdinand was again able to contemplate regaining at least some of the initiative.

Fortunately, having handsomely outmanoeuvred him, the French had troubles of their own, albeit they were likely to be only temporary. If anything Contades had been too successful. Until now his logistical tail had kept pace with his very methodical advance. Ironically, Fischer's dramatic coup at Minden now succeeded in dislocating it. The opportunity was too great to be passed up of course and the decision to relocate the French field army to the Minden area was undoubtedly correct, but Hameln was still in Hanoverian hands and Freytag's light troops were using it as a base from which to make a thorough nuisance of themselves. Until the fortress could be taken, the Weser could not be used by the French as a supply route. For the moment therefore Contades was wholly dependent upon a single road stretching over the hills to Herford, all of sixteen miles away. Therein lay Ferdinand's opportunity.

If that road could be cut Contades might be drawn out of his impregnable position at Minden, for reports from deserters indicated that his army was already growing hungry. The plan, as explained to King George on 26 July, was straightforward, albeit a little optimistic:[17]

> The garrison [four battalions] which was at Bremen, has marched on Vechta. I have ordered the Hessian hussars and jägers, as well as the regiment of Breidenbach, to join them. This detachment will march tomorrow to Vörde and the day after tomorrow to Osnabrück, so as to fall on the enemy detachment there. On the 29th, they … will join the Erbprinz at Rimsel. [Riemsloh]
>
> [The Erbprinz] marches tomorrow to Lübbecke, with a corps of 6-7000 men;[18] on the 29th he continues to Rimsel, where he will take over command of the whole corps. From Rimsel, this corps will take the enemy in the rear.
>
> On the 28th or 29th, I will take up a new position with the main army, so as to support the Erbprinz.
>
> I have also arranged for a move to be made from Hameln against St. Germain's corps at Schwöbber. Lieut. Colonel Freytag will undertake this task.
>
> The success of these moves depends very much on whether Münster will then still be holding out. I hope however to oblige the enemy either to leave his present position, or to accept battle.

As it happened, Münster had already fallen, surrendering to Armentiéres on 25 July. Fortunately, as the latter then proceeded south-east to take Lippstadt rather than immediately try to join Contades, he was not in a position to frustrate Ferdinand's plan.

The early signs were good. *Generalmajor* Karl Heinrich von Dreves swept down from Bremen and evicted the *Volontaires Etrangers de Clermont Prince* from Osnabruck.[19] Seemingly the hussars, under Hauptman von Schlieffen, accomplished it by themselves, taking a couple of cannon in the process, and then he and Dreves rendezvoused with the Erpbrinz exactly on schedule. Our anonymous British officer, takes up the story:

> On the 29th, he [the Erbprinz] marched to Rimsel, where he was joined by General Dreves from Osnabrug; on the 30th, he advanced towards Hervorden, and on the 31st he took post at Kirchlinegar, which lay in the road of the enemy's convoys from Paderborn.
>
> The Duke de Brisac, who commanded a detachment from the French army consisting of about 8,000 men, had the same evening taken post near Covelt [Gofeld], encamping with their left to that village, and their right towards the salt-pits, with the river Werra in their front. The Prince was determined to attack them next morning; but as their position was impregnable in front, there was no other way to come at them but by surrounding their left, for which purpose the following dispositions were made: Three attacks were formed, all of which were to depend on the success of that on the right; the troops destined for that attack consisted of a battalion of Diepenbroick, two of the Brunswick guards, two hundred volunteers, and four squadrons of Borck's dragoons; the four battalions of old Zastrow, Behr, Block and Canitz, and one squadron of Charles Breidenbach, with all the heavy cannon, composed the center [*sic*] the left was formed of three battalions, Block, Dreves and Zastrow, and of four squadrons of Busch: the troops of the center were designed to keep the enemy at bay, whilst those of the right should surround their left; those of our left were to march to the bridge near the salt pits, in order to prevent the enemy's retreat to Minden.
>
> The Hereditary Prince [Erbprinz] marched with the right, Count Kilmanseg was in the center, and M. De Dreves and M. de Borck brought up the left: they set out at three o'clock in the morning from their camp at Quernon. The enemy, on their part, likewise intended to attack us: as soon as Count Kilmanseg had come out of the defile of Beck, the enemy presented themselves before him, and a cannonade began on both sides; the right was to pass the Werra, in order to turn the enemy's left at the village of Kirchlinger, upon a very narrow bridge; this difficulty was, however, in some measure removed by the spirit of the troops, the infantry fording the river partly behind the horsemen, and partly in peasants' wagons.

By the passage of the Werra, the position of the enemy was entirely changed; the fire of the artillery was brisk on both sides, and lasted for two hours, though our's had always the superiority: at last, upon our shewing ourselves upon their rear, they immediately gave way, and in their filing off came upon the skirts of M. de Borck, who received them with a discharge of artillery, which was well supported; when, finding themselves entirely surrounded, they had no other resource but in flight. Five pieces of the enemy's cannon, with their baggage, fell into our hands; their loss in killed and wounded was very considerable, and a great number were made prisoners. Lieutenant-general Kilmanseg deserved the highest commendation: M. Otte, colonel of old Zastrow's, distinguished himself greatly at the head of his regiment, and repulsed the enemy's cavalry, that fell upon him, with considerable loss. Our loss was very slight; Captain Wegner of the artillery was wounded in the leg: and to him and Major Storck was owing the good service we had from the artillery.[20]

As our narrator ruefully remarked, 'however shining this action was in itself, yet it was in some measure eclipsed and swallowed up by that glorious and ever memorable victory gained on the same day over the combined armies of M. de Contades and the Duke de Broglio'.

The two battles were, however, intimately connected and so it is necessary to backtrack a little. At the outset of the adventure Ferdinand's main body was still encamped at Petershagen, a little to the north of Wangenheim's fortified position in front of Todtenhausen. Having sent off the Erbprinz, he waited there until the early hours of 29 July and then proceeded to march south-west to Hille, a village on the Bastau five miles upstream from the French left flank near Hahlen. He did so as ostentatiously as possible with the army formed in two parallel columns which marched across the plain with colours flying and bands playing.

Obviously enough, his progress was closely watched by the French but, as he had calculated, the difficulty of debouching quickly from their present position ruled out a hurried encounter battle and he was allowed to take up his new ground by Hille without interference. At the village there was a causeway over the Bastau marshes and from there a road to the gap in the Weihengebirge at Lübbecke, which Gilsa was immediately sent to occupy with three battalions.[21] Ferdinand was therefore well positioned either to receive a French attack should it come out of Minden, or to cross the hills by way of Lübbecke and join the Erbprinz, should the French be forced by shortage of supplies to evacuate Minden and fall back through the Porta Westfalica.

The advantages of his new position were very clear and indeed were intended to be so. By now aware that the Erbprinz was over the Weihengebirge and threatening their only supply line, Contades and Broglie divined that the purpose of the move was precisely in order to give Ferdinand that freedom of manoeuvre. Gilsa's occupation of Lübbecke only seemed to confirm this.

However, his Serene Highness was not content to await the French pleasure in deciding his next move. Instead he had actually prepared what he hoped was a massive trap. Wangenheim was deliberately left behind at Todtenhausen, not merely to continue covering Nienburg and its magazines, but was dangled as a tempting piece of bait to lure the French out of Minden.

In reality, Wangenheim, being far stronger than he looked, was intended to stand fast. The beauty of his position was its depth and the way in which a long low crest behind his forward line, and an old fortified embankment, the Land Wehr, shielded his actual camp from view. Only his grenadier brigade under the Prince of Bevern, which included Major Beckwith's British Grenadiers, remained with the guns and a few cavalry piquets in ostentatious occupation of his forward line. However, in addition to those six battalions of grenadiers, there were still another nine battalions of infantry and sixteen squadrons of heavy cavalry hidden to the north of Todtenhausen. He also had no fewer than twenty-six field guns – mostly 12-pounders – and a dozen more 3-pounders with his infantry.

Far from being quickly overrun, Ferdinand therefore reckoned on Wangenheim pinning down the French long enough for the main body of the Allied forces to come forward against them. Indeed, knowing how shockingly bad French staff work normally tended to be he also calculated that they might take so long crossing the Bastau stream from their own camp – in the dark – that he might actually be able to catch them in their flank.

All now depended on the enemy.

Chapter 7

The Battle of Minden

The French, as it turned out, were happy to oblige Ferdinand. Exactly as he hoped, Contades' took the bait and planned to first attack Wangenheim's isolated detachment and then swing around to attack the left flank of the Allied camp. This did not directly face towards Minden but stretched in a line north-east from Hille, sheltered behind the large village of Nord Hemmern and a stream called the Lander Beck. While by no means impassable, both obstacles would hamper movement and might together be sufficient to pin the Allies in place while the initial operations were carried out on their left, especially if a diversionary attack was simultaneously mounted by seizing the Eickhorst bridgehead opposite Hille.

Deployments

Whilst this proposed turning movement against Ferdinand's left seemed simple enough in concept, the French staff had some complicated work to do to accomplish it and for once they excelled themselves. Indeed Major General Kingsley afterwards described their orders as 'the best digested I have ever seen'.[1] In the first place the staff officers needed to pass the main body of the notoriously ill-disciplined army across the Bastau stream in the dark and form it up on the plain. At the same time Broglie's corps needed to be fetched from the far side of the Weser in order to deal with Wangenheim. In effect the two operations, although obviously very closely linked, were at one and the same time very sensibly planned to be run quite separately.

At 18.00 hours on 31 July 1759, Contades issued his orders. Some time previously two pontoon bridges had been thrown across the Weser just

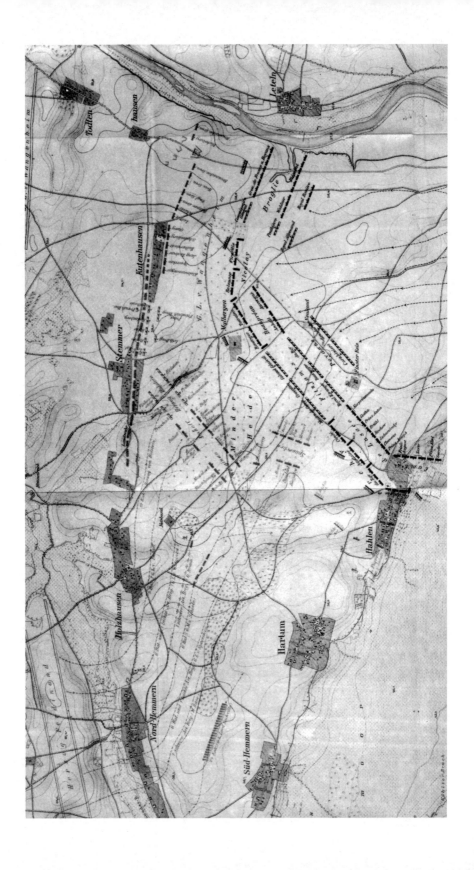

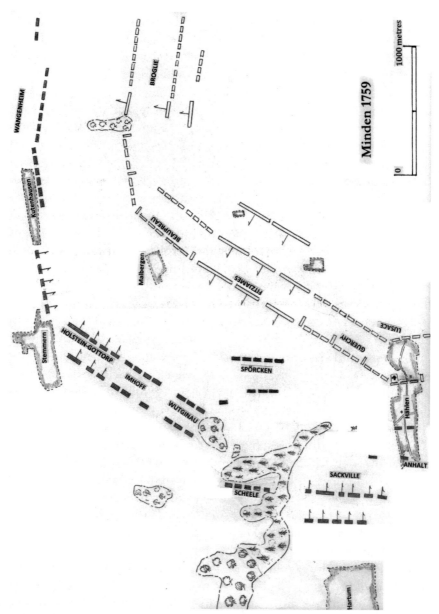

Opposite: Copy of the map of Minden c.6am from the German General Staff history of 1904.

Above: A tracing of the General Staff map, which has less detail but greater clarity and is modified by the addition of Sackville's cavalry and Scheele's infantry.

south of Minden in order to provide a good connection between Contades' corps on the left bank and Broglie's corps on the right. However, in order to avoid any danger of entanglement with Contades' own deployment, Broglie was instead to cross his corps over the Weser at dusk only by using the stone bridge, then pass straight through the town and exit by its north gate. Once reinforced by eight battalions of *Grenadiers de France* and *Grenadiers Royaux* under the Marquis de Saint-Pern, which were borrowed from Contades and some additional artillery, he was to assault Todtenhausen '*au point du jour*' – sunrise was due at 04.30 hours.

Meanwhile, the main body of the army was to move out of its camp in seven columns, crossing the Bastau by nineteen specially built bridges before wheeling round to form a north-westward facing battle-line stretching between the village of Hahlen on the left and Maulberg[2] on the right. The actual deployment was decidedly unorthodox but had a certain logic to it. Effectively the infantry was divided into two quite separate wings. On the left, around Hahlen, were sixteen French and fifteen Saxon battalions, supported by thirty guns under Lieutenant General Claude-Louis-François de Régnier, Comte de Guerchy and the Prince de Lusace respectively. On the right, by Maulberg, were a further sixteen battalions and thirty-four guns under Lieutenant General Jacques Bertrand, Marquis de Beaupréau. Next to him another division led by the Chevalier de Nicolai, comprising eight battalions, was to provide a link with Broglie's corps, and if necessary support the assault on Wangenheim's corps.

Unfortunately, although their deployment in this fashion was justified by the broad extent of the ground to be covered, it also meant that there was a gap of some 1,400 metres between the two wings, covered only by the fire of batteries established at either side. Contades therefore elected to post all of his cavalry in the centre, rather than hold them back in reserve. He was undoubtedly taking a risk in this, but if all went according to plan he would be justified by events. With Guerchy pinning Ferdinand's forces the cavalry would be very well placed and in sufficient strength to fully exploit the intended turning movement against the Allied left. Nevertheless, cautious as ever, Contades declared that once the deployment of all his forces was completed: '*Mr le Marechal en donnera les orders suivant les circonstances.*'[3]

No doubt this rider was intended to relate to timings and in particular on how quickly Broglie could deal with Wangenheim. Unfortunately, of course, as Helmuth von Moltke later declared, 'No plan of operations extends with any certainty beyond the first contact with the main hostile force'.[4] In this case, at the very outset of the battle the plans of *both* generals went very badly wrong indeed.

While Contades was doing exactly what Ferdinand hoped, the Prince's own plans depended on his army reacting very promptly to the anticipated French movement. Once the enemy came out there would obviously be a limited period in which to clear the significant obstacles in its immediate front and deploy forwards on to the battlefield. As with Contades' operation it was well planned. The army was to form in eight discrete columns, or divisions. Like the French, each column already had its own bridges thrown across the Lander Beck and lanes were ruthlessly cut through the hedges, fences and any other obstacles offered by the village. Once clear of Nord Hemmern the columns were then to march eastwards in order to form a battle-line lying between the villages of Hahlen on the right and Stemmern on the left.

The cavalry of the right wing, twenty-four squadrons (fourteen of them British) under Lord George Sackville, formed the first column. The heavy artillery of the right wing under Major Haase, of thirty guns and howitzers (nineteen British) and one infantry battalion[5], formed the second. The infantry of the right, eight battalions (six British) under General Spörcken and six battalions under General Scheele, comprised the third and fourth columns respectively. The heavy artillery of the centre under Colonel Braun – twenty-nine guns and howitzers (nine British) – formed the fifth. The infantry of the left wing, six battalions under General Wutginau and six battalions under Imhoff, comprised the sixth and seventh columns, while the eighth column consisted of the cavalry of the left wing, which amounted to nineteen squadrons under Holstein-Gottorp.

Depending on their starting positions in the camp this meant a march of between two and four miles in order to get into position. Guides were allocated, and the officers appointed to command the columns were also required to reconnoitre and familiarise themselves with the exact routes which were to be taken and the ground which their men were to occupy. And finally, precautionary orders were issued at 18.00 hours on the evening of 31 July requiring that 'at one o'clock to-morrow morning, the army shall be ready to march; the cavalry must be saddled, the artillery horses harnassed, and the infantry gatered. But the tents are not to be struck, nor the troops under arms till farther orders.'[6]

All Ferdinand could do now was wait, relying on the alertness of the strong chain of piquets thrown across his front to give him the timely warning he needed. 'The British [piquets] were posted in the village of

Hartum,' wrote our anonymous officer, 'the Hanoverian in Sud Hemmeren, the Hessian in the wood between Hartum and Halthausen, those of Brunswic in Stemmern, and the piquets of the cavalry in the woods, with a detachment upon the road from Hartum to Hahlen'.[7] As was customary, these piquets were commanded by the lieutenant general of the day. It had been Sackville's turn earlier but at about 17.00 hours the previous evening he handed over to Karl Leopold, Prinz von Anhalt-Bernburg. Unfortunately that night, according to Ferdinand, Anhalt completely failed in his duty.

Contades, on the other hand, had an unexpected stroke of luck; the first of his units were actually in place by midnight, but a very strong blustery wind blowing from the west not only masked the noise of the French movements but at the same time discouraged the Allied piquets from maintaining contact. This negligence was then compounded when a couple of French deserters came in and announced that an attack was imminent. However, for some reason, Anhalt attached no urgency to their story and did not alert Ferdinand immediately.[8] Consequently, it was not until 03.00 hours that his Serene Highness was belatedly awakened to the news that the French were already out. Sending off a flurry of orders to his equally somnolent division commanders he was anything but serene as he rode forward into the grey pre-dawn light to assess what was actually happening. It was not encouraging.

The Battle Begun

To begin with, Anhalt blandly assured Ferdinand that all was quiet – which cannot have helped his temper. Having ordered the hapless general to call in the piquets and employ them in securing Hahlen, Ferdinand pushed on. Almost immediately, however, he ran into a cavalry patrol which warned him that the French were already in occupation of the village. As will have been noted, Hahlen had the dubious honour of being earmarked as the southern anchor point of *both* armies and Contades' had got there first by pushing two battalions of light troops into the village almost as soon as it was dark. This was serious.

Despatching Estorff, his adjutant general, to make sure that Wangenheim had been alerted, Ferdinand carried on, accompanied only by his groom and a local guide. By now it was about 05.00 hours and there was sufficient daylight to see the plain was already filling with white-coated French soldiers. They were still extending northwards towards Kutenhausen, but beyond them he could already see the flash of artillery and smoke rising where Broglie had commenced his attack on Todtenhausen.

Although the blustery wind was still carrying the noise of that particular battle away from him, he was now able to hear artillery fire from behind him the direction of Hille. This was d'Havre occupying Eickhorst as noisily as possible. Ordinarily this might have been cause for concern, but with the main French army in plain sight before him, Ferdinand rightly dismissed the gunfire as the diversion it was. Two cannon were ordered to cover the Hille end of the causeway and Gilsa was summoned back from Lübbecke. Otherwise Ferdinand's priority was to get his own army out of its camp and facing in the right direction before Contades stormed forward. Ironically, he was greatly assisted in this by d'Havre's diversion for it would appear that the sound of the French cannon awakened most of Ferdinand's generals long before his messengers found them!

Fortunately, Contades' luck was beginning to run out and his carefully crafted plan was unravelling just as surely as Ferdinand's. It is one of the curiosities of the German war that while French tactical thinking at the time stressed the aggressive use of the bayonet, in practice their generals were all too often ruled by an excess of caution. In this case it was the normally dependable Broglie who effectively aborted the French offensive.

Wangenheim was just as oblivious as Anhalt to the threat assembling out in the darkness. Arguably, had Broglie stormed straight forward as soon as he was in position at 04.00 hours he might have carried Bevern's forward position in that first gallant rush, long before Wangenheim had time to react and bring forward the rest of his corps. Instead, at sunrise Broglie announced his presence with an artillery barrage. However, instead of softening up the Allied grenadier battalions, he was dismayed to find his guns immediately attracted a far heavier fire in exchange. Against his six field pieces and four howitzers Wangenheim was able to field twenty-six guns and two howitzers. The Hanoverian position was much stronger than it looked. Broglie immediately halted and waited for Nicolai's two brigades to come up. Then, going forward with them at about 06.00 hours, a personal reconnaissance revealed nine more Hanoverian battalions moving into position amongst the hedges of Kutenhausen and a substantial body of cavalry as well. It looked uncomfortably as if he might actually be outnumbered and indeed the speed with which the Allied cavalry were coming up led him to think he might be about to receive a counter-attack. Once again he halted any forward movement and this time galloped back to confer with Contades and seek reinforcements.

Ferdinand, in the meantime, was trying desperately to patch his own battle-line together. Most of his troops moved out of their camps between

04.00 hours and 05.00 hours. The sight of the great columns of men marching steadily towards the battlefield amidst huge clouds of dust kicked up from the sandy heath was evidently an impressive spectacle and many of the witnesses at Sackville's subsequent court martial were asked whether they had seen it. With only a relatively short distance to march, Holstein-Gottorp was probably approaching his designated battle position by Stemmer within the hour. Encouraging him to speed his march, and sending to Imhoff and Wutginau to likewise hurry up, the Prince was then dismayed to receive a message from Anhalt enquiring whether he should assault Hahlen!

On the face of it this seems to be another dereliction by Anhalt. Ferdinand believed he had ordered him to do so right at the start of the engagement. The Marquis of Granby would later testify to the clarity of Ferdinand's orders at Bergen and elsewhere, but those were his formal, scripted briefings. His verbal orders given in the heat of battle were a different matter entirely and often hurried, incomplete and consequently unclear. Ferdinand knew what he wanted, but when under pressure he evidently had difficulty in explaining himself clearly to others. At the time he ordered Anhalt to secure the village, neither general was aware that the French were already in occupation of the place. A display of soldierly initiative on Anhalt's part might have been appropriate at this point. However, after the Bergen affair there was something of a reluctance to do anything other than follow His Serene Highness' orders and Anhalt's hesitation was only part of a pattern that would be repeated by others throughout the morning.

In fairness, this particular job was no means as easy as Ferdinand seemed to assume. The long and relatively narrow village stretched for about 1,000 metres parallel to the Bastau and its marshes. The Brunswick piquets were too far away to help but Anhalt had three ad hoc battalions immediately available to him – one Hessian, one Hanoverian and one British battalion and he began by clearing the western end of the village with one battalion moving up either side of the main street and the third battalion in reserve.[9] Ferdinand had at least allocated him one of the British artillery brigades, comprising seven guns and two howitzers, by way of fire support, and Captain-lieutenant Edward Foy duly unlimbered them near a prominent windmill just a little to the north of the village. With Foy's help, clearing the French light troops out of the western half of the village was relatively easy as the attackers were aided by fires begun by the howitzers and fanned by that still blustery wind. In the middle of the village, however, there was a walled churchyard and there the defenders made a stand long enough for the *Champagne* Brigade to come up. That stopped the unfortunate Anhalt dead in his tracks and the French then appear to have remained in possession of the eastern end of the village throughout the battle. Worse, the four battalions of the *Champagne* brigade formed the left flank of the Comte de Guerchy's division and so the whole of the French left wing was now firmly anchored upon the village. This development, although surprisingly little remarked upon, was to seriously disrupt the deployment of Ferdinand's forces.

As we saw the Prince's original intention was to take up a position on a line running directly between Stemmer in the north and Hahlen in the south. Instead, with the French already formed in front of them, Holstein-Gottorp, Imhoff and Wutginau were, perforce, beginning the process of forming a new battle-line, refused or angled back south-westwards from Stemmer towards Hartum.

This meant that instead of taking up their fighting positions in open cornfields, on the right wing at least, the Allies were to find themselves as much as 1,200 metres further back than had been intended and in ground broken up by belts of trees and other obstacles. This was to have far-reaching and wholly unanticipated consequences.

Advance with Drums Beating

Meanwhile, the six British battalions had got off to a good start under General Spörcken. On receiving the orders to move, they formed up and promptly passed through their *debouchers*[10] at about 05.00 hours. Marching at a quick pace through the dust for about three miles, they seemingly outstripped Scheele's column on their left and were the first troops from the right wing to reach the battlefield. As soon as they emerged on to it, through a belt of woodland, an increasingly anxious Ferdinand gratefully pounced on them, despatching one of his aides, Johann Jacob, Graf von Taube, to 'tell General Spörcken to advance with the regiments he had, with drums beating, and attack whatever he might encounter'.[11]

Afterwards Ferdinand dishonestly contended he had merely instructed that 'if the troops advanced, they were to do so with drums beating' and so flatly denied ordering Spörcken to go forward and pitch into any enemy troops who got in his way. Yet, in the immediate context, Taube's version makes far more sense than the puzzling legend. In an army ruled by drum-beats, Ferdinand's version was wholly unnecessary and a nonsensical intervention at a time when he was desperately trying to regain control of a battle which appeared to be collapsing into chaos. The French had already formed their battle-line and indeed in this particular area were actually occupying the ground which Ferdinand had earmarked for his own troops. Only Holstein-Gottorp's cavalry on the extreme left were moving into their proper place. Imhoff, Wutginau and Scheele were probably not up yet and somehow it seemed he could not get his own orders obeyed. It was Bergen all over again and all he could do, just as at Bergen, was fling his troops straight in just as quickly as they came up.

At any rate, in prompt response to the order carried by Taube, Spörcken immediately deployed his leading brigade into line under Lieutenant General John Waldgrave – with Napier's 12th Foot on the right, Huske's Welch Fusiliers on the left and the junior battalion, Stewart's 37th, in the centre. Having done so, he very quickly stormed forward again, trailing behind him Major General William Kingsley's brigade and the two battalions of the Hanoverian *Füss-garde*.

On most maps depicting the crisis of the battle it misleadingly appears that Spörcken was not only plunging forward ahead of the rest of the army, but doing so at an eccentric angle, cutting across the front of Scheele's division on what should have been his left and so crowding him out. In actual fact nothing of the sort occurred, for in conformity to Ferdinand's immediate order as relayed by Taube, Spörcken was still advancing straight forward on his *original* line of march. He was still heading towards his division's previously allotted fighting position in a projected north-south battle-line which no longer existed. As Lieutenant General Kingsley afterwards bitterly complained: 'This order of battle was never form'd. It was indeed intended, but whether by the tardiness of, or obstacle to, the columns of the left in their marching, they never join'd the column of British and Hanoverian troops on the right till they alone had drove the enemy out of the field.'[12]

When Spörcken emerged from the woods he was evidently a little way ahead of Scheele's column. However, far from being crowded out by Spörcken's 'veering' to the left, Scheele was himself said to have been ordered by Ferdinand to move to the right and support Anhalt over by Hahlen. In fact, he eventually took up a position somewhere behind Spörcken and there stood fast, albeit one of his Hanoverian battalions, Hardenberg's Regiment, carried on forward regardless and eventually fell in with Spörcken's second line.[13]

Ferdinand's response to Spörcken's advance was ambiguous. By his own account he immediately sent word to halt so that they would not outstrip the other infantry coming up on their left, nor be out of breath when they faced the enemy. However, no-one was coming up on their left then or afterwards and this time, when Taube caught up with Spörcken, he recalled delivering a rather briefer message. It was not an instruction to halt and wait for everybody else, but simply to slow the pace in order not to get out of breath.[14]

If there was an order to halt, both Taube and Spörcken interpreted it as no more than an entirely sensible injunction to pause just long enough for Kingsley's brigade and the Hanoverian *Füss-garde* to catch up and properly deploy from column into line. When they did so, the latter may have moved forward on to the left of Waldgrave's brigade in the first line while Kingsley's brigade slotted in directly behind, with his own 20th Foot on the right, Home's 25th on the left and Brudenell's 51st in the centre.

As soon as all was arranged to his satisfaction, Spörcken's men shouldered arms once again and stepped out towards the enemy. As soon as they moved out of their final forming up point in a shallow swale they began to come under a heavy fire from a battery of French artillery, as Lieutenant Hugh Montgomery of Napier's 12th Foot explained:

> We marched from camp between 4 and 5 o'clock in the morning, about seven drew up in a valley, from thence marched about three hundred yards, when an eighteen pound ball came gently rolling up to us. Now began the most disagreeable march that I ever had in my life, for we advanced more than a quarter of a mile through a most furious fire from a most infernal battery of eighteen-pounders, which was at first upon our front, but as we proceeded, bore upon our flank, and at last upon our rear … At the beginning of the action I was almost knocked off my legs by my three right hand men, who were killed and drove against me by a cannon ball, the same ball also killed two men close to Ward, whose post was in the rear of my platoon.[15]

Lieutenant Thomas Thompson of the 20th Foot also recounted the cannon fire the infantry had to endure:

> On the immediate sight of us they opened a battery of eighteen heavy guns which from the nature of the ground, which was a plain, flanked this regiment in particular every foot we marched. Their cannon was ill-served at first, but they soon felt us and their shot took place so fast that every officer imagined the battalion would be taken off before we could

get up to give a fire, notwithstanding we were then within a quarter of a mile of their left wing. I saw heads, legs and arms taken off. My right-hand file of men, not more than a foot from me, were all by one ball dashed to pieces and their blood flying all over me, this I must confess staggered me not a little but, on receiving a confusion in the bend of my right arm by a spent musket shot, it steadied me immediately, all my apprehensions of hurt vanished, revenge and the care of the company I commanded took [their] place and I was *then* much more at ease than at this time [he was writing from hospital in Minden after the battle due to his injured arm]. All the time their left wing was pelting us with small arms, cannon and grape shot, and we were not suffered to fire, but stood tamely looking on whilst they at their leisure picked us off as you would small birds on a barn door. I cannot compare it with anything as their shot came full and thick, and had one quarter of them taken place [i.e. hit the target] there could not have been a man left.

In the meantime, having despatched Taube with his second message, Ferdinand had another problem to occupy him. His artillery chief, the Graf zu Schaumburg-Lippe, was absent with Wangenheim over by Todtenhausen. There he had earlier been engaged in a petty quarrel with the general over the tactical command of the latter's artillery and then when the battle began at dawn he had triumphantly asserted his authority by directing it in person. Consequently, Ferdinand now found his own artillery arriving on the battlefield with no-one on hand to deploy it. Consequently, leaving his other subordinates to fight their own battles, he decided to do the job himself and at that point it became clear there had been another breakdown in communications.

According to the later testimony of the officers concerned, the artillery did not move out of the camp until after 06.00 hours. More than half the guns in Major Haase' column were British, yet he had set off without passing down any orders to them and it was on Captain Forbes Macbean's initiative that they marched. Still ignorant of what was required of them, Captain David Williams was sent 'to see if I could find Lord George Sackville, or any other General Officer, that could tell me of any extraordinary orders relative to us; we were at a loss for orders; we were marching from the ground without any orders.' Equally uninformed as to where they should go, Sackville suggested they could do no wrong by going forward where he did not doubt they would find employment enough.[16]

This they did. Williams rode forward to find Foy warmly engaged in the task of 'cannonading' a French battery. When he returned, Captain Philips proposed they should join Foy, but:

> I made answer that we could be of no service there, for they did not see the enemy, nor did the enemy see them, that I know of. I told him, to the best of my knowledge, that we had best go to the left, which Captain Philips agreed to. A little before we entered the wood, we met Duke Ferdinand and the Duke of Richmond. The Duke of Richmond rode up to us, and gave an order, I don't know to whom in particular, but he spoke to anybody that heard; that it was Duke Ferdinand's orders that we should go there, pointing to the wood, which was then become to our right, and fire upon the enemy as fast as we could. I think I said it was impossible to go there, which I think Capt. Philips and Capt. Macbean agreed to. We marched on inclining to the left as we came out of the wood, without any farther orders that I know of.

Once through the trees they unlimbered their ten guns in one line, four commanded by Williams and six by Macbean with Philips in overall charge. Although interestingly Williams testified that while he believed Philips had given the order to open fire on the enemy, he was far from certain and believed it was by general consent![17]

It was also timely. In sticking doggedly to his original course, Spörcken was advancing straight towards the French cavalry drawn up immediately to his front. However, the British artillery now unlimbering on his right obligingly began shooting on to his objective by firing on the cavalry at a range of about 8-900 metres. As they did so they in turn came under fire from the same French battery which had been shooting up Spörcken's division. The British gunners turned on it and silenced it in short order. Williams recalled this took ten minutes, but to the best of Forbes Macbean's remembrance it was accomplished in only five minutes, and afterwards they resumed firing on the cavalry.[18]

It is often, if a little unkindly, alleged that cavalrymen saw their principal role in battle as 'adding tone to what would otherwise be just a vulgar brawl'. That might certainly be said of the French cavalry of l'ancien regime. Yet it was also equally axiomatic that cavalry cannot ride down resolute infantry and as Spörcken's infantry tramped determinedly towards them the realisation dawned on their commander, Lieutenant General Charles, Duc de Fitzjames, that his cavaliers must attempt to do just that.

The French front line comprised three brigades totalling twenty-three squadrons in all, and at his word of command two of the brigades, *Mestre de Camp* and *Royal Cravattes*, commanded by the Marquis de Castries, rode forward to their doom.[19] The British infantry halted. This was no time for a measured Alternate Firing by platoons, and at point blank range the volleys were delivered by battalions and both cavalry brigades were completely smashed:

> When we got within about 100 yards of the enemy, a large body of French cavalry galloped boldly down upon us; these our men by reserving their fire until they came within thirty yards, immediately ruined, but not without receiving some injury from them, for they rode down two companies on the right of our regiment, wounded three officers, took one of them prisoner with our artillery Lieutenant, and whipped off the Tumbrells. This cost them dear for it forced many of them into our rear, on whom the men faced about and five [?] of them did not return. These visitants being thus dismissed, without giving us a moment's time to recover the unavoidable disorder, down came upon us like lightning the glory of France in the persons of the Gens d'Armes. These we almost immediately dispersed without receiving hardly any mischief from the harmless creatures.[20]

Vivid though his story is, Lieutenant Montgomery manages to conflate two separate attacks, for having literally stopped Castries' charge dead in its tracks, it was Fitzjames' second line, comprising twenty squadrons of the *Royal Etranger*, *Bourgogne* and *du Roi* brigades under Chastellier-Du Mesnil, which rode through the wreckage of the first line and into the flank of Napier's regiment before being shot to pieces. Then came the French third line – the Marquis de Poyanne's *Carabiniers* and *Gendarmerie* – not charging straight forward as Montgomery implies, but hooking around Spörcken's left flank. This particular attack, although dangerous, was quickly disposed of for this time the French found themselves in a deadly crossfire and were badly shot up from all directions by Huske's 23rd Fusiliers, Hardenberg's Regiment and by both battalions of the Hanoverian *Garde*. Indeed, according to Spörcken the officers of the latter regiment afterwards armed themselves with swords taken from the fallen *Gendarmerie*.[21]

Far more dangerous was a simultaneous attack on the right flank by two of Guerchy's infantry brigades, *Aquitaine* and *Conde*:

We now discovered a large body of infantry consisting of seventeen regiments moving down directly on our flank in column, a very ugly situation; but Stewart's Regiment and ours wheeled, and showed them a front, which is a thing not to be expected from troops already twice attacked, but this must be placed to the credit of General Waldgrave and his aide-de-camp. We engaged this corps for about ten minutes, killed them a good many, and as the song says, 'the rest then ran away'. The next who made their appearance were some Regiments of the Grenadiers of France, as fine and terrible looking fellows as I ever saw. They stood us a tug, notwithstanding we beat them off to a distance, where they galled us much, they having rifled barrels, and our muskets would not reach them. To remedy this we advanced, they took the hint, and ran away. Now we were in hopes that we had done enough for one day's work, and that they would not disturb us more, but soon after a very large body of fresh infantry, the last resource of Contades, made the final attempt on us. With them we had a long but not very brisk engagement, at last made them retire almost out of reach, when the three English regiments of the rear line came up, and gave them one fire, which sent them off for good and all.[22]

Once again the actual course of events was a little more complicated than Montgomery suggests. It would appear that they first fought off one brigade and then engaged in a firefight with another. They were certainly not the *Grenadiers de France* as those gentry were being badly shot up to no purpose by Wangenheim's artillery over by Todtenhausen. However, if true, the rifle barrelled muskets may have been carried by some of the Saxon troops forming a second line behind Guerchy. At any rate the 'large body of fresh infantry' was certainly composed of Saxons and, as General Kingsley confirmed, they 'very gallantly attacked Kingsley's regiment, and which at first retreated, after losing a great number of men; but on the regiment's rallying again, and being supported by a fresh battalion of Hanoverian Guards, they were in their turn repulsed'.

Amongst the casualties was Kingsley himself. Stoutly refuting the story recounted in Entick's *Compleat History* that he had been wounded, had fallen off his horse, been taken prisoner and eventually rescued, he insisted that he, 'did not fall from his horse. His horse was shot in four places, fell with and died upon him. Neither was he taken prisoner, tho' the Saxon troops marched twice over him. They were twice going to shoot him, he did not discover himself, but at length disentangled himself from his horse and rejoined his regiment and brigade.'[23]

By then it was almost all over. The six British battalions, with a little help from the Hanoverian *Garde* had followed Ferdinand's orders to the letter, advancing with drums beating and attacking anything they encountered. To all intents and purposes by doing so they had won the battle by themselves and as Montgomery put it:

> It is astonishing, that this victory was gained by six English regiments of foot, without their grenadiers, unsupported by cavalry or cannon, not even their own battalion guns, in the face of a dreadful battery so near as to tear them with grape-shot, against forty battalions and thirty-six squadrons, which is directly the quantity of the enemy which fell to their share. It is true that two Hanoverian regiments were engaged on the left of the English, but so inconsiderably as to lose only fifty men between them. On the left of the army the grenadiers, who now form a separate body, withstood a furious cannonade. Of the English there was only killed one captain and one sergeant; some Prussian dragoons were engaged and did good service. Our artillery which was stationed in different places, also behaved well, but the grand attack on which depended the fate of the day, fell to the lot of the six English regiments of foot …
>
> The sufferings of our regiment will give you the best notion of the smartness of the action. We actually fought that day not more than 480 private and 27 officers, of the first 302 were killed and wounded, and of the latter 18. Three lieutenants were killed on the spot, the rest are only wounded, and all of them are in a good way except two.

The other regiments fared little better, indeed Kingsley's rather worse (see Appendix 3). While Napier's 12th lost seventy-seven rank and file killed and 175 wounded, Kingsley's 20th had seventy-nine rank and file killed and no fewer than 212 wounded out of about 440.[24] Little wonder then that Kingsley would complain, 'The Infantry of the center never came up. The attack was made by the British only; the Hanoverian guards sustained; the battle was over and the enemy beat before the center of the Infantry arrived.'

The battle was not yet over of course and it is important to appreciate that, notwithstanding the meticulous depiction of the two armies in the *Großer Generalstab* map of 1904 (and its numerous derivatives), it may be questioned whether everyone occupied the positions shown simultaneously. Wutginau's division appears to have reached the battlefield before Spörcken's action was over, but Imhoff came up later and was ordered to pitch straight in, to support another recent arrival in the shape of an artillery column under *Oberstleutnant* Braun. This was threatened first by Fitzjames' last uncommitted brigade, the *Colonel General*, and then the two infantry brigades of Beaupreau's front line. Imhoff ordered a bayonet charge by his front line, the four battalions of *Generalmajor* Victor August von Einsiedel's Brigade. This halted the French long enough for Holstein-Gottorp's cavalry to arrive and attack their rear.[25] The two French brigades immediately collapsed and became entangled with the wreckage of Fitzjames' cavalry division which was trying to sort itself out behind Maulbergen. A confused fight followed in which Beaupreau was wounded, captured and rescued, but in the end his second line under Saint-Germain, comprising the eight battalions of the *Auvergne* and *Anhalt* brigades held firm and covered the retreat of the rest.

Sackville and the British Cavalry

Suitably encouraged Wangenheim also went on to the offensive with both horse and foot. By now it was evident that the battle was lost and soon the whole French army was on the run, covered by Broglie. Over on the Allied right, however, something had gone badly wrong and the twenty-six squadrons of Sackville's cavalry division failed to get into the fight at all.

Ultimately this, rather than Spörcken's attack, would afterwards be remembered as the defining moment of the battle and almost entirely for political rather than military reasons. The legend, simply told, holds that Sackville was ordered to advance in order to complete the victory by riding down the retreating French – and that he refused to obey those orders, perhaps through cowardice. The facts are very different and at the outset it is necessary to assert that almost everything alleged against him by Ferdinand and by the Prince's personal staff was false. In proper compliance with the previous night's orders the cavalry were indeed saddled at 01.00 hours and when the alarm was belatedly raised the cavalry was swiftly formed up and moved out in good time – with Sackville at its head.

> Between five and six in the morning, I was waked by the firing of some cannon on the right of the camp; no orders had been sent to me, not had I any reason to imagine that the order to strike tents and march had been sent to the line; soon after I had a message from General Spörcken that the troops were getting under arms, and before my horses were brought out, Major Stubbs came to me from the line. I immediately galloped up with him, without even waiting for any of my Aids de Camp, and had the good

fortune to be at the head of the cavalry before any other general officer of that division had joined them.[26]

The problems began as the cavalry approached the battlefield. Whilst Sackville's earlier duties as lieutenant general of the day had offered little opportunity to reconnoitre his designated route, some of his aides had done so and his guide, a Herr Meyer, was familiar with it.[27] Had all gone as intended the column should have passed between Hahlen and its windmill and then deployed on to the open fields with the east end of the village on its right.

Instead, as we have seen, the French secured Hahlen during the night and Sackville now found himself hemmed in a very awkward position indeed. Not only was his intended path blocked by the Sachsen-Gotha Regiment, but there was artillery in action by the windmill and more infantry (Anhalt's piquets) engaged in attacking the village. As he put it himself: 'The cavalry had then upon its right the village of Hartum and inclosures, which run close upon the flank of the lines; on its left a long wood, and the country only open to the front, where the windmill, our original point of destination, stood; the particular spot where we halted was too narrow to contain the front; and Captain Smith having discovered that the ground widened to the right in the front, I advanced a little forwarder, and there halted again. I was by no means satisfied with this situation of the cavalry, thus separated from even the view of the rest of the army, hemmed in on both sides, and likely to be exposed during this Inaction to some batteries of the enemy.'[28]

It is worth strongly emphasising this point for the selective omission of this belt of woodland on many maps of the battle creates the quite erroneous impression that Sackville failed to act despite being 'well situated near Hartum' and in clear sight of the action and that he 'refused to advance despite repeated orders from Prince Ferdinand … Those magnificent regiments, burning for their opportunity, stayed near Hartum, within close distance of the desperate fighting of their fellow countrymen'.[29]

With all due respect to Sir Reginald Savory, this was nonsense for, in the first place, thanks to those woods Sackville had no opportunity to see what was happening on the other side, and whilst he may be criticised for not making greater efforts to find out, the fact of the matter is that his attention was fixed on the obstacles to his front in the direction he had been instructed to go.[30] Secondly, the orders which came to him were all too brief and to a degree contradictory.

Ferdinand first called for them as soon as he saw Fitzjames' cavalry coming forward. Taube was sent to hurry forward Wutginau's division, while a Hessian aide, Captain von Wintzingerode, rode to fetch Sackville. Within a few minutes, however, Ferdinand's impatience got the better of him and he despatched Captain Edward Ligonier to hurry him along. By now the French were clearly in confusion and Ferdinand naturally wanted the cavalry to come up quickly and exploit Spörken's success.

Sackville, as he afterwards stressed, was ready enough to obey, drew his sword and ordered the cavalry to advance. It was at this point things began to go wrong. One of Sackville's own aides, Lieutenant James Sutherland of the 23rd Fusiliers, had just returned from the front to report that the French had evacuated Hahlen. This was not due to any belated effort on the part of Anhalt, but rather part of a more general withdrawal by Guerchy and Lusace in the wake of their defeat by Spörcken. The way was at last clear for Sackville to move up with the cavalry and advance into the plain in accordance with his original instructions. The orders brought by Ligonier appeared to confirm this and Lord George began to advance straight forwards with drawn sword until Ligonier urgently told him he was not to go forward but required to move to the left. Sackville, by his own account, did not at first hear him over the beating of the dragoons' drums but at much the same time yet another of Ferdinand's aides, Lord Fitzroy, galloped up, not only confirming that the cavalry was to move to the left, but insisting that only the British cavalry were required.[31]

Perplexed, Sackville ordered all the cavalry to halt. Not only was he seemingly being required to move to the left, through the woods rather than advance to his front, but the new orders brought by Fitzroy not only required him to split his command but to do so in an awkward fashion for his two British cavalry brigades were posted on the right of his first and second lines. An ill-tempered argument then followed with both Ligonier and Fitzroy agreeing that the cavalry was required to move to the left, but flatly disputing whether all the cavalry were required, or only the British cavalry. In the end, hearing that Ferdinand himself was close at hand, Sackville decided to seek clarification from the great man himself.

However: 'As we galloped along, I saw the wood open to the plain more quickly than I imagined, and Col. Fitzroy continuing still very positive in his order, as reported to me, I sent back Capt. Smith with orders to bring up the British cavalry as fast as possible … When I came up to the Prince, I told him the state of the orders; he received me, as has been proved by many witnesses, with his usual civility, expressed to me no surprize at my not understanding the orders; but upon my pointing to him the head of the column of the cavalry of the second line, which was then in view coming out of the wood, gave me his own orders to form the cavalry on the heath, and sustain the infantry.'

There was no mention by then of pitching into or pursuing the French. It was too late for that and probably, given the time and space involved, it always was too late; and the opportunity far too fleeting. Ironically, however, had Sackville followed his first impulse by continuing to advance to his front in the direction of Hahlen he might indeed have emerged on to the plain in time to pitch into Guerchy's retreating infantry, just as Holstein-Gottorp had done on the left. Instead, by obeying Ferdinand's ill-digested commands and moving to his left, he was too late.

By now Spörcken had advanced to 'the hedges of Minden', where no doubt someone had the bright idea of plucking the famous roses from the gardens through which they passed and placing the on their hats and caps. He was well out of contact. Therefore, in obedience to the order to form a single line to sustain the infantry Sackville moved up behind 'a line of 7 or 8 battalions, commanded by Major Gen. Scheele, part of which belonged to the first, and part to the second line of the army'. The problem was that Scheele had no desire to move anywhere and claimed to have orders from Ferdinand to stay out of range of the fortress guns of Minden.

By that time, Ferdinand himself had moved off and was by now bringing forward Anhalt's piquets in a forlorn attempt to press the retreating French as they re-crossed the Bastau, so Sackville sent one of his aides, Captain Smith to 'acquaint the Prince, that the cavalry was halted in the rear of the infantry, where they could be of no service; and desired to know if he had any commands for them'.[32]

His Serene Highness did indeed, and called for the cavalry to come down, but once again it was too late. Early though the hour was, the hurly-burly was done; the battle lost and won. The French were not only in full retreat, but covered by their rearguards they were already safely out of danger.

Chapter 8

Afterwards

The French lost 7,086 men killed, wounded and taken at Minden. In addition to the prisoners, many of them wounded, the Allies also captured forty-three guns, ten infantry colours and seven cavalry standards. In return, Ferdinand lost 2,822 men, half of them belonging to the six British battalions. Arguably the victory might have been more complete had Sackville brought his squadrons of cavalry up in sufficient time to fight. Ferdinand certainly pretended this was the case and Savory's trenchant assertion that Sackville's supposed reluctance to move forward meant that 'one of the greatest opportunities for cavalry in the whole of military history was lost forever' is a wholly unjustified exercise in hyperbole.[1] If that formidable Prussian, Holstein-Gottorp, was unable to destroy the French right, it is wholly unrealistic to expect the relatively inexperienced Sackville to do better against their left.

Nevertheless, in spite of everything, the French were defeated and next day the victory required to be loudly proclaimed with a *feu de joie* and *Te Deum*, and a laudatory Order of the Day published. The latter was a disappointingly petulant affair in which Ferdinand heaped praise on a number of his subordinates, not all of whom deserved it, and pointedly omitted the names of Anhalt and Sackville. Neither, to be sure, had contributed anything substantive to the outcome, but in the case of the latter, the omission was emphasised by the writing of a personal letter of thanks to Forbes Macbean, who had been accidentally left off the acknowledgements, and more extraordinarily by a paragraph in the orders which read as follows: 'His Serene Highness further orders to be declared to Lieutenant General the Marquis of Granby [who had done nothing] that he is persuaded, that if he had the good fortune to have had him at the head of the cavalry of the right wing, his presence would have contributed to make the decision of that day more complete and more brilliant.'

Thus the assassination of Lord George Sackville began.[2] When all is said and done, he may not have been a particularly distinguished commander, but his real failing, as we saw in an earlier chapter, was political rather than military. Ferdinand's confidence in him was already fatally damaged by that warning of a possible British withdrawal and so his alleged unwillingness to co-operate at Minden meant that he made an admirable scapegoat for a battle that had so nearly ended in disaster. Sackville's downfall was a protracted affair which throws no credit on those involved, from Ferdinand on down – who from various motives of ambition, spite and politics contrived to force his recall and his replacement by the far more complaisant Lord Granby, who could be relied upon to make no difficulties of a political or financial nature. In the coming weeks a surprised and bewildered Sackville found his position become increasing uncomfortable to the point where both he and the British government recognised the need for his return home. The decision coincided with a blunt (and mendacious) letter to the King in which Ferdinand wrote: 'I dare to insist on the re-call of the said Lord George Sackville; I dare also very humbly hope that Your Majesty will give it serious attention by making this essential change at once. Otherwise I find myself obliged to state frankly that I will not be responsible for what might follow; and that, without this prompt change, I will be of no more use to this army.'[3] In other words it was either Sackville or Ferdinand. The ultimatum was unnecessary but vindictive as ever. King George immediately deprived Sackville of his regiment and announced that he had no further need of his services. He, for his part, demanded, and grudgingly received, the courtesy of a Court Martial, in which the generals appointed to sit in judgement bent over backwards to demonstrate their fairness and impartiality before eventually delivering a verdict of guilty on the bare charge of disobeying orders. As Lord George had hoped, to all intents and purposes the trial vindicated him, save in the eyes of partisan historians who seemingly never troubled themselves to actually read and evaluate the evidence presented.[4]

Sackville could certainly have performed better than he did, but his greatest fault on the battlefield was the simple fact that he was not bred up a cavalryman. Although periodically carried on the books of a number of cavalry regiments, his previous service had been in the infantry or as a staff officer. In both of these roles he had performed well and earned his position as commander of the British contingent in Germany, but he was no *beau sabreur*, although in the end it might be argued that it might have been better had he *not* obeyed those orders, but acted according to his own judgement.

Be that as it may, despite the short duration of the battle, the French admitted themselves beaten and badly beaten at that. The Erbprinz's simultaneous victory at Gofeld had cut the road to Paderborn and neither Contades nor Broglie had any stomach for fighting their way back into Westphalia; especially if the Erbprinz moved to block the Porta Westfalica. Instead, while Broglie held Minden Contades evacuated the camp behind the Bastau, withdrawing his army across the pontoon bridges on to the right or east bank of the Weser. As soon as this was done, Broglie then in turn abandoned Minden, blowing up the bridge behind him. By dawn on 2 August both generals were fleeing southwards for Frankfurt.

Ferdinand was slow to follow. To be sure the grim task of clearing the battlefield had to be performed and the surrender of Minden negotiated, but he at first made little effort to track the French retreat and was uncertain as to their destination. They were in fact making for Kassel down the right or east bank of the Weser, but Ferdinand, while hopeful of getting there first, also wanted to recover Münster and relieve Lippstadt and therefore marched through Westphalia. Lippstadt was safe but otherwise the operation was a failure. Münster was evacuated by the French on 2 August, but next day the *Volontaires Etrangers de Clermont Prince* re-occupied it. The original garrison was ordered back and it then took three-and-a-half months to dig them out. All in all, the end of the campaign was an anticlimactic affair. The French had been driven from Westphalia and the threat both to Ferdinand's beleaguered army and to Hanover itself was comprehensively banished, but the war was to go on for three more futile years.

If there was a solid achievement it was in the establishment of the British infantry as an elite force – by the most exacting European standards. Their reputation, deservedly, was now made and the buccaneering at Ste. Malo was far behind them. 'Twas a famous victory', and while still celebrated by the Minden regiments[5] it is a pity that their brigadiers, Kingsley and Waldgrave, and above all *General der Infantrie* August Friedrich von Spörcken, are not better remembered as well, for it was indeed an impossible victory.

Appendix I

Orders of Battle at Minden, 1 August 1759

Allied Order of Battle

Ferdinand's army did not form a continuous battle-line and is best enumerated by reference to the various columns which marched on to the field and deployed more or less independently of each other. The columns are described here by number starting with the First Column which was intended to form the right of the Allied army.

- First column: cavalry of the right wing
- Second column: artillery of the right wing
- Third and Fourth columns: infantry of the right wing
- Fifth column: artillery of the centre
- Sixth and Seventh column: infantry of the left wing
- Eighth column: cavalry of the left wing

It should be noted however that even then the deployments of the various units were not consistent. The cavalry of the first column under Sackville actually formed up behind the guns and escorting infantry of the Second column under Major Haase.

In addition to the troops under Prince Ferdinand's immediate command, Wangenheim's forces are also listed, but not the various detachments under the Erbprinz and Gilsa not actively engaged in the battle.

In describing the brigades individual units are listed where possible in order from the right.[1]

FIRST COLUMN:

Lieutenant General Lord George Sackville
Major General John Mostyn's Brigade[2] (right of first line)

Bland's 1st Dragoon Guards
Lieutenant Colonel Robert Sloper   3 sqdns
Red coat, faced blue; blue waistcoat and breeches, yellow lace with button
loops set in pairs.[3] Saddle-housings red edged yellow with blue stripe.
Cypher with crowned garter. Crowned cypher on holster caps.

Cholmondley's 6th Dragoons (Inniskillings)
Major Robert Hepburn[4]   2 sqdns
Red coat, faced yellow; yellow waistcoat and breeches, white lace with
loops set in pairs. Saddle-housings yellow edged white with blue stripe.
Triple-towered castle on green surrounded by wreath. Crowned cypher on
holster caps.

Royal Regiment of Horse Guards Blue.
Lieutenant Colonel James Johnston   3 sqdns
Dark blue coat, faced red; red waistcoat and breeches. Brass buttons on
coats and gold lace on hat. Saddle-housings red edged yellow with blue
stripe. Cypher within crowned garter. Holster caps same

Oberst **Georg Karl von Breidenbach's Brigade** (left of first line)

Grenadieren zu Pferde (Hanoverian)   1 sqdn
Red coat, faced black (red turnbacks); straw coloured waistcoat and
breeches. Black grenadier caps worn by troopers. Saddle-housings red with
border from inner edge out yellow-black-yellow-yellow-crimson zig-zag
then thick yellow line with black diamonds; gold Royal cypher crowned.
Holster caps the same.

Breidenbach *Dragooner* (Hanoverian)   4 sqdns
White coat, faced light blue; straw coloured waistcoat and breeches, white
lace. Grenadier troop with caps. Saddle-housings light blue border from
the inner edge out, lines of black-white-red-white-red-white-black; emblem
of a white horse on red ground over green turf in a white floral wreath
surmounted by a gold crown with red interior. Holster caps the same.

Garde du Corps (Hanoverian)   1 sqdn
Red coat, red cuffs and dark blue turnbacks; straw coloured waistcoat and

Above: Ferdinand of Brunswick (1721-92), commander in chief of His Britannic Majesty's Army in Germany from November 1757 to the war's end. Engraving after portrait by Georg Zeisnis depicting him in the buff-faced dark blue uniform of an officer of the Prussian Infantrie-Regiment Nr.39 adorned with the star of the Order of the Garter, awarded by King George II in recognition of his victory at Minden.

Left: Lord George Sackville (1716-85) after a portrait by Reynolds painted during the winter of 1758-1759 and which captures his character admirably. The fur-trimmed Hungarian-style coat is a personal affectation unsanctioned by any regulations. (Anne S.K. Brown Military Collection, Brown University Library)

Left: *General der Infantrie* August Friedrich von Spörcken (1698-1776). Seemingly regarded as a dependable, well-liked, but undistinguished officer, his action at Minden, in command of the British infantry, was undoubtedly the highlight of his career.

Major General William Kingsley (1698?-1769). According to the Dictionary of National Biography, 'He was an outspoken, independent Englishman, extremely popular with his soldiers, and an active freemason'.

A depiction of a British
infantryman after a
contemporary watercolour
sketch by Paul Sandby. While
18th century uniforms are often
characterised as tight and
impractical, this soldier, typical
of those who fought at Minden,
is clearly a comfortable and self-
reliant individual.

This British infantry officer appears in the 1759 Plan of Discipline for the County of Norfolk. He is identified as a militia officer by the lace loops on his coat, but otherwise gives a good impression of a typical subaltern of his day.

Above left: A contemporary engraving of an unknown British staff officer. Note the single-breasted coat with elaborately embroidered button-holes, indicating his status. (Anne S.K. Brown Military Collection, Brown University Library) Above right: A Grenadier of the Hanoverian *Garde* at Minden, by Richard Knotel. His appearance is slightly anachronistic in that the grenadier companies provided security for Ferdinand's headquarters and did not take part in Spörcken's action. However, an officer of Hardenberg's Regiment can be seen in the background.

Below left: Prussian Dragoons of the Regiment Holstein-Gottorp, by Knötel. This was one of the two Prussian dragoon regiments lent to Ferdinand, fighting on the right wing at Minden. Like all Prussian dragoons they wore light blue coats and in this case had light blue facings as well. Below right: A Hessian Grenadier of Regiment von Canitz. The musketier companies of this regiment served under the Erbprinz at Gofeld on 1 August 1759 but the grenadiers were with Wangenheim's corps at Minden.

Above left: 2nd Royal North British Dragoons. Distinguished famously by their grey horses and grenadier caps, the Greys served in the second line of Sackville's cavalry division on the left wing at Minden. Above right: A Trooper of the French cavalry regiment *Royal Allemand*, by Knötel. This German regiment was posted on the French right at Minden but its uniform is very similar to that of the *Royal Cravattes* which took part in the initial charge against Waldegrave's brigade. Note the bearskin cap worn by many foreign cavalry units in the French army.

Below left: Typical Hanoverian light troops depicted by Knötel. We can see a carabinier of Schiether's Freikorps in a white coat faced with green and, in the background, one of Luckner's Hussars, again in white but with a red pelisse and yellow boots. Below right: A Hussar of the *Chasseurs de Fischer* by Knötel. This particular regiment survived until the Revolution as the *Hussards de Conflans* and was the regiment of Conan Doyle's fictional Brigadier Gerard.

Left: An infantryman of the Chasseurs de Fischer, by Edmond Lajour.

Below: French infantry making ready to fire. The four-deep firing line depicted here, by Colonel Badouin, had been reduced to three ranks by 1759.

breeches, silver lace. Saddle-housings red edged silver, cypher in crowned garter. Holster caps same

Lieutenant General John Manners, Marquis of Granby (second line)
Major General Granville Elliot's Brigade[5] (right of second line)

Howard's 3rd Dragoon Guards
Lieutenant Colonel Flower Mocher   2 sqdns
Red coat, faced white; white waistcoat and breeches, yellow lace with loops set in pairs. Saddle-housings white edged yellow with central red stripe. Roman number in red surrounded by wreath. Crowned cypher on holster caps

Mordaunt's 10th Dragoons
Lieutenant Colonel William Augustus Pitt   2 sqdns
Red coat, deep yellow facings; yellow waistcoat and breeches, white lace with loops set three, four and five. Saddle-housings yellow edged white with green stripe. Roman number in red surrounded by wreath. Crowned cypher on holster caps

2nd Royal North British Dragoons
Lieutenant Colonel George Preston   2 sqdns
Red coat, dark blue facings; blue waistcoat and breeches, white lace with loops set in pairs. Grenadier caps. Belts white rather than buff. Saddle-housings blue edged yellow with blue stripe. Thistle on red within crowned strap of St. Andrew. Crowned cypher on holster caps.

Oberst **Ernst Wilhelm von Bock's Brigade** (left of second line)

Bremer *Kurassiere* (Hanoverian)   2 sqdns
White coat, apple green cuffs and turnbacks. Straw coloured waistcoat and breeches, white lace. Saddle housings apple green; border pattern of red, blue, yellow and white leaves; white horse on red ground over green turf within crowned garter. Holster caps same.

Weltheim *Kurassiere* (Hanoverian)   2 sqdns
White coat, bright blue cuffs and turnbacks. Straw coloured waistcoat and breeches, white lace. Saddle-housings bright blue; border from inner edge out red-yellow-red line, part discs yellow-red-yellow, wavy line checked dark blue/white, part discs red-yellow-red, yellow-red-yellow line; crowned cypher in white. Holster caps same.

SECOND COLUMN:

Major Haase (or Hasse), Hanoverian artillery

Twenty-eight pieces of artillery and two howitzers including British guns:

Captain Forbes MacBean[6]
ten medium 12-pounders manned by men of his own and Captain Phillips' companies

Captain-Lieutenant Edward Foy
four light 12-pounders, three light 6-pounders and two howitzers

Sachsen-Gotha *Infantrie* (Hanoverian)   1 Bn
Red coat, green facings; white waistcoat, straw coloured breeches, white lace – paired loops on coat. Black gaiters.

THIRD COLUMN:

General der Infantrie **August Friedrich von Spörcken**[7]
Lieutenant General John Waldegrave (first line)[8]

Napier's 12th Foot
Lieutenant Colonel William Robinson   1 Bn (541)[9]
Red coat, yellow facings; red waistcoat and breeches, white lace. Black or grey gaiters.

Stewart's 37th Foot
Lieutenant Colonel James Adolphus Oughton   1 Bn (460)
Red coat, brownish yellow facings, red waistcoat and breeches, white lace. Black or grey gaiters.

23rd Royal Welch Fusiliers
Lieutenant Colonel Edward Sacheverel Pole   1 Bn (548)
Red coat, dark blue facings, red waistcoat and breeches, white lace. Rank and file wearing fusilier caps. Black or grey gaiters.

Füss-garde (Hanoverian)   2 Bns*
Red coat, dark blue facings; blue waistcoat and straw coloured breeches, yellow lace. Yellow over white pom-pom in hat.
Probably black gaiters.
Grenadiers detached as Ferdinand's headquarters guard.

Major General William Kingsley's Brigade (second line)[10]

Kingsley's 20th Foot
Lieutenant Colonel John Beckwith   1 Bn (507)
Red coat, yellow facings; red waistcoat and breeches, white lace. Black or grey gaiters.

Brudenell's 51st Foot
Lieutenant Colonel Noel Fury   1 Bn (422)
Red coat, gosling-green facings; red waistcoat and green (?) breeches, white lace. Black or grey gaiters.

Home's 25th Foot
Lieutenant Colonel George Scott   1 Bn (513)
Red coat, yellow facings; red waistcoat and breeches, white lace. Black or grey gaiters.

FOURTH COLUMN:

Generalmajor **Johann Daniel Victor von Scheele** (first line)*

*This division was officially commanded by Generalleutnant *Karl Leopold, Prinz von Anhalt-Bernburg, but as he was acting as lieutenant general of the day, Scheele, as senior brigade commander, took over.*

IR Hardenberg (Hanoverian)   1 Bn
Red coat, orange facings; orange waistcoat and straw coloured breeches, white lace – paired loops on coat. Orange pom-pom in hat. Probably black gaiters.

IR Reden (Hanoverian)   1 Bn
Red coat, black facings and white turnbacks; white waistcoat and straw coloured breeches, white lace – paired loops on coat. Black over red pom-pom. Probably black gaiters.

IR Scheele (Hanoverian)   1 Bn
Red coat, straw coloured facings, waistcoat and breeches, white lace – paired loops on coat. Red over yellow pom-pom. Probably black gaiters.

Generalmajor **Heinrich von Wissenbach's Brigade** (second line)

IR Stolzenburg (Hanoverian)   1 Bn

Red coat, black facings and red turnbacks; straw coloured waistcoat and breeches, white lace – paired loops on coat. Red over black pom-pom. Probably black gaiters.

IR Estorff (Hanoverian)   1 Bn
Red coat, grass-green facings and turnbacks; grass-green waistcoat and straw coloured breeches, white lace – paired loops on coat. Red over green pom-pom. Probably black gaiters.

IR Erbprinz (Hessian)   1 Bn
Dark blue coat, yellow coloured facings and red turnbacks, straw coloured waistcoat; dark blue breeches, white lace – paired loops on coat. Yellow pom-pom. Black gaiters.

FIFTH COLUMN:

Oberstleutnant **Anton Ulrich Braun**, Hanoverian artillery

Sixteen pieces of artillery and four howitzers including British guns:

Captain-Lieutenant Duncan Drummond
two light 12-pounders, three light 6-pounders and four howitzers

SIXTH COLUMN:

Generalleutnant **Heinrich Wilhelm von Wutginau**
Generalmajor **Georg Heinrich von Toll's Brigade** (first line)

IR Wangenheim (Hanoverian)   1 Bn
Red coat, straw coloured facings; straw coloured waistcoat and breeches, white lace – paired loops on coat. Straw-coloured pom-pom. Probably black gaiters.

Leib-Garde zu Fuss (Hessian)   1 Bn
Dark blue coat faced red; straw coloured waistcoat, dark blue breeches, white lace – paired loops on coat. Red pom-pom with white centre spot. Black gaiters.

IR Toll (Hessian)   1 Bn
Dark blue coat, orange facings and red turnbacks; straw coloured waistcoat; dark blue breeches, white lace – paired loops on coat. Orange pom-pom. Black gaiters.

Schaumberg-Lippe Buckeburg Artillerie eight 6-pounders

Generalmajor **Friedrich August von Bischhausen's Brigade** (second line)

IR Anhalt (Hessian)   1 Bn
Dark blue coat, red facings; straw coloured waistcoat, dark blue breeches, white lace – paired loops on coat. Blue pom-pom with dark blue spot in centre. Black gaiters.

IR Bischhausen (Hessian)   1 Bn
Dark blue coat, straw coloured facings and red turnbacks; straw coloured waistcoat and dark blue breeches, white lace – paired loops on coat. Straw-coloured pom-pom. Black gaiters.

IR Mansbach (Hessian)   1 Bn
Dark blue coat, white facings and red turnbacks; straw coloured waistcoat, dark blue breeches, white lace – paired loops on coat. White pom-pom. Black gaiters.

SEVENTH COLUMN:
Generalleutnant **Philip Ernst von Imhoff**
Generalmajor **Victor August von Einsiedel's Brigade** (first line)

IR Gilsa (Hessian)   1 Bn
Dark blue coat, red facings; straw coloured waistcoat and breeches, white lace on hat but none on coat. Red pom-pom with white spot in centre. Black gaiters.

IR Prinz Wilhelm (Hessian)   1 Bn
Dark blue coat, dark rose red facings; straw coloured waistcoat and breeches, white lace – paired loops on coat. White pom-pom with dark rose spot in centre. Black gaiters.

Grenadieren Regiment (Hessian)   1 Bn
Dark blue coat, red facings; straw coloured waistcoat; dark blue breeches, white lace – paired loops on coat. Rank and file in tin-fronted grenadier caps with straw-coloured bag at rear. White pom-pom. Black gaiters.

IR Behr 2/*bataillon* (Brunswick)   1 Bn
Dark blue coat, red facings; white waistcoat and breeches, white lace. Red pom-pom topped white. Black gaiters.

Generalmajor **Johan Freidrich von Behr's Brigade** (second line)

Leib Regiment (Hessian)   1 Bn
Dark blue coat, red facings but no lapels; straw coloured waistcoat and dark blue breeches, yellow lace in paired loops on coat, white lace on hat. Yellow pom-pom. Black gaiters.

IR Imhoff (Brunswick)   2 Bns
Dark blue coat, white facings; white waistcoat and breeches, white lace. Blue pom-pom topped white. Black gaiters.

EIGHTH COLUMN:

George Lüdwig, Herzog von Holstein-Gottorp (front line)[11]

Hammerstein *Kurassiere* (Hanoverian)   2 sqdns

White single-breasted coat, dark green facings; straw coloured waistcoat and chamois breeches, yellow lace. White over green pom-pom.
Saddle-housings dark green with border from inner edge out red-yellow-red wavy line spiralling around similar white-red-white wavy line, outer line of diagonal stripes with the pattern blue-white-red-white-yellow-white-black-white-blue, etc. Royal cypher on red within crowned garter. Holster caps the same.

Leib-Regiment (Hessian)   2 sqdns
White coat, red collar, cuffs, lapels and turnbacks. Buff waistcoat and chamois breeches. Yellow lace. Saddle-housings red edged with a yellow braid decorated with a red stripe; a golden armed and crowned Hessian lion in the rear corner. Holster caps the same.

Reiter-Regiment Prinz Wilhelm (Hessian)   2 sqdns
White coat, blue collar, cuffs, lapels and turnbacks.Buff waistcoat and chamois breeches. Yellow lace. Saddle-housings blue edged with a white braid decorated with a blue stripe; a golden crowned and armed Hessian lion in the rear corner. Holster caps the same.

Holstein-Gottorp Dragoons (Prussian)   5 sqdns
Sky-blue coat, collar, cuffs and turnbacks. Straw coloured waistcoat and breeches. Thin white lace loops paired on coat. Black binding on hat. Saddle-housings blue with pointed corners; bordered with a wide white braid decorated with 2 thin red braids. Holster caps the same.

Generalmajor **Karl Ludwig von Urff aus Neiderurff's Brigade** (second line)

Reiter-Regiment von Miltitz (Hessian)   2 sqdns
White coat, green collar, cuffs, lapels and turnbacks. Buff waistcoat and
chamois breeches. Yellow lace. Saddle-housings green edged with a yellow
braid decorated with a medium green stripe; a golden armed and crowned
Hessian lion in the rear corner. Holster caps the same.

Reiter-Regiment von Prüscheck (Hessian)   2 sqdns
White coat, light blue collar, cuffs, lapels and turnbacks. Buff waistcoat and
breeches. White lace. Saddle-housings light blue edged with a white braid
decorated with a sky blue stripe; a golden crowned and armed Hessian lion
in the rear corner. Holster caps the same.

Finckenstein Dragoons (Prussian)   5 sqdn
Sky-blue coat, orange collar, cuffs and turnbacks. Straw coloured waistcoat
and breeches. Thin white lace loops paired on coat. Black binding on hat.
Saddle-housings orange with pointed corners; bordered with a wide white
braid. Holster caps the same.

GENERAL-LEUTNANT Georg August von Wangenheim's Corps[12]

This was drawn-up between the village of Kutenhausen and the Weser. Once
Ferdinand's own forces were in position his left wing under Holstein-Gottorp
was in contact with Wangenheim's right. The unusual deployment reflects the
obstacles created by Kutenhausen and by the entrenchments in front of
Todhausen.

Generalmajor Johann Wilhelm von Reden's Brigade (front line)

Leib-Dragooner (Hessian)   2 sqdns
Dark blue coat, red collar, cuffs, lapels and turnbacks. Buff waistcoat and
chamois breeches. Yellow lace on hat. Saddle-housings red with yellow
border decorated with a thin red stripe; the crowned cipher of Wilhelm VIII
in gold in the rear corner. Holster caps same.

Dragooner-Regiment Prinz Friedrich (Hessian)   2 sqdns
Dark blue coat, yellow collar, cuffs, lapels and turnbacks. Buff waistcoat
and breeches. White lace on hat. Saddle-housings yellow with white border
decorated with a thin yellow line. Holster caps the same.

Generalmajor Ernst Friedrich Carl von Hanstein's Brigade (second line)

Leib-Regiment Reiter (Hanoverian)   2 sqdns
White coat, yellow facings; straw waistcoat and chamois breeches. White

lace on hat. Red pom-poms. Saddle-housings yellow; border from inner edge out floral pattern of crimson, green, and white. Royal cypher on red within crowned garter. Holster caps the same.

Generalmajor **Ernst Philip Grothaus's Brigade** (second line)

Reden *Kurassiere* (Hanoverian) 2 sqdns
White coat, dark blue facings; straw waistcoat and chamois breeches. White lace on hat. Dark blue pom-pom Saddle-housings dark blue; border from inner edge out a crimson-green-white leaf pattern, border of white/yellow diagonal lines. White horse on red within crowned garter. Holster caps the same.

Heise *Kurassiere* (Hanoverian) 2 sqdns
White coat, orange facings; straw waistcoat and chamois breeches. White lace on hat. Red pom-pom. Saddle-housings orange; border from inner edge out yellow line, green line with yellow zig-zag superimposed, yellow-orange-yellow line, green line with yellow zig-zag superimposed, yellow line. White horse on red within crowned garter. Holster caps the same.

Hodenburg *Kurassiere* (Hanoverian) 2 sqdns
White coat, red facings; straw waistcoat and chamois breeches. White lace on hat. Blue pom-poms. Saddle-housings border from inner edge out lines of yellow-white-yellow-red-yellow-white-yellow. Cypher on red within crowned garter surrounded by white leaves. Holster caps the same.

Grothaus *Kurassiere* (Hanoverian) 2 sqdns
White coat, crimson facings; straw waistcoat and chamois breeches. White lace on hat. White over green pom-poms. Saddle-housings crimson, border a white chain pattern on red with a yellow and black line on each side. White horse on red within crowned garter. Holster caps the same.

(Third line) Ruesch *Husaren* (Hanoverian) 2 sqdns
Black dolman with white cords and trim; chamois breeches, red sash. Black *flügelmutze* with white skull and cross-bones

Infantrie (brigade commanders unknown)

IR Keilmannsegg (Hanoverian) 1 Bn
Red Coat, light green facings; straw coloured waistcoat and breeches, white lace. Red over green pom-pom. Probably black gaiters.

IR Spörcken (Hanoverian) 1 Bn

Red Coat, straw coloured facings; light green waistcoat and straw coloured breeches, yellow lace. Yellow over red pom-pom. Probably black gaiters.

IR Jung Zastrow (Hanoverian)   1 Bn
Red Coat, dark green facings; dark green waistcoat and straw coloured breeches, white lace. White over red pom-poms. Probably black gaiters.

IR Halberstadt (Hanoverian)   1 Bn
Red Coat, blue facings; blue waistcoat and straw coloured breeches, white lace. Red over yellow pom-poms. Probably black gaiters.

IR Schulenberg (Hanoverian)   1 Bn
Red Coat, black cuffs and lapels, straw coloured turnbacks; straw coloured waistcoat and breeches, white lace. Red over black pom-poms. Probably black gaiters.

IR Oberg (Hanoverian)   1 Bn
Red Coat, yellow facings; yellow waistcoat and straw coloured breeches, white lace. Yellow over red pom-pom. Probably black gaiters.

IR Laffert (Hanoverian)   1 Bn
Red Coat, deep yellow facings; deep yellow waistcoat and straw coloured breeches, white lace. Red over yellow pom-pom. Probably black gaiters.

IR Scheither (Hanoverian)   1 Bn
Red Coat, dark green facings; dark green waistcoat and straw coloured breeches, white lace. Green over red pom-pom. Probably black gaiters.

Prinz Friederich Karl Ferdinand von Bevern's *Grenadieren* Brigade[13]

Hanoverian *Grenadieren* Major von Wersebe   1 Bn

Spörcken Coy.
cap: brass front. Red bag over straw band. Yellow lace. Mixed yellow/red pom-pom.

Oberg Coy.
ap: yellow front; cypher within crowned garter. Red frontlet. Red bag over straw band; yellow lace. Mixed yellow/red pom-pom.

Keilmannsegg Coy.
cap: grass-green front and frontlet, cypher within crowned garter. Red bag over grass-green band; white lace. Mixed red/green pom-pom.

Jung-Zastrow Coy.
cap: dark green front, white horse on red within crowned garter. Red bag over green band; white lace. Mixed red/white pom-pom.

Scheither Coy.
cap: green front, with brass frontlet and brass royal arms. Red bag over dark green; white lace. Brass grenade badge to rear. Mixed red/green pom-pom.

Halberstadt Coy.
cap: yellow front with red frontlet, white horse on red within crowned garter. Red bag over yellow band, white lace. Mixed red/yellow pom-pom.

Laffert Coy.
cap: straw front with red frontlet, white horse on red within crowned garter over blue ribbon. Red bag over straw band, white lace. Mixed red/yellow pom-pom.

Schulenburg Coy.
cap: black front and frontlet. Brass royal arms on front and brass horse on frontlet. Red bag over black band. Brass grenade on rear and yellow lace. Mixed red/black pom-pom.

British Grenadiers

Major John Maxwell (20th Foot)   1 Bn

12th Foot
cap: yellow front embroidered with the King's cypher in red and a crown over it; a small red front flap with white horse. Red bag; yellow band wearing the number XII in red. White lace.

20th Foot
cap: pale yellow front embroidered with the King's cypher in red and a crown over it; a small red front flap with white horse. Red bag; yellow band wearing the number XX in red. White lace.

23rd Fusiliers
cap: dark blue front embroidered with three Prince of Wales feathers; a small red front flap with white horse. Red bag; dark blue band. White lace.

25th Foot
cap: deep yellow front embroidered with the King's cypher in red and a

crown over it; a small red front flap with white horse. Red bag; yellow band bearing the number XXV in red. White lace.

37th Foot
cap: pale yellow front embroidered with the King's cypher in red and a crown over it; a small red front flap with white horse. Red bag; yellow band bearing the number XXXVII in red. White lace.

51st Foot
cap: gosling-green front embroidered with the King's cypher in red and a crown over it; a small red front flap with white horse. Red bag; gosling green band. White lace.

Hessian *Grenadieren* von Donop	1 Bn
Hessian *Grenadieren* von Schlotheim	1 Bn
Brunswick *Grenadieren* von Stammer *Leib-Regiment* IR Imhoff brass plates on caps	1 Bn
Brunswick *Grenadiern* von Wittorff IR BehrIR Zastrow tin plates on caps	1 Bn

Artillerie under Graf zu Schaumburg-Lippe-Buckeburg[14]
Hessian *Artillerie* (3 coys) under *Oberst-leutnant* Heinrich Wilhelm von Huth

Sixteen 12-pounders
Four 6-pounders
Two 3-pounders
Two howitzers

Schaumburg-Lippe-Bückeburg *Artillerie*

Six 6-pounders
Ten 3-pounders

Schaumburg-Lippe-Buckeburg *Infantrie*(escorting artillery)	1 Bn

Blue coat, red facings; white waistcoat and breeches. White lace. Grenadier company (not detached) distinguished by blue cuffs and Prussian-style fusilier cap with dark blue conical bag and low brass front.

2 French Order of Battle

Main Army under *Maréchal* de Contades deployed in front of the fortress of Minden

Left Wing Infantry (deployed around Hahlen)

Lieutenant General Claude-Louis-François de Régnier, Comte de Guerchy (first line)

Thirty pieces of artillery

Champagne **Brigade** (in Hahlen)

Regiment *Champagne*   4 Bns
White coat, cuffs and lining; red waistcoat and white breeches. Gold lace on hat. White gaiters.

Du Roi **Brigade**

Regiment *du Roi*   4 Bns
White coat, blue cuffs and lining with light orange buttonhole loops in three closely set groups of three on front, and three individual loops on each cuff and pocket; blue waistcoat with individual loops, and blue breeches. Gold lace on hat. White gaiters.

Aquitaine **Brigade**

Regiment *Aquitaine*   2 Bns
White coat and lining, blue cuffs and collar; blue waistcoat and white breeches. Gold lace on hat. White gaiters.

Regiment *Vastan*   2 Bns
White coat, cuffs and lining, black collar; red waistcoat and white breeches. Gold lace on hat. White gaiters.

Condé **Brigade**

Regiment *Condé*   2 Bns
White coat and lining, red cuffs and collar; red waistcoat and white breeches. Gold lace on hat. White gaiters.

Regiment *Enghien*   2 Bns

White coat and lining, red cuffs and collar; red waistcoat and white breeches. Silver lace on hat. White gaiters.

Saxon Contingent: Lieutenant General Comte de Lusace (Prinz Xaver Franz of Saxony)

First Saxon Brigade (second line, behind Hahlen)

Garde   1 Bn
White coat, red collar, cuffs, lapels and lining; red waistcoat and white breeches. White lace on hat with red over white pom-pom. Black gaiters.

IR Prinz Karl Maximilian   1 Bn
White coat, green collar, cuffs, lapels and lining; green waistcoat and white breeches. White lace on hat with green over white pom-pom. Black gaiters.

IR Prinz Xaver   2 Bns
White coat, light blue collar, lapels cuffs and lining; light blue waistcoat and white breeches. White lace on hat with light blue over white pom-pom. Black gaiters.

IR Prinz Friedrich August   2 Bns
White coat, yellow collar, lapels, cuffs and lining; yellow waistcoat and white breeches. White lace on hat with yellow over white pom-pom. Black gaiters.

IR Prinz Josef   1 Bn
White coat, no lapels, crimson collar, cuffs and lining; crimson waistcoat and white breeches. White lace on hat with crimson over white pom-pom. Black gaiters.

IR Prinz Clemens   1 Bn
White coat, light blue collar, lapels, cuffs and lining; light blue waistcoat and white breeches. White lace on hat with light blue over white pom-pom. Black gaiters.

IR Fürst Lubomirski   1 Bn
White coat, yellow collar, lapels, cuffs and lining; yellow waistcoat and white breeches. White lace on hat with yellow over white pom-pom. Black gaiters.

Second Saxon Brigade (second line on right of First Brigade)

Fus. Regt. Rochow   1 Bn

Uncertain. Original regiment which surrendered at Pirna had green coats faced with red.

IR Graf Bruhl 1 Bn
White coat, red collar, cuffs, lapels and lining; red waistcoat and white breeches. White lace on hat with red over white pom-pom. Black gaiters.

IR Prinz Anton 1 Bn
White coat, sky blue collar, cuffs, lapels and lining; sky blue waistcoat and white breeches. White lace on hat with sky blue over white pom-pom.

IR Prinz Sachsen-Gotha 1 Bn
White coat, light blue collar, cuffs lapels and lining; light blue waistcoat and white breeches. White lace on hat with light blue over white pom-pom. Black gaiters.

IR Kurprinzessin 2 Bns
White coat, mid-blue collar, cuffs, lapels and lining; mid-blue waistcoat and white breeches. White lace on hat with light blue over white pom-pom. Black gaiters.

Centre (cavalry) Lieutenant General Charles, Duc de Fitz-James Lieutenant General, Charles Eugene Gabriel, Marquis de Castries (front line)

Mestre-de-Camp Brigade

Mestre-de-Camp General Cavallerie 2 sqdns
Iron grey coat and lining, black cuffs and lapels, white button-hole lace; buff waistcoat and breeches. Gold lace on hat. Yellow carbine belt. Saddle-housings red edged with a yellow and orange striped braid decorated with an embroidered stack of 5 standards. Holster caps the same.

Fumel Cavallerie 2 sqdns
White coat, red cuffs, lapels and lining; buff waistcoat and breeches. Silver lace on hat. Buff carbine belt. Blue saddle housings edged yellow with red central stripe.

Espinchal Cavallerie 2 sqdns
White coat, red lapels, cuffs and lining; buff waistcoat and breeches. Gold lace on hat. Buff carbine belt. Blue saddle-housings edged green with white central stripe.

Poly Cavallerie   2 sqdns
White coat, red lapels, cuffs and lining; buff waistcoat and red breeches.
Silver lace on hat. Yellow carbine belt. Blue saddle-housings edged yellow
with black central stripe.

Royal Cravattes **Brigade**

Royal Cravattes Cavallerie   2 sqdns
Blue coat and lining, red cuffs and lapels, white button-hole lace; buff
waistcoat and breeches. Bearskin cap with red bag. White carbine belt. Blue
saddle housings edged with orange braid with blue, white, red squares.

La Rochefoucault de Surgeré Cavallerie   2 sqdns
White coat, red collar, cuffs, lapels and lining; buff waistcoat and breeches.
Silver lace on hat. Buff carbine belt. Blue saddle housings edged black with
buff central stripe.

Talleyrand Cavallerie   2 sqdns
White coat, red lapels, cuffs and lining; buff waistcoat and breeches. Gold
lace on hat. Buff carbine belt. Blue saddle-housings edged with coffee and
green squares.

Colonel-General **Brigade**

Colonel-General Cavallerie   3 sqdns
Red coat and lining, black cuffs and lapels; buff waistcoat and breeches.
Gold lace on hat. White carbine belt. Red saddle housings edged with black
and white checks.

Marcieu Cavallerie   2 sqdns
White coat, red cuffs, lapels and lining; buff waistcoat and breeches. Silver
lace on hat. Yellow carbine belt. Blue saddle housings edged blue with buff
stripe.

Vogue Cavallerie   2 sqdns
White coat, red lapels, cuffs and lining; buff waistcoat and breeches. Gold
lace on hat. Yellow carbine belt. Blue saddle-housings edged green with red
stripe.

Conde Cavallerie   2 sqdns
White coat, red cuffs, lapels and lining; buff waistcoat and breeches. Silver
lace on hat. White carbine belt. Blue saddle housings edged with crimson.

Lieutenant General Charles-Louis Joachim, Marquis of Chastellier-Du Mesnil (second line)

Royal Etranger **Brigade**

Royal Etranger Cavallerie   2 sqdns
Blue coat, red cuffs and lapels, blue lining; buff waistcoat and breeches. Gold lace on hat. White carbine belt. Saddle-housings blue, edged with orange with blue chain alternately filled white and yellow.

Crussol Cavallerie   2 sqdns
White coat, red cuffs, lapels and lining; buff waistcoat and breeches. Silver lace on hat. Yellow carbine belt. Blue saddle housings edged with violet and white squares.

Noailles Cavallerie   2 sqdns
Red coat, red lapels, cuffs and lining; buff waistcoat and breeches. Silver lace on hat. Yellow carbine belt. Blue saddle-housings edged green with violet and yellow squares.

Bourgogne **Brigade**

Bourgogne Cavallerie   2 sqdns
Blue coat, red cuffs and lapels, blue lining; buff waistcoat and breeches. Silver lace. White carbine belt. Blue saddle housings edged with orange yellow braid with small white squares

Cavallerie Liégeoise   2 sqdns
Blue coat, yellow cuffs, lapels and lining, white lace buttonholes; yellow waistcoat with white lace buttonholes and buff breeches. Bearskin cap. Buff carbine belt. Blue saddle housings edged white.

Archiac Cavallerie   2 sqdns
White coat, red lapels, cuffs and white lining; buff waistcoat and breeches. Silver lace on hat. Yellow carbine belt. Blue saddle-housings edged with yellow with green stripe

Du Roi **Brigade**

Du Roi Cavallerie   2 sqdns
Blue coat, red cuffs and blue lining; buff waistcoat and breeches. Gold lace on hat. Buff carbine belt. Blue saddle housings edged crimson with white chain

Henrichemont Cavallerie   2 sqdns

White coat, red cuffs, lapels and white lining; buff waistcoat and breeches. Silver lace on hat. Yellow carbine belt. Blue saddle housings edged with red and white squares

Moustiers Cavallerie   2 sqdns

White coat, red lapels, cuffs and lining; buff waistcoat and breeches. Gold lace on hat. Yellow carbine belt. Blue saddle-housings edged violet with white stripe

Noé Cavallerie   2 sqdns

White coat, red cuffs, lapels and lining; buff waistcoat and breeches. Silver lace on hat. Yellow carbine belt. Blue saddle housings edged blue with red stripe

Charles Léonard de Baylenx, Marquis de Poyanne (third line)

Gendarmerie de France

NB: The Gendarmerie were organised in companies, which were in turn paired to form squadrons as noted below. All wore the same basic uniform of scarlet coat, cuffed and lined in the same, edged with varying amounts of silver lace; buff coats and red breeches. Saddle housings were also red edged with silver. Company distinctions were the quantity and arrangement of the lace, the colour of the carbine belt (edged silver) and badges on the saddle-housings and holster caps. It will be noted that the companies were paired into squadrons by carbine-belt colour.

Gendarmes Écossais	1 sqdn	Yellow carbine belt; very rich lace
Gendarmes de Bourgogne		Yellow carbine belt
Gendarmes Anglais	1 sqdn	Purple carbine belt
Chevau-legeres de Bourgogne		Purple carbine belt
Gendarmes Bourguignons	1 sqdn	Green carbine belt
Gendarmes d'Aquitaine		Green carbine belt
Gendarmes de Flandre	1 sqdn	Light orange carbine belt
Chevau-legeres d'Aquitaine		Light orange carbine belt
Gendarmes de la Reine	1 sqdn	Red carbine belt
Gendarmes de Berry		Red carbine belt
Cheveau-legeres de la Reine	1 sqdn	Cherry red carbine belt
Cheveau-legeres de Berry		Cherry red carbine belt

Gendarmes du Dauphin	1 sqdn	Blue carbine belt
Gendarmes d'Orleans		Blue carbine belt

Cheveau-legeres du Dauphin	1 sqdn	Light blue red carbine belt
Cheveau-legeres d'Orleans		Light blue carbine belt

Carabiniers Brigade

Carabiniers de Monsieur 10 sqdns
Blue coat, red collar, cuffs and lining (collar and cuffs edged silver); buff waistcoat and breeches. Silver laced hat.White bandolier edged silver. Saddle-housings blue edged white.

Left Wing Infantry (deployed behind Maulbergen)

Lieutenant General Jacques Bertrand de Marquis de Beaupréau (first line)

Thirty-four pieces of artillery

Touraine **Brigade** (deployed facing north-west behind Malbergen)

Regiment *Touraine* 2 Bns
White coat, clue facings; blue waistcoat, white breeches. Gold lace on hat. White gaiters.

Regiment *d'Aumont* 2 Bns
White coat, white facings; red waistcoat. White breeches. Gold lace on hat. White gaiters.

Rouergue **Brigade** (deployed facing north-west behind Malbergen)

Regiment *Rouergue* 2 Bns
White coat, red facings; red waistcoat, white breeches. Gold lace on hat. White gaiters.

Regiment *Comte de la Marche* 1 Bn
White coat, blue facings; white waistcoat. White breeches. Gold lace on hat. White gaiters.

Regiment *Tournasis* 1 Bn
White coat, red facings; white waistcoat and breeches. Gold lace on hat. White gaiters.

Comte de Saint-Germain (second line)

Anhalt Brigade

Regiment *Anhalt* (German)   2 Bns
Blue coat, yellow facings including lapels; yellow waistcoat and breeches.
Silver lace on hat. White gaiters.

Regiment *Saint-Germain* (German)   1 Bn
Blue coat with yellow collar and lining; blue waistcoat and breeches. Gold
lace on hat. White gaiters.

Regiment *Bergh* (German)   1 Bn
Blue coat, red facings; white waistcoat and breeches. Gold lace on hat.
White gaiters.

Auvergne Brigade

Regiment *Auvergne*   4 Bns
White coat and lining, violet collar and cuffs; white waistcoat, white
breeches. Gold lace on hat. White gaiters.

Chevalier de Nicolai (front line)

Picardie Brigade (deployed facing north opposite Kutenhausen)

Regiment *Picardie*   4 Bns
White coat, white facings; red waistcoat, white breeches. Gold lace on hat.
White gaiters.

Regiment *La Marche*   1 Bn
White coat, red facings; red waistcoat. White breeches. Gold lace on hat.
White gaiters.

Belzunce Brigade (deployed facing north opposite Kutenhausen)

Regiment *Belzunce*   4 Bns
White coat, violet facings; violet waistcoat, white breeches. Gold lace on
hat. White gaiters.

Victor-Francois, Duc de Broglie's Corps

The corps was originally deployed as listed below, but after being ordered to stand fast, facing Todtenhausen, the infantry was redeployed in three lines with the infantry resting its right flank on the Weser, and each of the three lines flanked by cavalry on the left. Exactly how this was accomplished is a little unclear.

Advance Guard
Grenadiers de France Brigade: Vincent-Judes, Marquis de Saint-Pern

Grenadiers de France   4 Bns
Blue coat and cuffs, red collar, lapels and lining, white lace button loops; blue waistcoat and breeches. Fur cap. White gaiters.

3/*Grenadiers-Royaux* Chevalier de Modéne   2 Bns
White coat, cuffs and lining, blue collar; white waistcoat and breeches. Hats (not caps) laced white. White gaiters.

6/*Grenadiers-Royaux* Chevalier de Chantilly   2 Bns
White coat, cuffs and lining, blue collar; white waistcoat and breeches. Hats (not caps) laced white. White gaiters.

Artillery:

Six 12-pounders
Four howitzers
Twelve other cannon – probably light Rostaing guns

Louis Nicolas Victor de Félix d'Ollières, Chevalier du Muy (first line)

Piédmont Brigade

Regiment *Piédmont*   4 Bns
White coat and lining, black cuffs; white waistcoat and breeches. Gold lace in hat. White gaiters.

Regiment *Dauphin*   2 Bns
White coat and lining, blue cuffs and collar; blue waistcoat and white breeches. Gold lace in hat. White gaiters.

Royal-Bavière Brigade

Regiment *Royal-Deux-Ponts* (German)   2 Bns
White coat and lining, red collar and cuffs; white waistcoat and breeches. Silver lace in hat. White gaiters.

Regiment *Royal Bavière* (German)   2 Bns
Blue coat, black collar, cuffs and lapels edged with white lace, white lining; blue waistcoat and breeches. Silver lace in hat. White gaiters.

Waldner Brigade

Regiment *Waldner* (Swiss)   2 Bns
Red coat, blue collar, cuffs and lining, silver-laced buttonholes in threes; blue waistcoat with white lace on buttonholes, and blue breeches. Silver lace on hat. White gaiters.

Regiment *Planta* (Swiss)   2 Bns
Red coat, blue collar, cuffs and lining, silver-laced buttonholes; blue waistcoat with while lace buttonholes and edging, and blue breeches. Silver lace on hat. White gaiters.

Lieutenant General Prince Camille* (second line)

* *Louis Camille de Lorraine, Prince de Marsan*[15]

Commissaire-General Brigade

Commissaire-General Cavallerie   2 sqdns
White coat and lining, black cuffs and lapels; buff waistcoat and breeches. Gold lace. White carbine belt. Blue saddle housings edged with red and yellow squares

Lameth Cavallerie   2 sqdns
White coat, red cuffs, lapels and lining; buff waistcoat and breeches. Silver lace. Yellow carbine belt. Blue saddle housings edged violet with central buff stripe.

De Salles Cavallerie   2 sqdns
White coat and lining, red cuffs and lapels; buff waistcoat and breeches. Silver lace on hat. Yellow carbine belt. Blue saddle-housings edged with black with red stripe

Penthieve Brigade

Penthieve Cavallerie   2 sqdns
White coat, red cuffs, lapels and lining; buff waistcoat and breeches. Fur cap. White carbine belt. Blue saddle housings edged with blue with yellow stripe.

Toustain Cavallerie   2 sqdns
White coat and lining, red cuffs and lapels; buff waistcoat and breeches. Silver lace. Buff carbine belt.
Blue saddle housings edged with red and white squares.

Royal-Allemand Brigade

Royal-Allemand Cavallerie (German)   2 sqdns
Blue coat in long 'Polish' style with small red cuffs and red lining, and white brandenburgs; red waistcoat edged white and buff breeches. Fur cap with red bag. Yellow carbine belt. Blue saddle housings edged with blue with orange yellow chain filled with red.

Nassau-Saarbruck Cavallerie (German)   2 sqdns
Blue coat, buff cuffs, lapels and lining; buff waistcoat and breeches. Bearskin cap. Buff carbine belt. Blue saddle housings edged with red and black squares.

Wurtemburg Cavallerie (German)   2 sqdns
White coat, red cuffs, lapels and lining; buff waistcoat and breeches. Bearskin cap.Yellow carbine belt. Blue saddle-housings edged with green and violet squares.

In addition to the above Broglie had a number of light troops under his command, presumably on the other side of the Weser, where they would have been in a position to outflank Wangenheim's position.

Apchon Dragoons   4 sqdns
Red coat and lining with sky-blue cuffs, white lace button loops; red waistcoat with small sky-blue lapels and white button-loops. Red breeches. Red cap with sky-blue bag. Silver lace on hat if worn.
Red saddle housings edged with sky-blue blue with orange yellow.

Volontaires de Schomberg (German)   3 sqdns
Green coat, red cuffs, collar lapels and lining; buff waistcoat and breeches. Brass "classical" helmet trimmed with sealskin, black horsehair mane. Wolfskin shabraque.

Royal-Nassau Hussards (German)   4 sqdns
Blue dolman with buff collar and cuffs and white cords. Scarlet pelisse edged with white cords and black fur edging. Red sash, dark blue breeches. Black cap with orange and white lace to wing.
Red saddle-housings with orange lion and orange and white edging.

Garrison of Minden under *Maréchal de camp* de Bisson

Loewendahl Brigade

Regiment *Loewendahl*(German)   2 Bns
Blue coat and lining, white collar and cuffs; blue waistcoat with white lace
button-loops in pairs, and white breeches. Gold lace on hat. White gaiters.

Regiment *Bouillon*(Walloon)   2 Bns
White coat and lining, black collar, cuffs and lapels; white button-loops in
pairs – eight on lapels and four below. White waistcoat and breeches. Silver
lace on hat. White gaiters.

Duc d'Havré diversionary force Eickhorst to the left, opposing Hille.

Four guns

Navarre Brigade
Regiment *Navarre*   4 Bns
White coat and lining, white cuffs; red waistcoat and white breeches. Gold
lace in hat. White gaiters.

Light Troops

Volontaires du Dauphiné
Mixed corps of infantry and dragoons. Blue coat, lining and breeches. Buff
collar cuffs and waistcoat, white buttonhole lace on left for infantry and
both sides for dragoons. Hats laced with silver for infantry, blue caps
trimmed with brown fur for cavalry. Blue saddle-housings for latter laced
white.

Volontaires Liegeois
Mixed corps of infantry and dragoons. Blue coat, lining, waistcoat and
breeches, white buttonhole lace. Hats laced with silver for infantry, brass
helmets for dragoons. White sheepskin saddle-housings for latter.[16]

Volontaires de Muret
ad hoc temporary corps formed of infantry volunteers

British Casualties at Minden 1759[1]

Napier's 12th Foot

Killed: Lieutenants William Falkingham, Henry Probyn, and George Townshend, 4 sergeants, 1 drummer and 77 rank and file.

Wounded: Lieutenant Colonel William Robinson; Captains Mathias Murray, William Cloudesley, Peter Campbell; Captain-lieutenant Peter Dunbar; Lieutenants Thomas Fletcher, William Barlow, Thomas Lawless, Edward Freeman, John Campbell and George Rose; Ensigns John Forbes, David Parkill and John Kay; 11 sergeants, 4 drummers, 175 rank and file.

Missing: Captain Peter Chabbert and Robert Ackland and 11 rank and file.[2]

Kingsley's 20th Foot

Killed: Captains Joseph Frierson, Walter Stewart and William Cawley; Lieutenants Edward Brown and George Norbury; Ensign John Crawford, 1 sergeant and 79 rank and file.

Wounded: Captains Charles Grey, John Parr and Alexander Tennant; Captain-lieutenant David Parry; Lieutenants Luke Nugent, John Thompson, George Denshire and W. Boswell; Ensigns N. Irwin, William Dent and William Renton; 12 sergeants and 212 rank and file.

Huske's 23rd Fusiliers

Killed: 4 sergeants and 31 rank and file.

Wounded: Lieutenant Colonel Edward Sacheverel Pole; Captains William Fowler and John Fox; Captain-lieutenant Richard Bolton; Lieutenants Charles Reynell, Joseph Patterson,

Arthur Barber, Grey Groves and George Orpin; Second Lieutenant David Ferguson; and 6 sergeants, 3 drummers and 153 rank and file.

Missing: 10 rank and file.

Home's 25th Foot

Killed: 1 sergeant and 18 rank and file.

Wounded: Captain Francis Gore; Lieutenants Alexander Campbell, Henry Stirrup[3] and Wilson[4]; Ensigns Samuel Pintard, Thomas Edgar and Lockhart; 4 sergeants and 115 rank and file.

Missing: 9 rank and file.

Stuart's 37th Foot

Killed: Lieutenant Green[5]; 1 sergeant and 42 rank and file.

Died of wounds: Captain-lieutenant Hutchinson and Lieutenant Brome.

Wounded: Captains Loftus Cliffe[6], Bayley, Blunt, Graeme, Parkhurst, and Joshua Allen Viscount Allen; Lieutenants John Smith, Barbutt, Boyle Spencer, Slorach and John Hamilton; Ensign James Elliot; 4 sergeants, 4 drummers and 180 rank and file.

Missing: 22 rank and file.

Brudenell's 51st Foot

Killed: Lieutenant Widdows[7] and 20 rank and file.

Wounded: Lieutenant Colonel Noel Fury[8]; Captains Richard Montgomerie, Blair, Donnellan and Walker; Lieutenants Gordon, Samuel Knollis, and Thomas Green; Ensign Peake; 3 sergeants and 745 rank and file.

Missing: 1 sergeant and 4 rank and file.

Royal Artillery

Killed: 2 rank and file.

Wounded: Lieutenants Rogers and Harrington; 1 sergeant and 9 rank and file.

Missing: Lieutenant Carden and two rank and file.

TOTALS:

Killed
3 Captains
7 Lieutenants
1 Ensign
11 Sergeants
1 Drummer
269 rank and file

Wounded   3 Lieutenant Colonels
23 Captains
27 Lieutenants
12 Ensigns
41 Sergeants
11 Drummers
919 Rank and File

Died of   1 Captain-Lieutenant
Wounds   2 Lieutenants

Missing   2 Captains
2 Lieutenants
1 Sergeant
58 Rank and File

Appendix III

Lord George Sackville's Account of Minden

The passage below forms a part of Sackville's defence in his court martial, as set out in pages 286-313 of the published transcript[1], and is presented here as a continuous narrative, by redacting only a number of digressions discussing the reliability of certain witnesses:

Immediately upon the army's marching into the camp at Hille on the 29th of July, the Generals were required in the public orders to reconnoitre the nine debouchers leading into the plain of Minden, and I was at the same time appointed Lieutenant General of the day. In that duty I attended at head quarters all the morning of the 30th, and remained there till I went in the afternoon to relieve Lieut. Gen. Imhoff in the command of the picquets of the army. The next day in visiting the posts of the picquets I reconnoitred the ground as far as an officer of my command ought to have gone. The Prince of Anhalt relieved me about five in the evening, and in my return to head quarters to make my report, I sent off Col. Watson, Deputy Quarter-master General, and Capt. [James] Smith, with directions to reconnoitre the avenues from the camp into the plain of Minden, that I had no opportunity of visiting. I remained some time at head quarters to make my report, and when I arrived at my own, Colonel Hotham[2], Adjutant General of the British troops, brought me the order that had been given only at six o'clock that evening (the supposed neglect of which was made the introduction to the charge against men) for the troops to be in readiness at one in the morning, the horses of the cavalry to be then saddled, but not to strike tents, or march till further orders, and for the Generals to make themselves acquainted with the avenues leading from the camp into the plain of Minden. The orders concerning the troops he had sent to the brigades, those relating to the Generals I had already anticipated, as far as the duty of the picquets would permit me to reconnoitre, and the night made it impossible for me to do more.

145

Neither these orders nor any other circumstance at that time could give me the least suspicion of an engagement next morning. The orders for saddling had been frequently given to the army for a fortnight before, and the silence of the Prince when I reported to him the state of the picquets where everything was quiet, left me no reason to imagine that any signs of the enemy's intending to attack us had appeared that afternoon.

Between five and six in the morning, I was waked by the firing of some cannon on the right of the camp; no orders had been sent to me, not had I any reason to imagine that the order to strike tents and march had been sent to the line; soon after I had a message from General Spörcken that the troops were getting under arms, and before my horses were brought out, Major Stubbs[3] came to me from the line. I immediately galloped up with him, without even waiting for any of my Aids de Camp, and had the good fortune to be at the head of the cavalry before any other general officer of that division had joined them; I call it my good fortune, because it might have happened in the confusion of that morning to me, as it did to other people, not to have been so early at my post; and yet I think I should not have deserved any blame from H.S.H.

When I came up to the line all was ready for the march, and the infantry, which I passed, not more ready than the cavalry; I had no reason then to enquire, whether the orders sent to the brigades for saddling at one had been obeyed; it is certain now that they had; but though they had not yet, as the cavalry was equally ready with the rest of the army, I should not have chosen to throw upon the field officers, whose duty it was to attend to the immediate execution of such orders; the charge of neglect in this duty, which has since been so unjustly imputed to me.

I immediately formed the cavalry in column, and as the guide appointed for it was arrived, I marched a considerable time before the orders to march, which amidst the hurry of the morning had somehow miscarried, were delivered to Colonel Hotham. Upon the march, the other Generals and my Aids de Camp came up. Major Estorff[4] soon brought me an order to form into squadron, which was done directly. The march proceeded after this at such a pace as was proper for bringing the whole column up in good order; the account given of it by Capt. Smith, the only witness who saw the line pass, proves the squadrons were hurried in the rear, yet I am accused by one witness of the slowness of this march; a strong instance how imperfect a representation is commonly given of each circumstance of an action, when officers attached by their duty to a particular post, pretend to form an opinion of what is, or may be done in other places.

The circumstance is otherwise of no moment, for in spite of the confusion of orders the cavalry arrived at its ground a considerable time before the column of infantry had entered the plain. With whatever promptitude then H.S.H's orders were obeyed by the rest of the army, I must beg leave to say, that the cavalry of the right wing under my command was intitled to equal praise.

The guide who conducted the column was ordered to lead it to the windmill near Halen, as we were marching thither. Captain Malhortie[5] came up, ordered me to form in two lines, which was immediately done, near the village of Hartum, and there to wait for further orders.

The cavalry had then upon its right the village of Hartum and inclosures, which run close upon the flank of the lines; on its left a long wood, and the country only open to the front, where the windmill, our original point of destination, stood; the particular spot where we halted was too narrow to contain the front; and Captain Smith having discovered that the ground widened to the right in the front, I advanced a little forwarder, and there halted again. I was by no means satisfied with this situation of the cavalry, thus separated from even the view of the rest of the army, hemmed in on both sides, and likely to be exposed during this Inaction to some batteries of the enemy; while I was waiting impatiently for orders to advance, Capt. Williams of the artillery came to me from Capt. Philips, to acquaint me that the heavy brigade of the artillery had marched from its ground without any orders, and desired to know, if I had any particular directions for them. As I imagined they might have been forgot in that hurry, which always attends the surprise of an army, and was certain there could be no design of leaving the British artillery behind, I took upon me, without sending to his Serene Highness to order them to advance in front, where I did not doubt they would find employment, and where afterwards they did such signal service; the only way they could advance was by following the Hanoverian artillery along the left flank, through the intervals of the cavalry till they came into the wood. Every circumstance of my situation at that time, when I was left to form the best judgement I could of the state of affairs, conspired to persuade me that the cavalry could have no way to act but by moving forward. The intelligence of the guide, the difficulties of the ground towards the right and left, and the knowledge I had, that the ground beyond the windmill, which I had reconnoitred, was open and extensive, all led me to this supposition. The first object that appeared to me was a body of infantry in the front towards the right, which for a little was cannonaded by the enemy, but soon afterwards made a movement to the village of Halen, and seemed beginning to attack it, I immediately concluded that the future operations of the cavalry might depend upon the success of that attack, and therefore sent Lieut. Sutherland[6] to reconnoitre it, but soon after that Capt. Winschingrode[7] came up to me full gallop, and in great haste delivered me an order in French; his hurry made him express it indistinctly, and I desired him to repeat it; and he then said, as I understood, "That it was the Duke's order to form the cavalry in one line, making a third to sustain the infantry, and to advance." I had no difficulty to comprehend the general intention of this order, when it was repeated, as it agreed with every observation I had been able to make. The attack on the village of Halen by our troops, the firing chiefly in front, an open country there, inclosures and obstructions upon every other quarter, made it impossible for me to doubt, that the intention of the orders was that the cavalry should move forwards, which indeed the word advance sufficiently of itself expressed. Captain Winschingrode having repeated his orders galloped off; and I immediately made the dispositions necessary for putting the order in execution…

[At this point Sackville entered into a very lengthy discussion of the contradictory evidence of the witnesses and supposed witnesses to this exchange]

… I now return to shew, what were the measures I took for putting into execution the order to form the cavalry into one line, making a third to sustain the infantry, and to advance: the literal obedience to it required me to attempt forming the two lines into one, as a third to sustain the infantry, and then I was to advance. The Court remembering the position of the cavalry at that time, surrounded on each side by woods and inclosures, will easily conceive, that the situation of the wood on the left, which must have intersected such a line, might create a reasonable hesitation in any man as to the manner of advancing. I resolved to take the steps I thought most necessary for the execution of the order; I immediately ordered Captain Hugo[8] to clear my front of the Saxe-Gotha regiment, which would, till it was removed, prevent our advancing: I ordered Capt. Brome to go forward to reconnoitre the position of the enemy, and I sent Capt. [Richard] Lloyd, another Aid de Camp, to find out our infantry, and report to me their situation, that I might then judge in what manner, and by what movements, I could best fulfil his Serene Highness's intentions; for I could never think I should have done my duty, had I precipitately marched the cavalry into a wood, without knowing whether it led from, or towards its destination. I would not be understood in the least to insinuate, as if I imagined the difficulty of obeying the order literally, a sufficient excuse for not carrying the spirit of the orders into execution; but I must think, that taking every step that could enable me to form my own judgement of the state of facts, from whence alone I could be enabled to act according to the spirit of the order, was paying all possible obedience to it. In my apprehension then, it became my first duty to procure all the necessary information I could; when I had discharg'd that duty, I should then, if I had found it necessary, have risked the literal disobedience of my orders, and have advanced with the cavalry, formed as they were, in two lines, as far as the plain beyond the wood, and then to have made the necessary movement for sustaining the infantry, where the ground would not have best allowed it.

Whether the measures I took were the most proper, or whether I have acted with the same ability as many before whom I now stand, would have done in the like situation, I shall not presume to say; but I hope nobody can think after the steps I did take, that I can be suspected of having intentionally disobeyed the orders I received; and I must further observe, that had I by hastily obeying the orders of Capt. Winschingrode, brought any misfortune upon our cavalry (if the intention had been taken of blaming me) I might now have been standing at your bar for having given too much credit to orders brought by an officer not properly authorised to deliver them to the British troops. But suppose the orders of Capt. Winschingrode were, as has been asserted, to move to the left, and that there had been no obstruction neither from the wood nor the artillery; let any one consider only what was the space of time in which I was to act, and what was the extent of the lines I was to put in motion. The interval of time that elapsed between Capt. Winschingrode's leaving me, and the cavalry's advancing, is ascertained by the most undoubted evidence, not to have exceeded seven or eight minutes, Col. Hotham says, it was between five and ten minutes, Lieut. Bisset[9] says about seven or eight minutes; all the witnesses in general (excepting indeed Col. Sloper[10], who makes it at one occasion half an hour, and on another a quarter) are of the same opinion; but the incertainty of any opinion with regard to time, so strongly appearing in all the depositions, has determined me upon every material interval, to endeavour to obtain a more convincing proof; Capt. Hugo, who during this space, galloped about 200 paces, delivered an order, and return, swears from the knowledge of what he then did, that the time was not above seven or eight minutes; Capt. Lloyd from the like reason, gives the same evidence. If this concurrence of facts and opinion could leave the smallest doubt in any mind, Capt. Winschingrode's evidence, who says that galloping from me he met Col. Fitzroy galloping towards me, who joined me, as everybody knows, after the cavalry was in motion, proves to demonstration, that there could not have been above six or eight minutes in which I was to act. The lines which were to be put in motion during that time, consisted of twenty-four squadrons, and had the order been given for marching from the left immediately upon Capt. Winschingrode's leaving me, the squadrons upon the right could not have begun to move before the arrival of a different order. The generals, who understand the movement of lines, will know I am right in this assertion. Hitherto I have not supposed the Saxe-

Gotha regiment any obstruction to moving forwards, nor desired any allowance of time upon that account; it has been admitted however, that five minutes might be necessary for that purpose, when it was treated as the most trifling obstruction; supposing it to have employed no longer time, (and whatever time was employed I am not to be blamed, as I immediately gave the proper order) it is sufficient to account for the whole interval in which I am accused of having remained inactive; for Capt. Hugo immediately returned after delivering his orders, and before the front was quite clear of that regiment, the first line was in motion. Immediately after Capt. Hugo's return, Capt. Ligonier[11] arrived with Capt. Lloyd, whom a few minutes before I had sent to reconnoitre the position of the infantry; the orders that Capt. Ligonier delivered to me, are fully stated in Col. Hotham's deposition, that his serene Highness ordered the cavalry to advance, and he added as the reason of the order, the enemy is retiring or in confusion, *et il vous prie d'en profiter*: the other officers who were near me, understood the orders in the same manner. But it is unnecessary to trouble the Court with referring to their depositions; for Col. Ligonier himself agrees with Col. Hotham, and says, that the orders he brought, was to advance with the cavalry, in order to profit from the disorder which appeared in the enemy's cavalry.

Col. Sloper, as usual, differs from all the other witnesses, and asserts that Capt. Ligonier said to me "It was the Duke's orders that I should advance immediately with the cavalry under my command, and that the movement was to the left;" but it must be clear to the Court, that there was no mention of the left in the order itself which Capt. Ligonier delivered.

This order removed every doubt that had attended the former, was not accompanied with any difficulty in the execution, but was perfectly clear and explicit. Did I endeavour to raise any objections? Did I even question Capt. Ligonier upon it? Did I then hesitate one moment to obey? Captain Ligonier has said that without making an answer, I immediately drew my sword, gave the word to march, and the troops advanced. So sudden an obedience demonstrates what disposition I had to obey every order I understood, and the Court may judge from hence that I would have obeyed every other order with equal alacrity, had they been equally clear. Thus far, there is not the least appearance of contradiction in the evidence (excepting always Col. Sloper) with regard to Capt. Ligonier's order, but Capt. Ligonier then says, that when the troops had moved a few paces forwards, he told me it was to the left I was to march. This explanation of his order was not heard or understood by any of the officers about me, as is clear from Lieutenant Sutherland's deposition, Capt. Lloyd, Capt. Bisset, and Captain Hugo, who all understood at the time that Capt. Ligonier had expressed himself no otherwise with regard to his orders, than by saying the whole cavalry was to advance.

It will appear also by what passed afterwards, that this explanation was not heard or understood by me, and yet it is not improbable that Capt. Ligonier at the time he mentions may have said something about going to the left; he spoke it by his own account after the line had advanced a few paces: the drums were then beating, for they had continued so by Capt. Smith's deposition, till the halt. Capt. Ligonier's order had not occasioned me a moment's reflection, and it might very naturally happen in that situation, that he might have said something about going to the left, which neither I, not any person about me, heard.

In a very short time after the cavalry was in motion, Col. Fitzroy[12] arrived, and delivered me an order to advance with the British cavalry only to the left. I immediately halted the cavalry, and was, I confess, astonished to receive an order so contradictory to every idea, that either from former orders, or from my own observation, I had formed of the service of the cavalry that day, and I could imagine besides no possible reason for dividing the cavalry, and bringing up the British only.

The Court will easily enter into the doubts, which at that time perplexed me, for I think there has never yet been any tolerable reason assigned for this difference in the orders. The enemy, as every body knew, was greatly superior to us in cavalry; the attack had not begun when Col. Fitzroy was sent off, consequently the enemy's cavalry was not then weakened; why then send for an inferior body of cavalry? Was it to avoid delay? As has sometimes been given out. Why then send for the British cavalry? Which being posted on the right, were at least half a mile more distant from the infantry than the Hanoverian. I could not but imagine at first, that there was a mistake in the delivery of the orders. I saw Col. Fitzroy out of breath and much hurried; I desired him not to be in a hurry, to recollect himself, and deliver his orders distinctly. He then repeated his orders again; I expressed my surprize, and told him, that I had but just received orders from Capt. Ligonier to advance with the whole cavalry, and that I could not imagine that the Prince meant to divide them, Col. Fitzroy then said, that Capt. Ligonier and he left the Prince at the same time, and brought the same order; I then asked for Capt. Ligonier, he came up and asserted in the strongest terms that his order was right, and said that he could answer for it with his honour and his commission; Col. Fitzroy continued equally positive that his orders were right, and insisted that they brought the same orders, and left the Prince at the same time; I desired that they would agree what their orders were, and that I was ready to execute either of them; they both continued equally positive; I saw no method from them of clearing up that confusion, and I asked whether the Prince was at hand? And where they had left him? Col. Fitzroy answered, that he had left him just on the other side of the wood not a great way off, and coming towards us. I immediately determined, what every man I believe in the like situation would, to have an explanation of these orders, when it could be obtained by going so little a way, and when the trifling delay that could occasion, must have been of much less prejudice to the service, than an improper obedience ...

I have already said, that Col. Fitzroy having told me, that the Prince was not a great way off, I desired to be conducted to him. As we galloped along, I saw the wood open to the plain more quickly than I imagined, and Col. Fitzroy continuing still very positive in his order, as reported to me, I sent back Capt. Smith with orders to bring up the British cavalry as fast as possible. The place from whence I sent him back, was not distant from the nearest part of the cavalry above 50 or 200 yards by Col. Fitzroy's account, and by the account so often given of the extent of the wood at that part of it, could not have been many hundred yards from the left of the British cavalry, so that the delay occasioned by my desiring to go to the Prince, could only be the time it might take to gallop twice that distance. Capt. Smith, as he passed by the left towards Gen. Mostyn, made the cavalry wheel by quarter ranks, so that all possible expedition was used, and they were marched in that order: I observed, it was asked with some appearance of surprize, how the woods opening could occasion my sending back for the British cavalry only? A moment's reflection made that question unnecessary; the wood's opening soon to the heath reconciled me a little to the movement being made to the left; if that was to be done, then Col. Fitzroy's order, and not Capt. Ligonier's was to be followed, (for I understood nothing from the last of this movement) and of consequence the British cavalry only were to be brought up. This, together with Col. Fitzroy's positiveness, and Capt. Ligonier's absence, who had gone from me, when I set out towards the Prince, induced me, tho' I own without being convinced to give the order I did to Capt. Smith.

When I came up to the Prince, I told him the state of the orders; he received me, as has been proved by many witnesses, with his usual civility, expressed to me no surprize at my not understanding the orders; but upon my pointing to him the head of the column of the cavalry of the second line, which was then in view coming out of the wood, gave me his own orders to form the cavalry on the heath, and sustain the infantry. I should greatly wrong the Prince, if I should suppose it necessary to take much notice of what has been told the Court, of his expressing his surprize at my doubt upon the orders, not by words, but by his looks and actions. The orders he gave me were materially different in their object from either Capt. Ligonier's, or Col. Fitzroy's; these orders alone were a confirmation of my doubts, and his manner seemed to me to correspond with his words. But it has been observed, that before Col. Fitzroy came up, the Prince expressed his dissatisfaction at my conduct, for when he sent

Mr. Derenthal[13] to hasten me; he said, looking towards the cavalry, that he did not know, what Lord George Sackville was doing there. If his Serene Highness was dissatisfied with any body then it could not be me, for the cavalry he saw at that time was the second line; but the expression does not seem to import any blame, but only shews his surprize, that the cavalry appeared so much to the rear, where to be sure he did not expect them; and where, if he had known, they were obliged by going to the left to place themselves, he probably would not have chosen they could have made that movement.

The orders I received, pointed out to me the object I was to have in view, sustaining the infantry, by a formed body of cavalry. There was nothing mentioned of attack or pursuit, nor any thing that could in the least induce me by advancing in a hurry to hazard any disorder or confusion in the cavalry, which would have made it totally unfit to sustain infantry: had pursuit then been the object, his Serene Highness would undoubtedly have ordered the cavalry, which first appeared, to have advanced instantly, without ordering me to form the whole. I immediately dispatched Capt. Lloyd to order the cavalry to form in line, and followed him myself.

The second line, it is certain, was got upon the heath sooner, but not a great deal sooner than the first. Capt. Smith met Lord Granby at the entrance of the wood from the ground where the cavalry was first formed, and the cavalry marching from the left, and , and their flank being close to the wood, sufficiently proves how short a time they could have been in motion. From thence he went very fast to Gen. Mostyn, who was not far off; the cavalry marched immediately by quarter ranks, which across the wood was by much the quickest way, and they marched at a very good pace. The cavalry that I shewed to the Prince, was the second line; but at, or soon after that time, the first line appeared also, for Lieut. Sutherland, who was then by me, says, the first cavalry that he distinguished coming out of the wood was the Blues.

I sent Capt. Hugo then to the Hanoverian cavalry of the first line, that I had left on the other side of the wood, because it was very clear now, the Prince's intentions were not, that the British cavalry only should advance upon the heath. I then set about forming the cavalry as the ground would best admit, taking the most expeditious and effectual method of fulfilling his Serene Highness's intentions. Here it may undoubtedly be said, there was a halt. That is to say, the squadrons that first formed, stopped till the others could form up with them in line, and without such a halt, it was impossible the cavalry could form at all. But the whole body was never halted, and some part of it always in motion.

How much time was employed in this manoeuvre, is not ascertained by the evidence; no particular time can be said to be necessary for such movements, as the making of them slower or faster, must always depend upon the adroitness of the troops, and their readily comprehending the orders they receive. Capt. Smith's evidence shews, that the Hanoverian squadrons on the left formed too near to the wood, and instead of inclining to the left in advancing, as I ordered them, wheeled to the left. This mistake I was obliged to set right, and some time was lost by it; Col. Pitt[14] is the only witness, who has an opinion as to the time employed in forming the line; he thinks it was about a quarter of an hour that the brigade, in which he was, halted in forming the line; but he also thinks, that when the brigade alone formed at their first coming out of the wood with Lord Granby, the halt was about ten minutes, so that five minutes more, supposing his calculation just, was no extraordinary time for forming a line, which consisted of more than double the number of squadrons of which he speaks.

If it was upon this occasion that Lord Granby found fault with my manoeuvres, I flatter myself, his Lordship would not have blamed them, had he known, that I was acting under the orders of the Prince. The intention, of which I am persuaded he would have agreed with me, could not have been otherwise satisfied, than by advancing with a well-formed line of cavalry fit to sustain.

Before the line was quite formed, the left moved, the inconvenience of the squadrons that first formed having taken up too little ground, soon appeared, for as we came up to the fir grove so often mentioned, Bland's and the Inniskillings, were thrown out of the line entirely: even this obstruction did not make me halt the line, tho' I was obliged upon that account to move a little slower, and to incline the squadrons to the left; afterwards we moved on, without any sort of stop, except occasional ones to dress the line, till we came in the rear of the infantry, and there the cavalry was halted, as this undoubtedly was the object pointed out by the Prince's orders.

In order to explain a little more fully to the Court the movements of the cavalry at that time, I must beg they would consider a moment what was then known with regard to the state of the action. No officer of the cavalry, I believe, imagined that the engagement was over before we came upon the heath; nor had his Serene Highness any idea that the success of the few battalions that had engaged could determine the event of the day, as is plain from the orders he gave to sustain the infantry; it appears now indeed, that the action must have been over at that time. Mr Derenthal had before that congratulated the Prince upon the success of the infantry, and we know that after that success the French never returned to the charge. But as I hope not to be censured upon circumstances that I could not know, neither shall I attempt to excuse myself by them. Let my conduct be judged only according to the views I was enabled to form at that time; ordered to sustain the infantry, could I have been justified had I not paid the utmost attention to bringing up the cavalry in line? Was that not essentially necessary to the object of the order? The slowness of the movement is here again found fault with. The march, at particular times, might be slow in particular parts of the line; but whenever I could bring them up regularly, it was sufficiently fast through the whole line. Capt. Smith proves that he met me advancing at a full trot as I came towards the place where the action had begun. With regard to the halts that I made, it is now clear from the whole evidence, that there were but two halts after the cavalry came upon the heath; the one was that which was first made to form in line; the other when they halted in the rear of the infantry. This appeared very clear both from Col. Pitt and Col. Hotham's deposition. And what in other parts of the evidence might have been mistaken for halts, are explained by this last deposition to have been only occasional halts for dressing the line. I need make no apology for these, as every officer knows the necessity of them. The first halt could not be avoided, and the last was in obedience to the order I received.

Some doubts seem to have arisen whether that infantry behind, which I then halted, was the infantry I was ordered by the Prince to sustain. It must be very clear to every one, that at the first line of infantry I came up to, it was my duty, in execution of my order, to halt. The infantry behind which I halted, are proved to the Court to have been a line of 7 or 8 battalions, commanded by Major Gen. Scheele, part of which belonged to the first, and part to the second line of the army; if we can credit the plan of Lieut. Roy[15], so much relied on, it is difficult to say precisely what part of the line of infantry his Serene Highness intended the cavalry should have sustained; the events of the day totally changed all lines and dispositions. But I think it is certain, that had the cavalry been in a situation originally to have formed as a third line to sustain the infantry, it must have formed behind some of these very regiments; and after the orders were received, this was the only line of infantry upon the plains of Minden that ever appeared for the cavalry to have sustained.

I soon saw that no service could be done in this situation, I thought in all probability there might elsewhere; for no action that ever I had known, had been decided in so short a time, and by the fate of a single attack. I sent an Aid de Camp to acquaint His Serene Highness, that the cavalry could do no service where it was, and to desire to know if he had any commands for them? The Court will scarcely suppose, that this would have been the conduct of a person who had any disinclination to obey.

It will now be proper (having gone through the particular movements of the cavalry) to take notice of a general object of enquiry that has been pursued through the course of the trial, whether the cavalry attacked any enemy, or sustained any infantry that ever was engaged? As to the first attacking the enemy, never was the object of any order I received excepting Col. Ligonier's, and with what readiness I obeyed that order, till I was stopped by Col. Fitzroy's, the Court already knows. As to sustaining infantry that was engaged with the enemy, if there was a proper relation of the action before the Court, it would at once appear, how impractical that was. It was for this reason that I wished to have asked a few questions of the officers of the infantry; but as the Court had had the trouble of so long an attendance, I could not wonder, that they wished to shorten the examination, and I very readily submitted to their opinion. I must beg leave therefore to mention a fact or two, not in the depositions, but so publickly known, and so confessedly true, that it is impossible to call them into question. I mean only this, Capt. Winschingrode has said, that when he left the Prince the infantry had moved about 100 paces towards the enemy, Col. Fitzroy says, that when he came off, the infantry was advancing briskly; I desire only to add to this what every body knows, that the British brigade of infantry on the right, advanced with the utmost impetuosity, before any line of battle was formed, or before any artillery could be brought to oppose the enemy's batteries, attacked the French line, and after a very short conflict, sustained and assisted only by the second brigade of British, and the two battalions of Hanoverian guards, defeated it, and put it to flight.

Capt. Derenthal proves the short duration of the action; he left Brudenell's regiment after the success of the infantry, and had been with the Prince sometime before Col. Fitzroy returned to him with me; after which there was no firing of small arms heard. I desire only now to remind the Court, that the only part of the army that did engage the French line were the six British regiments, the two battalions of Hanoverian guards, and perhaps Hardenberg's regiment. The evidence will shew how far they had rushed on pursuing their victory.

Lieut. Sutherland, and Capt. Lloyd, after they had delivered the orders from me, for the cavalry to form, galloped across the plain towards the infantry. Lieut. Sutherland came up first with the Hanoverian guards and a little more advanced be found the British; the enemy was then close to the walls of Minden. Lieut. Lloyd saw the French cavalry at such a distance as just to distinguish it to be cavalry, and that was all. They both think the infantry that had engaged were above a mile, Lieut. Sutherland thinks near two from where they left the cavalry forming.

Lieut. Bisset left me, while I was receiving the Prince's order, and in going towards the infantry, met the wounded officers coming off. He then came towards me, and immediately returned to his regiment, when he found the enemy out of sight, but as it was imagined they were forming behind the houses, he returned to desire my permission to join his regiment, which had lost a great many officers; he immediately returned to his regiment, and never saw the enemy more till they afterwards appeared in the hedges of Minden. Capt. Smith likewise galloped on to the infantry, as the cavalry began to advance, and found the Hanoverian guards and the British amongst the inclosures of Minden, and the enemy that had engaged them distinguishable only by a cloud of dust what they had raised towards Minden; and the officers of the British infantry asked him where the rest of the army was, for they had not seen any more of it than two battalions of the Hanoverian guards all that day.

Against these facts there is only the opinion of one or two cavalry officers, founded upon conjecture, not observation, that the cavalry might have sustained the body of infantry that was engaged. I leave it to the Court to form the conclusion, whether it was possible for the cavalry to have sustained that infantry, which not even the remainder of the first, nor any other part of the second line ever came up to, to sustain, or to have shared with them the glory of the day.

Appendix IV

Contemporary Accounts of the Battle of Minden

Though excerpts from the following accounts have, in some instances, been included in the main body of this book, they are reproduced at length below.

Lieutenant Hugh Montgomery
12th Regiment of Foot to His Mother
Quoted in H.C. Wylly's *History of the King's Own Yorkshire Light Infantry*.

Dear madam – The pursuit of the enemy, who have retired with the greatest precipitation, prevents me from giving you so exact an account of the late most glorious victory over the French army as I would, had I almost any leisure, however here goes as much as I can. We marched from camp between 4 and 5 o'clock in the morning, about seven drew up in a valley, from thence marched about three hundred yards, when an eighteen pound ball came gently rolling up to us. Now began the most disagreeable march that I ever had in my life, for we advanced more than a quarter of a mile through a most furious fire from a most infernal battery of eighteen-pounders, which was at first upon our front, but as we proceeded, bore upon our flank, and at last upon our rear. It might be imagined, that this cannonade would render the regiments incapable of bearing the shock of unhurt troops drawn up long before on ground of their own choosing, but firmness and resolution will surmount almost any difficulty. When we got within about 100 yards of the enemy, a large body of French cavalry galloped boldly down upon us; these our men by reserving their fire until they came within thirty yards, immediately ruined, but not without receiving some injury from them, for they rode down two companies on the right of our regiment, wounded three officers, took one of them prisoner with our artillery Lieutenant, and whipped off the Tumbrells. This cost them dear for it forced many of them

158

into our rear, on whom the men faced about and five of them did not return. These visitants being thus dismissed, without giving us a moment's time to recover the unavoidable disorder, down came upon us like lightning the glory of France in the persons of the Gens d'Armes. These we almost immediately dispersed without receiving hardly any mischief from the harmless creatures. We now discovered a large body of infantry consisting of seventeen regiments moving down directly on our flank in column, a very ugly situation; but Stewart's Regiment and ours wheeled, and showed them a front, which is a thing not to be expected from troops already twice attacked, but this must be placed to the credit of General Waldgrave and his aide-de-camp. We engaged this corps for about ten minutes, killed them a good many, and as the song says, 'the rest then ran away'. The next who made their appearance were some Regiments of the Grenadiers of France, as fine and terrible looking fellows as I ever saw. They stood us a tug, notwithstanding we beat them off to a distance, where they galled us much, they having rifled barrels, and our muskets would not reach them. To remedy this we advanced, they took the hint, and ran away. Now we were in hopes that we had done enough for one day's work, and that they would not disturb us more, but soon after a very large body of fresh infantry, the last resource of Contades, made the final attempt on us. With them we had a long but not very brisk engagement, at last made them retire almost out of reach, when the three English regiments of the rear line came up, and gave them one fire, which sent them off for good and all. But what is wonderful to tell, we ourselves after all this success at the very same time also retired, but indeed we did not then know that victory was ours. However we rallied, but all that could now be mustered was about 13 files private with our Colonel and four other officers one of which I was so fortunate to be. With this remnant we returned again to the charge, but to our unspeakable joy no opponents could be found. It is astonishing, that this victory was gained by six English regiments of foot, without their grenadiers, unsupported by cavalry or cannon, not even their own battalion guns, in the face of a dreadful battery so near as to tear them with grape-shot, against forty battalions and thirty-six squadrons, which is directly the quantity of the enemy which fell to their share. It is true that two Hanoverian regiments were engaged on the left of the English, but so inconsiderably as to lose only 50 men between them. On the left of the army the grenadiers, who now form a separate body, withstood a furious cannonade. Of the English there was only killed one captain and one sergeant; some Prussian dragoons were engaged and did good service. Our artillery which was stationed in different places, also behaved well, but the grand attack on which depended the fate of the day, fell to the lot of the six English regiments of foot. From this account the Prince might be accused of misconduct for trusting the issue of so great an event to so small a body, but this affair you will have soon enough explained to the disadvantage of a great men whose easy part, had it been properly acted, must have occasioned to France one of the greatest overthrows it ever met with. The sufferings of our regiment will give you the best notion of the smartness of the action. We actually fought that day not more than 480 private and 27 officers, of the first 302 were killed and wounded, and of the latter 18. Three lieutenants were killed on the spot, the rest are only wounded, and all of them are in a good way except two. Of the officers who escaped there are only four who cannot show some marks of the enemy's good intentions, and as perhaps you may be desirous to know any little risks that I might have run, I will mention those of which I was sensible. At the beginning of the action I was almost knocked off my legs by my three right hand men, who were killed and drove against me by a cannon ball, the same ball also killed two men close to Ward, whose post was in the rear of my platoon, and in this place I will assure you that he behaved with the greatest bravery, which I suppose you will make known to his father and friends. Some time after I received from a spent ball just such a rap on my collar-bone as I have frequently from that once most dreadful weapon, your crooked headed stick; it just welled and grew red enough to convince the neighbours that I was not fibbing when I mentioned it. I got another of these also on one of my legs, which gave me about as much pain, as would a tap of Miss Mathews's fan. The last and greatest misfortune of all fell to the share of my poor old coat for a musket ball entered into the right skirt of it and made three holes. I had almost forgot to tell you that my spontoon was shot through a little below my hand; this disabled it, but a French one now does duty in its room. The consequences of this affair are very great, we found by the papers, that the world began to give us up, and the French had swallowed us up in their imaginations. We have now pursued them above 100 miles with the advanced armies of the hereditary prince, Wanganheim, and Urff in our front, of whose success in taking prisoners and baggage, and receiving deserters, Francis Joy will give you a better account than I can at present. They are now entrenching themselves at Cassel, and you may depend on it they will not show us their faces again during this campaign. I have the pleasure of being able to tell you that Captain Rainey is well; he is at present in advance with the Grenadiers plundering French baggage and taking prisoners. I would venture to give him forty ducats for his share of prize money. I have now contrary to my expectations and in spite of many interruptions wrote you a long letter, this paper I have carried this week past in my pocket for the purpose, but could not attempt it before. We marched into this camp yesterday evening, and shall quit it early in the morning. I wrote you a note just informing you that I was well the day after the battle; I hope you will receive it in due time. Be pleased to give my most affectionate duty to my uncles and aunts ... The noise of the battle frightened our sutler's wife into labour the next morning. She was brought to bed of a son, and we have had him christened by the name of Ferdinand.

Unknown Officer
12th Foot

This somewhat bombastic account appears in R.T. Higgins *The Records of the King's Own Borderers or Old Edinburgh Regiment*, pp.98-100, and is also attributed to an officer in Napier's 12th Foot. The references to the capture of the French baggage and to the French wounded dying by the roadsides indicate that it too was written some days afterwards.

We have gained one of the most glorious battles that ever was fought, against an Army at least twice our number. Prince Ferdinand has during the whole Campaign, notwithstanding all disadvantages, displayed the most masterly skill in generalship; but the last *coup d'éclat* has raised his reputation above the reach of detraction. Foreseeing that the Electorate of Hanover would be quite exposed should he retreat farther, he determined to bring the Enemy to battle, notwithstanding their superiority. He knew them too well to expect they would attack without a manifest advantage; and to endeavour to force their camp and intrenchments was to take the bull by the horns. For these reasons, he resolved to play off a stratagem against M. Contades, in order to draw him out into the open field; as he suspected the camp to be swarming with spies, he communicated his plan only to the General Officers.

On the 29th and 30th July he made several marches and countermarches with the Army, which was divided into three bodies, chiefly with the design of amusing the Enemy. On the 31st he filed off with the main body to the right, quite out of sight, leaving General Wangenheim in the Camp with eighteen thousand men; he then posted small bodies in proper places, who, by signals conveyed from one to another, could give him immediate intelligence of the least motion of the French. These dispositions being made, he waited the event of his scheme, which was answered to his wish.

Betwixt four and five in the morning of the 1st August, M. Contades poured out his troops, in order to fall on Wangenheim, whom he expected to crush in a twinkling. That brave General received them with the greatest firmness and resolution. The onset of the French Army was extremely furious, rushing with the greatest impetuosity, like a deluge, threatening to sweep all before it. But the undauntedness and good disposition of our Troops checked their career, and made them reel back again; however they soon rallied, and returned to the charge, and Wangenheim must have been overpowered, had not Prince Ferdinand, most unexpectedly and disagreeably for the French, advanced with the main body. He immediately fell upon their left wing with great vigour, and saluted them with a most terrible discharge of his Artillery, which did prodigious execution, and put them into the utmost disorder; but fresh troops coming up, the most desperate conflict was renewed.

Prince Ferdinand rode up and down through the lines, exhorting his soldiers to behave gallantly. He detached reinforcements wherever there was occasion; he animated the Troops by his example, exposing his person like a young Officer, and at the same time putting in practice all the arts of a most consummate General.

Our British Infantry, headed by Generals Waldegrave and Kingsley, fought with the greatest ardour and intrepity, sustaining and repelling the repeated attacks of the Enemy with the most romantic bravery. The soldiers, so far from being daunted by their falling comrades, breathed nothing but revenge; for my part, though at the beginning of the Engagement I felt a kind of trepidation, yet I was so animated by the brave example of all around me, that when I received a slight wound by a musket ball slanting on my left side, it served only to exasperate me the more, and had I then received orders, I would with the greatest pleasure have rushed into the thickest of the Enemy. We fought, in short, like British to outshine themselves. Interest, honour, glory, and emulation, conspired to render the Battle of Thorhausen famous to posterity.

The French Officers did all they could to wrest the victory from us; often did they rally their broken troops and return to the charge, and as often were they beat off with the greatest havoc. Our Artillery was handsomely served. At last, after the most obstinate dispute of six hours, the French gave way on all hands, in spite of the utmost endeavours of their Commanders, whom they hurried along in the flight it was, and not a retreat. Thousands jumped into the water, and many were forced into it by the crowds pressing hard behind, and the roads were all strewed with those who lay expiring of their wounds: a dismal sight! The loss of the French is computed at seven thousand killed on the field and in the pursuit; about twice as many wounded; four thousand drowned; and it is said we have made about five thousand prisoners. We have taken fifty-two pieces of cannon, sixteen pairs of colours, nine standards, and their whole baggage.

Our loss, in killed and wounded and missing, is about fourteen hundred, among whom is no officer of note. The Hanoverians have lost near two thousand.

Major General William Kingsley's notes.

Kingsley did not, so far as is known, write a narrative account of the battle, but what follows are a series of marginal notes which he added to a copy of Entick's *Compleat History of the Late War*. Those passages in italics below are the extracts from the text to which Kingsley's notes refer.

On the 31st [of July] in the evening, the Prince further ordered that at one o'clock the next morning the army should be ready to march …

Kingsley: This had been ordered for several nights before, so that P. Ferdinand had not more reason to think of an action the next day than for several others before.

On the 31st, at 6 in the evening, a grand Council of War was held at Marshal de Contades' quarters … The Marshal gave the Generals the order of the march.

Kingsley: The best digested I ever saw. We received none from P. Ferdinand, nor did he seem to put that confidence in Generals to be so explicit, as he seldom or never intrusted any with the order of battle. Let those reconcile this conduct who can.

Marshal Contades formed the whole plan of the action upon a supposition that D. Ferdinand, having removed the greatest part of his army so far to the right of Hill, was at too great a distance from Wangenheim to succour him.

Kingsley: There was no part of the army to the right of Hill, nor no other regiments [which were Napier's and Kingsley's] near it, and which covered the Duke's quarters.

The whole French army was marching into the plain of Minden by five o'clock in the morning.

Kingsley: The enemy were well formed by three in the morning. Had they instantly marched forward, our whole army had been surprized and must have been totally destroyed. The Prince of Anhalt, General of that day, lost two hours by not sending the deserters who gave him intimation of the enemy's being in motion to Prince Ferdinand sooner, not putting confidence in them.

I before mentioned that the Duke gave orders in the evening of the 31st of July, for the army to be ready to march at one o'clock the next morning … By some mistake the order was not brought to Lord George Sackville, so that instead of the horses being saddled at one o'clock … they were not saddled before four.

Kingsley: Nor, I believe, to any other general officer.

The order speedily was put in execution, although it was not brought to Lord George Sackville by another mistake, so that the army was drawn up in lines before he knew anything of the matter; but the French having raised a battery at Eichhorst, which played early in the morning on some out posts on the right of the Hanoverian army ... the firing waked his Lordship, and being informed that the army was formed, he immediately repaired to the head of the line.

Kingsley: Hill, Prince Ferdinand's quarters, covered with Kingsley's and Napier s regiments, three miles from camp. The firing did not wake his Lordship. The moment I heard it, I sent to know whether his Lordship heard, or what orders he had received. The messenger brought me back word that no orders were come, as the Serjeant of his Lordship's guard told him that everything was quiet, and his Lordship in bed. But it is certain he was in time at his post.

Between six and seven, the whole allied army drew up in order of battle, having its right, consisting of cavalry under Lord George Sackville, extended toward the village of Hartum; its centre was composed of infantry, and its left of General Wangenheim's corps and some German cavalry.

Kingsley: This order of battle was never form'd. It was indeed intended, but whether by the tardiness of, or obstacle to, the columns of the left in their marching, they never join'd the column of Brittish and Hanoverian troops on the right till they alone had drove the enemy out of the field.

About seven o'clock, the French began to fire upon a battery in the front of the right wing of the allied army, from one in front of their left wing, but as soon as the English artillery was prepared, it returned their fire, and in less than ten minutes silenced those guns of the enemy's.

Kingsley: The English artillery did not silence those guns till toward the end of the action.

In the meantime, D. Ferdinand ... ordered the infantry of his centre to advance against the centre of the French, which consisted of the flower of their cavalry, and who anticipated the shock of the Allies by attacking their infantry.

Kingsley: The Infantry of the centre never came up. The attack was made by the British only; the Hanoverian guards sustained; the battle was over and the enemy beat before the centre of the Infantry arrived.

Such was the unshaken firmness of these troops ... that nothing could stop them; they cut to pieces several bodies of the enemy's cavalry, and entirely routed the whole of it. The Saxon foot, which were on the left of the French horse, made a show of coming down on those conquering regiments ... but they vanished before the English infantry.

Kingsley: They did actually come down, and very gallantly attacked Kingsley's regiment, and which at first retreated, after losing a great number of men; but on the regiment's rallying again, and being supported by a fresh battalion of Hanoverian Guards, they were in their turn repulsed. The enemy's cavalry were at this time beat out of the field.

The English regiments, Kingsley's, Napier's, Stuart's, Huske's and Brudenel's [and Home's, inserted by Kingsley], *but especially the three former, the Hanoverian Guards and Hardenberg's regiment, all behaved to admiration.*

Kingsley: I never saw Hardenberg's in the action, nor were the Hanoverians in the heat of it; as they march'd in the rear of the right column they could not be up time enough to assist but in supporting. Their loss will shew this.

Kingsley was wounded at the head of his brave regiment and fell off his horse; a squadron of French cavalry rode over him without his receiving any hurt; as he was lying on the ground, a French soldier was going to run him through with his bayonet, but he discovered himself, was taken prisoner, and afterward retaken by his own men

Kingsley: Kingsley did not fall from his horse. His horse was shot in four places, fell with and died upon him. Neither was he taken prisoner, tho' the Saxon troops marched twice over him. They were twice going to shoot him, he did not discover himself, but at length disentangled himself from his horse and rejoined his regiment and brigade.

Unknown Officer

The Operations of the Allied Army: Under the Command of His Serene Highness Prince Ferdinand, Duke of Brunswic and Luneberg, During the Greatest Part of Six Campaigns, Beginning in the Year 1757, and Ending in the Year 1762. By an Officer who served in the British Forces, T. Jeffreys, London, 1764.

The author of this work is unknown but his extensive and detailed knowledge of the operations points to the likelihood of his being Colonel Robert Boyd, the British Commissary attached to Ferdinand's headquarters. If so, however, although evidently well informed Boyd was not an eyewitness, since he was besieged in Lippstadt at the time. The redacted passages refer to the simultaneous operations by Gilsa and the Erbprinz:

[Extract pp.96-103] The 29th [of July], the army marched in three columns by the right from Petershagen camp to that of Hille; Prince Ferdinand led the first column, composed of the first line, the heavy artillery, conducted by Count la Lippe Buckebourg, formed the second column, and General Sporcken led the third, composed of the second line. The army took its camp between Hille and Fredewald, having the villages of Nord, Hemmern, and Holthausen in its front; the head-quarters were at Hille, and covered by the regiments of Napier and Kingsley. A disposition was made of the piquets of the army; the British were posted in the village of

Hartum, the Hanoverian in Sud Hemmeren, the Hessian in the wood between Hartum and Halthausen, those of Brunswic in Stemmern, and the piquets of the cavalry in the woods, with a detachment upon the road from Hartum to Hahlen.

The two brigades of light British artillery assigned to the piquets, and the Generals of the day, were ordered to Hartum.

In order to conceal the march of the army, General Wangenheim's corps was formed under arms near the batteries Count Buckebourg had erected before Thonhausen [Todtenhausen]; and when those troops went back to camp, the regiments of Buckebourg, with the brigade of heavy artillery of the left wing, encamped in the front of the line.

This day his Serene Highness desired all the general officers to inform themselves very exactly of the several passages and routs through which the army was to march into the plain of Minden, and to make themselves perfect in them, in case the army should be ordered to advance.

The 30th in the afternoon, the three battalions of Linstow, Prince Charles, and the first of Behr, (Brunswick) marched from camp, under the command of General Gilsoe, to take post at Lubec, where they were joined the next day by a detachment of 300 horse of the right wing.

The 31st in the afternoon, his Serene Highness renewed his orders to all the generals, who were to lead the columns, to examine in person those routs which their respective columns were to take in order to get into the plain of Minden, and particularly to examine the ground between the windmill of Hahlen and the village of Stammeren, where the army was to form in order of battle.

July 31st, M. de Contades, who had wrote to Paris for that purpose, obtained leave to engage the Allied Army, and having considered their situation, judged it to be a convenient juncture to attack the corps under General Wangenheim, which he thought he should be able to effect before it could be supported by the main body, from which it was detached above two leagues; he also knew the Allied Army was weakened by the large detachment under the Hereditary Prince; he therefore determined to pass the defile at Minden, contrary to the advice of the Duke de Broglio, and for that purpose the enemy were taken up all that day in throwing eight bridges over the rivulets which run between the morass and the town of Minden; about midnight they came out of their camp in eight columns: at the same time the Duke de Broglio's corps repassed the Weser at Minden, and formed the ninth column upon the right of their army...

About five o'clock in the morning of the 1st of August, the whole French army was formed in order of battle upon the plain. The Duke de Broglio's reserve came close to the Weser: the cavalry occupied the heath in the center, and the infantry of the left extended to the morass near the village of Hahlen. His Serene Highness Prince Ferdinand (who had ordered his army to hold itself ready to march at one o'clock in the morning) began to move out of his camp in eight columns about five. The cavalry of the right wing formed the first, the heavy artillery of the right wing the second, the infantry of the right the third and fourth, the heavy artillery of the center the fifth, the infantry of the left wing the sixth and seventh, and the eighth column consisted of the cavalry of the left wing.

General Wangenheim's corps, having moved out of its camp much about the same time through the openings already made in the dyke of the Landwehr, was soon formed in order of battle. The grenadiers were posted upon the right of the batteries of Thonhausen, the eight battalions of infantry in the hedges of Kutenhausen upon the right of the grenadiers, and the eighteen squadrons of cavalry in the open fields upon the right of the infantry.

At three in the morning, the enemy began with cannonading the village of Hille, where Prince Ferdinand had his head-quarters, from a battery of six pieces of cannon, erected the day before on the causeway of Eickhorst, which led through the morass to Hille. Opposite to this place they also had posted some troops with orders to make a false attack on that side, with an intent to favour their real one on our left, but not on any account to pass the morass until our army should give way. They were, however, disappointed in their scheme of drawing our attention to that quarter; for his Serene Highness, judging their intention, contented himself with sending thither two pieces of heavy cannon, and enjoining the officers of the piquets posted at Hille to defend it till the last extremity.; and at the same time General Gilsoe, who was posted at Lubec, was to attack the enemy at Eickhorst.

While the army was to march to form itself, the enemy began to cannonade the batteries of Thonhausen and General Wangenheim's corps.

Between six and seven o'clock, the Allied Army began to take up its ground in order of battle, having its right to the inclosures between the villages of Hartum and Hahlen, and its left towards Stemmeren.

The piquets of the army, under the command of the Prince of Anhalt, as lieutenant general of the day, were drawn up in the front of the cavalry of the right wing near to Hahlen; and from them were detached the piquets of the infantry, with two howitzers, to get possession of Hahlen, where the enemy had thrown two battalions during the night.

About seven o'clock, after the cavalry of the right wing was formed, the French began to fire from a battery, which raked our column of artillery upon its march.

As soon as the infantry of the right wing was drawn up behind a fir wood, the two brigades of British foot, the Hanoverian guards, and Hardenberg's regiment, marched forward to attack the left of the enemy's cavalry, having bore for about 150 paces a very smart cannonading from a large battery of the enemy, the fire of which was crossed by another battery at Malbergen: but notwithstanding the loss they sustained before they could get up to the enemy, notwithstanding the repeated attacks of the enemy's cavalry, notwithstanding a fire of musketry well kept up by the enemy's infantry, notwithstanding their being exposed in front and flank, such was the unshaken firmness of those troops that nothing could stop them; and the whole body of the French cavalry was totally routed.

The Saxon troops, which were on the left of the French cavalry, near their large battery, made a shew of coming down upon these conquering regiments, after the French horse had gone off; but the good countenance of the British foot, and the sharp fire they kept upon them, soon obliged the Saxons to fly. The brigade of infantry, commanded by Major-general Schiele, detached from the center of the army by order of his Serene Highness to support the piquets in the village of Hahlen, with Wangenheim's battalion and Hessian guards, likewise detached to support the English, at the conclusion of this attack, came in near the right of the British infantry, and also fired upon the Saxons.

During this attack upon our right one of our batteries silenced that of the enemy which had so much annoyed our infantry, and obliged it to be withdrawn. At the same time, the attack upon our left was concluded with like success, and the enemy's batteries at Malbergen were taken. In this attack the regiments du corps and Hammerstein (Hanoverian horse), the regiment of Holstein (Prussian), and the Hessian horse and battalions of grenadiers, signalised themselves prodigiously.

General Wangenheim's corps maintained pretty nearly the same position during the whole action.

The batteries erected under the care of the Count de la Lippe de Buckebourg, grand master of the artillery, in the front of Thonhausen, contributed greatly to decide the fortune of the day; he having by that battery which was before the grenadiers, totally extinguished the fire of the enemy's batteries on their right, at the same time, great havock among the Swiss and grenadiers de France.

About nine o'clock in the morning the enemy began to give way, a general confusion soon followed, and about ten the whole French army fled in disorder, part took shelter under cover of the cannon of Minden, and the rest made the best of their way over the bridges they had thrown over the rivulets between that town and the morass, every one of which they broke down as soon as they had passed over for fear of being pursued.

The Duke de Broglio covered the retreat; he occupied with his infantry the gardens near Minden, soon after which his cavalry followed the main body of their army.

Towards the end of the battle the artillery of the right was pushed forward as close as possible to the enemy posted near the wood of Dutzen, who were part of those battalions our piquets had drove out of the village of Hahlen, to which, in their retreat, they had set fire.

Part of the French army having retired into its old camp, his Serene Highness commanded the British artillery to advance as near the morass as possible to dislodge them; this order was executed, and the enemy was, in consequence thereof, obliged to retire behind the high ground whereon stands the windmill of Dutzen, with their right extending towards the Weser…

The cavalry which was posted on our right did not engage this day, as they were destined to support the infantry of the left line. When the enemy began to retreat, they were ordered to move forward, to pursue the flying troops of the enemy; but through some mistake they did not come up in time, and were thereby prevented from reaping that share of the glory which they might otherwise have done.

The victorious army encamped the same night upon the field of battle, the head-quarters being fixed at Suderhemmen. The loss of the Allies in this action amounted to about 2,800 killed and wounded, of which the British troops alone made 1394. We lost no officers of distinction. That of the French consisted in between 7 and 8000 killed, wounded, and made prisoners in the action; the Prince de Camille was amongst the number of the slain; the Count de Lutzelbourg, and the Marquis de Monit, Marechaux de Camp, with several other officers of principal rank, were among that of the prisoners. The trophies gained were forty-three pieces of cannon, ten pair of colours, and seven standards. Such was the signal and glorious victory of Thonhausen, where the intrepid bravery of the troops, their resolute and undaunted countenances during the whole action, (not one platoon giving way) gained them immortal honour.

Appendix V

Testimony of Royal Artillery Officers at the Sackville Court Martial

A s noted in the narrative, the testimony of the two artillery officers called as witnesses during Lord George Sackville's court martial is particularly illuminating. Presided over by General Onlsow, the trial commenced on 29 February 1760, the court itself comprising no fewer than ten lieutenant generals, including Lord De la Warre and Lord Cholmondley, and three major generals. Fortunately for history, a fourth major general, William Belford of the Royal Artillery, was objected to by Sackville as the two men had clashed while Sackville was Lieutenant General of the Ordnance.

Having considered the matter the court was of the opinion that this was insufficient to debar Belford from sitting, but as the latter declined to sit he was excused that duty. As it turned out, his absence, although not otherwise significant, meant that none of the otherwise august military officers remaining had any notion of artillery matters.

Whilst the various other staff officers and cavalry officers testified to the court as to who said what and when, and what orders may or may not have been given, received or understood, Captains Williams and Macbean of the Royal Artillery provided a picture of the wider battlefield beyond the trees which so hemmed in the other actors, and also provided some fascinating detail as to how the Royal Artillery operated in more general terms.

It is an intriguing series of exchanges in which certain members of the court showed themselves to be astonishingly ignorant of artillery matters and the two artillery officers proved at times at times to be deliberately obtuse and at others their testimony was bordering on downright insolence.

The following is taken from the published record of the court martial.

Captain David Williams

Lieutenant General Sackville: At what time did the British Artillery march from the camp on the 1st of August?

Williams: Something after six o'clock.

Question: Who was the commanding officer in camp, when the artillery was put in motion?

Answer: I believe it was Capt. *Macbean* that put them in motion. But I think Capt. *Philips* arrived before they were off the ground.

Q: Do you know that there was any order for the artillery to march at that time?

A: I do not know that they had any; Capt. *Macbean* can best inform the Court of that.

Q: Was you sent to me with any, and what message from Capt. *Philips*, the Captain of the artillery, during the march?

A: To the best of my knowledge, I was sent by Capt. *Philips* to see if I could find Lord *George Sackville*, or any other General Officer, that could tell me of any extraordinary orders relative to us; we were at a loss for orders; we were marching from the ground without any orders. I then rose off, and the first General Officer I met was Gen. *Elliott*; I asked him if he knew of any orders relating to us. He told me he did not, but that he would send an Aid de Camp to Lord *George Sackville*. I then begged to know where Lord *George Sackville* was; he told me in the front of the first line: upon which I told him, I believed I could be there sooner than the Aid de Camp. I then rode up to Lord *George Sackville*. My Lord *George*, before I had time to speak to him, asked me what I wanted. I told him that Capt. *Philips* had marched from the ground with our heavy brigade of artillery; that he had sent me to his Lordship, to know if he had any extraordinary orders for us. I think my Lord seemed surprized at our not having received any orders; he therefore ordered me back to hasten Capt. *Philips* up as soon as possible. I was sensible that Capt. *Philips* would not want to he hurried up, and therefore rode off to the front to reconnoitre the ground there.

I must observe, that I believe Lord George thought I was gone back directly to Capt. *Philips*.

I went to Capt. *Foy* to where his artillery was. I passed by them. He was with the light brigade of artillery. I did not go designedly to him, but to reconnoitre the ground. I asked him some questions. I do not know very well what they were; but I believe they were tending to know how the enemy was situated. He made me little or no answer. As I was very well acquainted with the situation of the ground there, and had seen the direction of the enemy's cannon-shot, I rode back as fast as I could to Capt. *Philips*, informed him of what had passed between men and my Lord *George*, as also what I had done. Then I returned to the artillery.

Q: Did I say anything more to you, than to bid Capt. *Philips* advance? Did I give any other order?

A: To the best of my knowledge Lord *George's* expression was this: We shall find something for you to do in the front.

Q: Did you advance as fast as possible with the artillery?

A: I think we did.

Q: Which way did you advance to the front? What road did you take?

A: We marched pretty near in a direct line as far as the wood, and in the same road I think that the *Hanoverian* artillery marched, and through the intervals of the cavalry of the right.

Q: Did you pass through both lines?

A: We did.

Q: When you had passed the front line of cavalry, which way did you then go?

A: I believe we marched straight on for 100 yards, and then turned to the left, and went through the wood; after we got through the wood, we inclined a little to the right, and near that wood unlimbered, took the fore-wheels from the carriages. We loaded our guns as soon as we could, and fired upon the enemy.

Q: Are you particularly acquainted with the wood, and the ground about it?

A: I think I have a perfect idea of it.

Q: Had you frequently reconnoitred that ground, and about it?

A: Yes.

Q: What sort of a wood was it?

A: The wood to the right of us in front of the cavalry – I have a sketch of it in my pocket; I do not know how to express my ideas, without looking at it – The wood to the right of where we passed through was thick.

Q: Do you mean in front of the cavalry?

A: I mean the wood to the front of the cavalry, and the left also. I cannot speak so well to it, as from the sketch.

President: You may look at the sketch to refresh your memory.

[*Witness produces it*]

This shews my idea of the wood, and what I mean by the front, and the left, and the road we passed through with the cavalry.

L.G. Sackville: What sort of a wood was it upon the left of the cavalry, and towards the front of the cavalry?

A: Thick tall trees. It was with some difficulty that we got through with our cannon.

Q: Did you march more than one carriage, or one gun abreast?

A: I believe not.

Q: Did you imagine that cavalry could march through it without breaking?

A: I am not a judge of what cavalry could do, but I think they could not have marched above three or four horses abreast.

172

Q: Have you ever seen a survey of that ground?

A: I have.

Q: Where did you see it?

A: Count *La Lippe Buckeburg* gave it me.

Q: Does that survey answer your own observation?

[*Looks at the survey*]¹

A: It does, the best of any I have seen.

Q: Does it lay down the wood as you have described it?

A: I think it does, only upon a smaller scale.

Q: What did you observe upon your first getting out of the wood?

A: I think it was our infantry that was to the left of us on the heath, and, to the best of my knowledge, the *French* cavalry marching up to charge our infantry.

Q: How long was it, after you got upon the heath, before you opened the first *English* battery? How long did you take in unlimbering and preparing?

A: I believe we began to fire about half an hour after we passed through the cavalry.

Q: Upon what did your battery first fire?

A: I only answer for four guns, which I commanded. We fired a few shot, I think upon the cavalry of the enemy, and then turned them upon a *French* battery that fired at us; when that battery was silenced, we turned the fire upon the cavalry and the infantry both.

Q: How long was it before you silenced the enemy's battery?

A: I cannot exactly say, but I believe they were silenced in about ten minutes.

Q: Did you afterwards advance?

A: When we found the enemy retreated we did.

Q: At what time of day did the enemy retreat?

A: To the best of my knowledge about twenty minutes after eight.

Q: How far did you afterwards advance?

A: We advanced with the whole ten medium twelve-pounders, which was the whole. We came to a marsh, or rather a meadow, that was there at the bottom; two of the guns of the four that I commanded went about fifty or one hundred yards, for what I know, into the meadow. I was ordered to cease firing, and these guns brought back to the edge of the marsh.

Q: Who ordered you to halt there?

A: I cannot justly say, but I was told it was by Duke Ferdinand's orders. [At this point Sackville asked whether Williams thought the cavalry could have come into action more quickly by the windmill or through the woods. Williams declined to comment, although as we shall see Lord De la Warre shortly took it up again. Sackville then asked him (as

173

with other witnesses) as to whether 'he saw any thing in my looks manner or behaviour, during the whole of that day, different from what it was on other days?' To this Williams very firmly answered in the negative, 'especially as I received my orders very distinctly from Lord George.' Sackville having no other questions, it was then the turn of the Judge Advocate and other members of the court.]

Judge Adv.: It cannot be supposed that I am acquainted with matters relating to the artillery, therefore I will only ask a question or two.

Q: With respect to the few shot that you mentioned to have fired from the guns under your command, did you perceive that they had any effect upon the enemy's cavalry?

A: I cannot say. I believe they took place, as I pointed most of them myself. But I did not perceive any thing remarkable.

L. Delawar: I will ask a question for my own information. In one of your answers you gave an account that you marched straight forwards about one hundred yards, then you turned to the left through the wood, after that you went a little to the right near the wood, unlimbered, loaded and fired upon the enemy, and then you say our infantry was to the left, and the *French* cavalry marched up to charge them. Then you was asked, on your knowledge of the ground, whether it was nearer for the cavalry to join the infantry by the windmill, or by going through the wood to the left, and you say you are not certain as to the position of the enemy; but as they were obliged to retreat by *Minden*, the windmill was the nearest way. Now I shall be glad to know, as to that part of the enemy you saw and fired upon, was it nearer for the cavalry to join them by the windmill, or by going through the wood?

A: I do not know through what part of the wood the cavalry went, and every moment of time, when troops are in motion, they alter their distance.

L. R. Bertie: From the situation the cavalry were in as you passed through the two lines, was it nearer to have gone by the windmill to the enemy you first fired upon, or was it nearer to have marched to the left through the wood to them?

A: I must beg leave to observe, that I am not a judge of what the cavalry might have done, nor do I know which way they marched. I can tell how I should have gone with a single horse.

Q: But as to the road?

A: I know of no road.

Q: If you had gone through with a horse?

A: The way the artillery went, I should have left the windmill a little to the right. Upon a single horse I should have gone a little to the left of the windmill, which I think is the shortest way.

Q: Is that the shortest way?

A: Yes, if there had been no impediment.

President: Who gave you the orders for drawing up the artillery, and firing upon the enemy?

A: I do not know. I believe it was Capt. *Philips*. I am not certain; but I believe it was by general consent. There were ten guns in one line. Capt. *Macbean* had six, and I had four.

Q: How far was it from the position the cavalry was in, when you passed them, to the spot where you unlimbered, from the left of the cavalry?

A: I believe it was between five and six hundred yards from the left of the cavalry.

Q: How far was it from the ground where you unlimbered, to the enemy's cavalry that you fired upon?

A: It is impossible for me to ascertain how far.

Q: How far do you think?

A: I think it was between nine hundred and one thousand yards.

Q: How near was the enemy's cavalry to our infantry at the time of your firing upon them?

A: I cannot give any kind of guess, as the French battery engaged my attention a good deal at that time.

L. Harrington: How long was it from the time of your passing through the cavalry to your seeing them again on the plain of *Minden*?

A: As the enemy retired, we with the artillery advanced, and fired when we had opportunity. I do not remember that I ever in particular looked back till we ceased firing, then I think the cavalry was in the rear of the infantry, both which were four or five hundred yards behind the artillery. I am not certain but I think so.

Q: Where were they?

A: In the rear of our artillery.

Q: What sort of ground was it after you passed through the wood?

A: When we first passed through the wood, I believe there was a small field of corn; to our left was heath, when we first came out of the wood.

Q: Did you then march with more than one gun in front, after you was through the wood?

A: No; there were troops and baggage to the left. I believe they were the *Hanoverian* waggons, which even prevented our own ammunition waggons coming up abreast.

Q: Did you ever upon a march advance with more than one gun in front?

A: It is the rule with us, where the ground will admit of it, in order to shorten the line of march, to march two, three, four, five, six, seven, eight, nine, or ten in front.

President: Who gave you the order for the artillery to march to the heath?

A: When I went back to Capt. *Philips*, I told him that Capt. *Foy* was

175

warmly engaged (or words to that effect) with a French battery cannonading. Capt. *Philips* said, we shall go and relieve him. I made answer that we could be of no service there, for they did not see the enemy, nor did the enemy see them, that I know of. I told him, to the best of my knowledge, that we had best go to the left, which Capt. *Philips* agreed to. A little before we entred the wood, we met Duke *Ferdinand* and the Duke of *Richmond*. The Duke of *Richmond* rode up to us, and gave an order, I don't know to whom in particular, but he spoke to anybody that heard; that it was Duke *Ferdinand's* orders that we should go there, pointing to the woo, which was then become to our right, and fire upon the enemy as fast as we could. I think I said it was impossible to go there, which I think Capt. *Philips* and Capt. *Macbean* agreed to. We marched on inkling to the left as we came out of the wood, without any farther orders that I know of.

Gen. Cholmondley: You have said it is the rule with the artillery, that when they can they double up, as far as from two or three to ten. These were twelve-pounders. Did you ever see this put in execution?

A: I am not certain to the number of ten; but I believe I have. I remember that day, when the French retreated, we marched with as many abreast as we could, thirty or forty foot from each other, in order for the pursuit.

Q: From your own knowledge, how many is the greatest number of cannon you ever have marched with abreast, of what calibres, by whom commanded, and where?

Witness: I should be glad to know whether the question means in the field, or where?

Q: I do not mean upon the parade. I mean in an enemy's country, where you are likely to come to action.

A: I think, to the best of my knowledge, when I commanded a brigade of artillery under the Hereditary Prince, where we expected the enemy every hour, that I marched them to the number of six or eight, I believe. I cannot tell in whose country it was.

Q: The calibres?

A: Twelve and six pounders, I think; I am not positive; if I had time I could recollect. Capt. *Philips* and Capt. *Macbean* have made use of the same method when they commanded.

Q: I make a difference between artillery upon the march, and artillery doubling up to a line and forming; therefore when you expected the enemy, was you ready drawn up and formed., or did you form them from one to six upon the march?

A: I formed them from one to six upon the march.

Q: At the time you mentioned, did you march with six pieces ready formed, or did you form them upon the march?

A: I really do not know what is meant by forming. I said the reason we did it was to shorten the line of march.

Q: Forming is a military term from quarter to half ranks, and so to squadrons; so you form from one gun to ten. I ask whether these six guns were ready formed, or did you form them upon the march from one to six?

A: I said from one to six upon the march; when we come to action we take the fore-wheels off.

Q: But the day you marched under the Hereditary Prince, when you was marching up, had you the cannon then regularly formed six pieces abreast, or was you marching up with one single cannon, and as you marched along doubled up?

A: I say we were marching one behind another, and upon the march, in order to shorten the march, we doubled up into six.

Q: How far did you march with six cannon in front:

A: It is impossible for me to ascertain the distance. It is as the ground will admit of it.

Q: But at that time?

A: I cannot tell whether it was five hundred yards or fifty.

Q: Did you serve in the last war in *Flanders*?

A: I did not serve in the last war in *Flanders*. I was in *Germany* in the year 1743, and was frequently with the army.

Captain Forbes Macbean

L. G. Sackville: Did you give orders for the march of the British artillery on the first of August from the camp?

A: I did.

Q: Had you any order for so doing?

A: There was no direct order from his Serene Highness that morning for so doing.

Q: Do you remember any body, and whom, being sent to me from Capt. *Philips* during the march, in relation to the artillery?

A: Yes. I was not present, but Capt. Philips told me immediately after, that he had sent Capt. *Williams* to Lord *George Sackville*, at the head of the cavalry.

Q: Did you know the answer he brought?

A: Yes

Q: Did you advance as fast as possible afterwards?

A: Yes

Q: Did you pass through the lines of cavalry?

A: To the best of my memory we did.

Q: When you had passed the front line of cavalry, how did you get into the plain?

A: We advanced a little to the left, where we heard the biggest cannonading.

Q: Did you go through the wood?

A: Yes.

Q: Was there a road or track through it?

A: Yes; to the best of my knowledge, a track made by the *Hanoverian* artillery that went before us.

Q: Have you a plan or survey of the wood?

A: No

Q: Have you seen any that you take to be accurate?

A: Yes.

Q: In whose hands is it?

A: Capt. *Williams's*.

Q: What did you observe upon your first getting out of the wood?

A: I observed, a little advanced to our left, a body of troops closely engaged, and a battery in our front.

Q: When did you open the first *English* battery, that which you commanded?

A: I cannot recollect the time.

Q: Did you not open it as soon as you could unlimber?

A: Immediately.

Q: Upon what did it play?

A: We played upon a battery which was opposed to us in our front.

Q: How soon did it silence that of the enemy?

A: To the best of my remembrance, in about 5 minutes' time.

Q: Upon which part of the enemy's army was your fire directed after you had silenced that battery?

A: Upon the body of cavalry.

Q: How soon did you advance after you had silenced the enemy's battery?

A: I cannot say exactly the time; but, when we found that the enemy's battery was silenced, we advanced.

Q: How far did you advance afterwards in the course of the day? Please to mention the different steps you took.

A: When we kept advancing, the first body of troops which we discovered as a proper object, was two large columns of infantry; we immediately unlimbered, and began playing upon them; they very soon broke and dispersed: it was afterwards said they were *Saxon* troops. We then still advanced nearer to *Minden*, till we were fired upon from the ramparts, after having played for some time upon the rearguard of the *French* army.

Q: Who ordered you to halt?

A: His Serene Highness the Duke.

Q: Did any, and what troops support your battery?

A: There were no troops near us: there was a regiment allotted for the service of the artillery; but upon our first coming into the field and unlimbering, I presume they were otherwise disposed of; they gave us twenty men to assist us, and we saw no more of them: it was a regiment of *Saxe-Gotha*.

Q: Did Capt. *Philips* send you to apply to any body, and whom, for that purpose, for supporting the artillery?

A: Yes, he sent me to apply to any General Officer at the nearest part of the line.

Q: To whom did you apply, and what passed?

A: I found Major-General *Scheele* of the *Hanoverian* troops, who commanded a brigade, I think, in our rear at a distance.

Q: What passed?

A: I acquainted the General, that I was sent by Capt. *Philips* to inform him, that we were advancing to fire upon the enemy wherever we saw them; and as his brigade was the nearest troops to us, that he might support us. His answer was that he had orders from his Serene Highness the Duke to remain there, and not expose his brigade to the cannon of *Minden*, towards which place we were then advancing, to fire on the scattered remains of the *French* troops. Major Gen. *Scheele*, at the same time, desired I would acquaint Capt. *Philips* of it, that he might not expose himself to the fire of the town.

Q: Did you go by day-break next morning after the battle towards *Minden*?

A: I went, to the best of my remembrance, between 4 and 5 o'clock next morning.

Q: Whom did you meet coming out of the town?

A: I met a French officer accompanied by a trumpet.

Q: Who was that officer?

A: He informed me that he was Aid de Camp to the Quartermaster-General of the *French* army.

Q: What did he shew and describe to you in coming along?

A: He gave me a general account of the order and disposition for battle by Marshal *Contades*, the particulars of which I cannot remember, only that he was sent by Marshal *Contades* to conduct the Duke *De Broglio* to his post; that the whole *French* army had orders to be on the field of battle, upon the ground assigned to them, at midnight; that the right of the *French* army was to be near to a red house, which he then shewed to me; the army was to be drawn up at midnight, and to the best of my remembrance, he said they were there.

Q: Did you speak to me during the action?

A: No.

L. G. Sackville: Then I shall not ask him the general question.

Judge Adv.: If the latter part of this evidence should appear to be material, I hope to be indulged with examining it hereafter; I cannot see a possibility of its being so at present: I would not anticipate his Lordship's defence.

L. G. Sackville: The other day I asked what instructions were given by Prince *Ferdinand* previous to the engagement: I ask these questions now, to shew that the *French* army was there so early that there was not time for giving any.

Judge Adv.: You say that you have seen a survey, which you believe to be accurate, and which Capt. *Williams* had: when you speak of the accuracy of this plan or survey, do you mean that it is accurate as to that part of the wood through which you passed or marched with the artillery; or are you acquainted enough with the wood to speak to the accuracy of the plan through the whole wood?

A: I only mean that part which we marched through.

Q: You observed a battery and a body of troops closely engaged: what part of the *French* army was that body of troops?

A: I believe they were the *French* cavalry engaged with the *British* infantry.

Gen. Cholmondely: Please to describe that part of the wood you marched through, and the other part that you observed in marching through.

A: I have but a very faint idea of the wood in general, but that part we marched through was thick enough to prevent our marching with the artillery to the spot proposed; therefore we were obliged to follow the track which the *Hanoverian* artillery had made before us, and were thereby obliged to make a little detour to the left.

Q: Did you think that that was the thickest part of the wood where you marched through?

A: As I have but a very faint idea of the wood in general, I cannot tell that.

Q: Could you march more than one a breast through the wood?

A: No.

Q: When you came out of the wood upon the plain, did you double up with any of your cannon?

A: Yes, we drew them up in a line.

Q: How many in a line?

A: Ten guns.

Q: Did you then advance with ten guns in front?

A: No.

Q: I should be glad to know, when you are marching up to an enemy with one gun in front, what is the greatest number that you have doubled up to, kept advancing with, of what calibre, where and by whom commanded?

A: All batteries in the field are drawn up in a line.

Q: How many can you double up to and advance with?

A: We never march with more than one gun in front: as soon as we come within sight of the enemy, we draw all the guns we have or as many as the ground will admit of, in a line.

Q: In your practice how many have you seen them double up to?

A: All the guns we have: that is the general practice.

Q: From your experience at any engagement, or any spot, how many have you doubled up to, and have you kept marching forward with them, let the number be five or ten, or any number.

A: The largest brigade I ever belonged to was this on the 1st of *August*; we were twelve-pounders, that was the calibre. It was my brigade; but as Capt. *Phillips* was the senior officer, he commanded it on that occasion.

Q: Now, as to marching forward, you have seen them double up to ten, did they all march forward in line?

A: No, that cannot be with heavy guns; but it is usual with lighter guns or battalion guns.

Q: How many guns were there at that time?

A: The brigade consisted of ten.

Q: Did you ever know of six twelve-pounders marching in front and advancing?

A: I cannot say I have.

Q: How many horses had you at each gun?

A: Five, as I remember; it is the government's allowance.

Q: Were five horses able to draw these twelve pounders through the wood?

A: Yes.

Lord Albemarle: Did the *British* artillery lead the first column?

A: No.

Q: To what column did the artillery belong?

A: The heavy artillery of the right of the army formed a column of themselves.

Q: In other marches, did not the *British* artillery always follow that column, the heavy artillery of the right, unless there were particular orders to the contrary?

A: In general, when the army marched to the right, the British heavy brigade of artillery led the column; but, when the army marched to the left, we brought up the rear.

Q: Where were the guides, at the head of the *British* or Hanoverian *artillery*?

A: I presume they were at the head of the *Hanoverian* artillery; we saw nothing of them.

Q: Was there a guide always at the head of the *British* artillery when they led the column.

A: Yes.

Q: How near was the right wing of cavalry to the body of troops that you saw engaged when you passed them?

A: I cannot tell; for the wood already spoken of intercepted the view of them.

Q: You may recollect how far it was from the wood to the spot of ground where you unlimbered?

A: We were then just before the wood.

Q: How far was it from that spot of ground to the ground you saw the *British* infantry engaged upon?

A: The distance to the best of my remembrance was between 800 and 1,000 yards.

Gen. Cholmondely: Did you see the two lines of cavalry of the right wing formed?

A: In marching up to the field of battle, I remember passing through the intervals of the cavalry of the right wing; whether they were at that time drawn up in one or two lines, I cannot recollect.

Q: Did you see them in either one or two lines halt? Did you see the cavalry drawn up and halted?

A: They were halted when we passed through them.

Q: What was the distance between the cavalry when drawn up that you passed through their intervals, to the wood that was upon their left?

A: I cannot say.

Q: Did you not march through the cavalry and go to that wood?

A: Yes.

Q: You marched with the artillery, and very slowly, and you do not know the distance between the cavalry and the wood?

A: No.

Q: Was there any thing in particular that would hinder you knowing that distance?

A: No, not that I remember.

Q: Was there any thing that more particularly pointed out the distance between the place where you first unlimbered, and the place where you saw the troops engaged, than pointed out the distance that I have asked about, between the place where the cavalry was formed and the wood?

A: Yes, there being the enemy, which alone we looked for.

Q: I should be glad to know, whether judging of distance is not of the greatest use to people concerned in artillery, and what they greatly study to make themselves masters of?

A: Yes, of very great use: in the field we make no use of instruments to ascertain distances, and only judge by the eye.

At this point the President of the Court, Sir Charles Howard, probably rather wisely, adjourned the proceedings until next morning. Neither artillery officer was called again.

Appendix VI

The British Army in the Seven Years War

L ike all European armies of the day the British army comprised horse, foot and guns as outlined in Chapter 2, and like all of them it had its own idiosyncrasies and a distinct character which shaped how it behaved upon the battlefield.

In administrative terms there were in effect two British armies at this period. The variable numbers of regiments serving in mainland Britain and abroad were carried on the English or British Establishment, reluctantly paid for by the British exchequer and administered by the Secretary at War (a government official) with the advice of the Commander-in-Chief at Horse Guards in London.

The 15,000 men established as a permanent garrison for Ireland were on the other hand paid for through the quite separate Irish exchequer and administered by the Lord Lieutenant or viceroy's staff in Dublin Castle. Apart from four regiments of 'Irish Horse' no units were permanently assigned to the Irish Establishment and any units ordered on service automatically transferred back to the British Establishment. Unfortunately the Dublin Castle regime was a byword for inefficiency and corruption and the political necessity of frequently dispersing units on minor policing duties meant it was notorious that good regiments sent there rapidly went to the dogs.

Yet Ireland served a useful purpose in that the 15,000-man establishment was fixed, unlike the British one which fluctuated at the whim of parliament and it thus provided a refuge for regimental cadres which might otherwise be disbanded in peacetime. On the outbreak of war with the regiments on the British Establishment justifying their existence by already being usefully employed, it usually fell to the Irish ones to be hurried off on active service first.[1]

In terms of organisation British regiments were broadly similar to their continental counterparts. With very few exceptions British infantry

183

regiments comprised only a single battalion and the two terms were therefore synonymous. Each infantry battalion mustered ten companies in wartime[2], one of them designated as grenadiers and formed not of the tallest, but of the steadiest and most reliable soldiers in the battalion.[3] Each company was commanded by three officers; a captain, lieutenant and ensign (or a second lieutenant for the grenadiers), and comprised three sergeants, three corporals, two drummers and a notional seventy men. One man in each company was nominated as a pioneer and formed into an independent section under a corporal. Three of the regiment's ten captains also ranked as field officers; of whom the colonel was normally but an absent patron.[4] Normally this left the lieutenant colonel and major in actual command, although it was common enough to find one or the other absent, either on leave or holding a staff or other appointment and it was even possible from time to time to find the battalion commanded by the senior captain.

Administration of the battalion was the responsibility of the Major and the Adjutant. The latter, often an ex-ranker, was an office held by one of the company officers – usually a lieutenant – assisted by the senior sergeant or sergeant major and at least one clerk. Similarly the paymaster's job was performed part time by one of the captains. The chaplain was a mythical beast rarely if ever encountered on active service. Basic medical services were provided by a surgeon and his mate, and everything else by the quartermaster, quartermaster sergeant and their assistants, all once again drawn from their companies. Both surgeon and quartermaster also drew heavily upon the regimental women. Officially six women per company were carried on the ration strength, but in practice there were usually considerably more and were employed as nurses, laundresses, cooks and other support staff.

Cavalry regiments were variously designated as Dragoon Guards and Dragoons. Confusingly the former were neither dragoons nor guards. Until 1746 they had been regiments of Horse but in that year by way of a cost-cutting measure all but the Blues and four regiments of Horse serving in Ireland (and so separately paid for) were nominally re-designated - and paid - as dragoons while at the same time granted the title of Dragoon Guards in recognition of their former status.[5] They also retained certain distinctions as to their uniforms. As Horse for example they had worn full-length lapels on their coats. Dragoons by contrast had no lapels. As they were now neither horse nor dragoons they adopted half-lapels like those worn by the infantry.

Whatever their designation, cavalry regiments were broadly similar in organisation to the infantry save that companies were designated as troops and that there were usually only six of them, with three being joined together to form a squadron. As mentioned elsewhere an additional Light troop was formed in each regiment in 1758, but none accompanied their parent units to Germany and until the arrival of the 15th Dragoons and 87th/88th Highlanders in 1760 the British contingent included no light troops.

Recruits for all these regiments were mostly enlisted at country markets and hiring fairs by small regimental parties in possession of a "beating order", which was effectively a licence issued by the government's War Office. This not only permitted them to quite literally beat a drum by way of advertisement and seek recruits for their own regiments within a specified area, but also required local officials such as magistrates, justices and constables to provide them with all necessary assistance. This requirement was frequently taken by those officials as an open invitation to empty the local jails. Just as frequently however such kind offers were politely declined since recruiting officers were earnestly, if a little optimistically, recommended to take only such as 'were born in the Neighbourhood of the place where they are Inlisted in and of whom you can get and give a good account' and positively instructed that no 'Strollers, Vagabonds, Tinkers, Chimney Sweepers, Colliers, or Saylors to be Inlisted.'[6] Instead its recruits were normally young men either lacking family ties or occasionally running away from the prospect of them. They were also disproportionately found from amongst the labouring poor and from amongst weavers and other cloth-workers, both of whom were vulnerable to unemployment during the periodic economic depressions of the day.

In an entirely typical example only seven out of eighty-nine men enlisted into Captain Hamilton Maxwell's company were aged over thirty and of the rest no fewer than fifty-nine fell into the comparatively narrow sixteen to twenty age band. As to occupations, whilst a broad scatter of occupations was represented, no fewer than sixty-two of them were recorded as labourers – albeit this was a broad term encompassing anyone who did not declare a more specific trade.[7]

Enlistment was in theory for life. There are documented cases of old men serving in the ranks such as John Tovey, then all of fifty-nine years old, who had his jaw shot away at Culloden in 1746.[8] Otherwise the dramatic reductions in the size of the Army which invariably followed the happy outbreak of peace meant that discharges were to be had for the asking and consequently most men retired by their forties if not before. Contrary to widespread belief, although it obviously had its hard bargains, the eighteenth century British Army was not some species of ambulant penal institution.

In the eighteenth century the term an officer and a gentleman was normally interpreted literally. A study by P. J. Razzell of the social origins and backgrounds of British officers found that in 1780 some twenty-four per cent were members of the titled aristocracy (albeit usually younger sons) and a further sixteen per cent were drawn from the untitled landed gentry.[9] Although accounting for forty per cent of the total even the most cursory examination of the annual *Army List* reveals that the aristocrats such as Sackville and Granby were quite disproportionately concentrated in the socially elite Guards and cavalry. Consequently, far more than sixty per cent of the officers serving in the ordinary infantry regiments, and particularly the captains and other company officers belonged to what might be termed the middling classes. That is to say an ill-defined spectrum of 'private gentlemen' drawn from the lesser landed families and from the families of professionals and even tradesmen, but generally speaking were the sons of doctors, clergymen, farmers and the like, and above all the sons of soldiers. Some had the money with which to purchase their commissions, or at least sufficient credit to obtain a loan, but all too often they lacked it and had to rely on the patronage and 'interest' of others to begin and progress their careers. It was very much an old boys' network.

The rapid rise of well-connected individuals such as Sackville belies a much slower progression for most officers. On average in 1759, the year of Minden, it was taking ten years for an officer to reach the rank of captain and seventeen years' service was commonly required for a major. Very typically a Captain Robert Bannatyne declared that same year that: 'My father [a Scottish clergyman] had no great Estate and dying whilst his children were young you May guess whether five of us did not find use for small inheritance.'[10] In this case it was Bannatyne's stepfather, another clergyman, who not only got his own son, Forbes McBean, into the Royal Artillery but obtained a commission in the East India Company service for Robert and a commission in the regular 13th Foot for his younger brother William. Once they were actually serving in the army however the all-important interest was exercised by other officers; hence Sackville's dismay at being denied unfettered powers of promotion on taking over as commander-in-chief of the British forces in Germany since that interest was naturally mirrored by grateful obligations.

Notwithstanding the supposed requirement for commissions to be purchased, there were always free commissions to be had, not least because commissions were firmly ruled not to be heritable property and therefore the death of an officer automatically offered a free promotion to the most senior man below him and so on down until ultimately creating a non-purchase vacancy for a new entrant as an ensign or second lieutenant. It was thus possible for a deserving senior NCO to gain a commission in this way, although on active service such vacancies frequently went to what were termed 'volunteers'. These were otherwise suitable young gentlemen who lacked the funding to purchase a commission and so instead served in the ranks until such time as they might be recommended to such a vacancy – usually by the general commanding on the spot.[11]

The end result was that like their men the British officer corps was a very great deal more diverse in origin and character than popular legend allows, and probably a good deal more diverse than its German and French counterparts. While the high command might be dominated by undoubted aristocrats such as Sackville, the lower ranks were often of a coarser mould and included men such as William Dawkins, a lieutenant in the 39th who once threatened to cut his major's throat! It was perhaps understandable that their German colleagues might sometimes be a little wary of British officers.

Appendix VII

His Britannic Majesty's Army in Germany

While it is usually convenient to refer to the Allied Army, the core of His Britannic Majesty's Army in Germany were his Hanoverian troops. Until the arrival of the British contingent they accounted for more than all of the rest put together and in effect first Cumberland and then Ferdinand commanded the *Hanoverian* Army and its auxiliaries.[1]

Hanover

Infantry regiments normally had only a single battalion, although the *Füss-garde* (Footguards) boasted two. Ordinarily a battalion comprised seven companies each notionally mustering 122 officers and men. There was no permanent grenadier company as such but eight men in each company were designated as grenadiers and on active service were formed into a temporary one. The *Füss-garde* grenadiers were employed as a headquarters guard, but those belonging to the line regiments were formed into three consolidated grenadier battalions. In all, at the outset of the war, there were two battalions of *Füss-garde*, twenty-four *musketier* battalions and three grenadier battalions. Two further *musketier* battalions were raised in 1758 but seemingly had only five companies apiece. None of the men in the new units were designated as grenadiers since by then the consolidated grenadier battalions had become permanent formations and were no longer sustained by their parent regiments.

All Hanoverian infantry wore red coats with regimentally-coloured facings displayed on the cuffs, lapels and linings of the coat, and usually on the waistcoat as well. Breeches were normally straw coloured and grenadiers had red cloth mitre caps displaying the facing colour on the front in the British fashion.

The cavalry comprised two household regiments; the *Garde du Corps* and the *Grenadieren zu Pferde* (Horse Grenadiers) although both were small units mustering only a single squadron apiece. The line regiments were divided between *Kürassiere* and Dragoons of which the former numbered eight regiments each of two squadrons and the latter four regiments with four squadrons apiece. Otherwise in practical terms there was no other difference between them and the *Kürassiere* regiments and the dragoons were both employed as heavy cavalry. No additional units were raised during the course of the war.

All of the cavalry wore white coats, except the two household regiments who were in red, with the latter in the inevitable mitre caps. The *Kürassiere*, oddly enough, had no armour but were clearly distinguished from the dragoons (and the *Grenadieren zu Pferde*) by being armed with carbines and having no lapels on their coats, whilst the latter in spite of their heavy cavalry role were burdened with muskets and infantry accoutrements instead.

At the outset the artillery comprised six companies each of sixty-seven officers and men, but under Prince Ferdinand it was expanded into four field brigades each of two or three companies. Unusually, Hanoverian artillerymen had steel grey coats rather than the dark blue traditionally worn by gunners across most of Europe.

There were no light troops prior to the war, but in May 1757 a small *Jäger* corps with a strength of just two companies was formed by Graf von Schulenburg. As was not uncommon, one of the companies was mounted and at about much the same time a Captain Lückner and fifty-four of his *Frei-husaren* (then in the Dutch service) were also hired. Not surprisingly this force was wholly inadequate to face the far more numerous light troops fielded by the French right from the very beginning. Consequently a dramatic expansion took place and by 1760 Lückner's Hussars had four squadrons with a notional strength of 32 officers and 632 men. The *Jäger*, taken over by the Colonel Freytag who unsuccessfully defended the Obensberg, saw an equally substantial if less spectacular expansion, rising at one point to six companies apiece of *Jäger zu Füss* and *Jäger zu Pferde*. Not surprisingly this proved unsustainable in the long run and in 1762 Freytag's corps was amalgamated with another raised by a Major von Stockhausen to make a single battalion of just four companies.

In addition there was another major unit known as Scheither's Freikorps formed in May 1758. This was an interestingly mixed corps. When first raised it had three companies, of which one, designated as *karabiniers*, was a conventionally dressed light cavalry unit; the second was designated as grenadiers and the third as *Jäger*. By 1762 it too had expanded to muster four companies of *karabiniers* and two of fur-capped grenadiers, and although there was still only one *Jäger* company, the corps also acquired an artillery detachment.

Hesse-Kassel

Next in order of size, if we except the British contingent, were those troops hired from Hesse-Kassel.[2] The infantry amounted to a *Lieb-Garde zu Füss*, eleven regiments of the line (one of which was a *Grenadiere* regiment)[3] and two consolidated grenadier battalions. Initially all Hessian infantry regiments mustered a single battalion, in this case with ten companies, and just as in the Hanoverian service eight men in each company were designated as grenadiers and drawn off into the consolidated grenadier battalions on active service. Under a new *Landgraf* in 1760[4], a major re-organisation took place along Prussian lines, which saw the regimental establishment first reduced to eight companies and then divided into two battalions each of four companies, without actually increasing the number of men in the regiment. The seniorities and designations of the regiments also changed quite confusingly, two of them for example becoming fusiliers, however as this did not take place until after Minden its complexities need not detain us. All were dressed in dark blue coats distinguished as usual by regimentally coloured facings, with straw coloured waistcoats and probably dark blue breeches[5]. Grenadiers wore mitre caps with a polished tin front and a facing coloured cloth 'bag' at the rear.

The cavalry were very similar in organisation to their Hanoverian colleagues. There was a *Leib-Regiment* and four regiments of heavy cavalry, this time designated as *Reiters* and each mustering two squadrons. There were also two regiments of dragoons each with four squadrons. The former wore white coats and the latter dark blue. The Prussian-inspired reforms in 1760 saw the *Reiters* converted to *Kürassiere* but unlike the infantry this merely entailed a change of uniform[6], not of organisation.

Originally the Hessian artillery had an establishment of two companies, but this was increased to three in 1757, with a total of fifteen officers, twenty-seven NCOs and 385 men including the necessary drivers, with two more companies being added in the 1760 re-organisation. Hessian gunners were distinguished by the traditional dark blue uniform, faced with red and for practicality's sake had dark blue waistcoats and breeches as well.

There were surprisingly few light troops in the Hessian army, with just two companies of *Jäger zu Füss* in 1757 and two more of *Jäger zu Pferde* by August 1759, dressed naturally enough in hunting green. There was also a regiment of Hussars comprising only two squadrons and although the 1760 reorganisation saw the notional establishment doubled to four squadrons, as with the infantry there was no corresponding increase in the regiment's actual strength.

Brunswick

The Brunswick continent amounted to four infantry regiments, formed of two battalions each consisting of five *musketier* companies and a discrete grenadier company. The latter were however permanently detached on mobilisation and formed into two grenadier battalions, for a total of ten battalions. All were dressed in dark blue coats with the usual varied facing colours but easily distinguished from the Hessians by wearing white waistcoats and breeches. Similarly although the grenadiers had metal-fronted caps the rear bag was dark blue rather than facing coloured. Oddly enough two of the regiments had brass-fronted caps and two tin and their companies were brigaded accordingly. As in the Hanoverian army both grenadier battalions became independent of their parent units in 1759 and one was divided to provide the cadre for a third, bringing the Brunswick total up to eleven battalions.

Oddly enough to all intents and purposes there were no Brunswick cavalry. In 1757 there was only a small regiment of red-coated dragoons mustering four companies each of three officers and sixty-six men, but it did not form part of the Allied army until after Minden. At that time it was re-designated as *karabiniere*, increased in size to three squadrons and given a completely new buff coloured uniform closely resembling that of Prussian *kürassiere* – including a black breastplate.

The artillery arm was equally small, with no heavy guns and its three companies assigned exclusively to manning the light pieces organic to the infantry regiments. While they wore the traditional dark blue gunners' coats this limited role was reflected by their wearing straw-coloured waistcoats and breeches.

The Brunswick contingent was at first equally deficient in light troops. Neither hussars nor *Jäger* were raised until late 1759, after the Minden campaign was over, although it did eventually contribute a battalion to the Chasseur brigade in 1762. Whilst out-with the scope of this study it is also worth remarking that later that year the most exotic of all Freikorps units, the *Volontaires Auxiliares de Bronswick* was formed by a Colonel von Rauch. This mustered three mounted and three infantry companies, of which the former comprised a company apiece of *Husaren, Grenadieren zu Pferde* and *Bosniaks* – the latter being kaftan-clad uhlans or lancers. The three infantry companies were officially designated as grenadiers but apparently more commonly referred to as 'Turcos' – Turks. All or most of them, both mounted and un-mounted appear to have been Balkan prisoners of war and deserters from the Imperial armies trafficked by the Prussians!

Prussia
As we saw earlier, three Prussian *Füsiliere* regiments, each of two battalions, took part in the earliest operations, but were recalled in early July of 1757 and never replaced. All three had dark blue coats, straw coloured waistcoats and a distinctive cap, similar to a grenadier one but with a lower front plate and separate 'bag'.

Early in 1758 Ferdinand received the welcome addition of two Prussian dragoon regiments mustering five squadrons each and another five squadrons of hussars. The dragoons, dressed in light blue coats, were very reluctantly returned in 1760, but the hussars, a mixed detachment comprising; three squadrons of Regiment No.5 in black, and two squadrons of No.7 in yellow, served until the end of the war.

Other Contingents

Buckeburg, ruled by the Duke of Schaumburg-Lippe, at first provided a single blue-coated infantry battalion with an establishment of 820 officers and men and a company of steel grey-coated artillery with just two light cannon. As a 'spare' unit the infantry battalion was assigned as an escort battalion for the Allied artillery train and when Ferdinand resolved to increase the number and weight of his guns, by 1759 they had also provided the personnel to man eight 12-pounder cannon. In addition Lippe also raised a small troop of *Karabiniere*, dashingly dressed and mounted in black. Despite their light cavalry role they were given black armour and helmets dating back in style to the Thirty Years War. A company of *Jäger* were more conventionally dressed in green.

Sachsen-Gotha also provided a single infantry battalion, hired into Hanoverian service at the beginning of the war. Although it fought at Mehr in 1758 it too was largely employed as an escort for the artillery and retained that role even after being taken into the Hanoverian army proper in January 1759. At that time it also exchanged its original white coats for red ones.

In addition to the above there were a number of independent units in British and Prussian pay including a very colourfully uniformed five battalion-strong *Legion Britannique* raised in 1760, largely comprised of Germans but including Swiss, Dutch and at least one Russian. Each of its battalions also boasted an integral company of dragoons but these were grouped into a consolidated regiment. Officially classed as light troops they were frequently employed in a conventional role.

Appendix VIII

The French Army and its Allies in the Seven Years War

From beginning to end French troops, albeit many of them recruited in Germany, Switzerland, Belgium, Ireland, Hungary and even Poland, formed the overwhelming majority of those opposed to His Britannic Majesty's forces, there was a division comprised of Saxon troops and from time to time some Imperial troops which were occasionally Austrian regulars but more usually drawn from a variety of minor south German states.

The French

Oddly enough in some ways the French Army might be said to have had more in common with their British counterparts than the British had with their German allies. As in the British Army, most French soldiers were recruited by voluntary enlistment. Where British ones supposedly enlisted for life, Frenchmen did so for a relatively short period of only six years, albeit it could be arbitrarily extended by a couple of years at need.[1] However a proportion of those liable for militia service were not only conscripted (by ballot) into proper battalions for second line service but were also liable to be drafted as replacements into regular regiments of the line.

French officers, like their British colleagues normally purchased their commissions, although there were some differences in emphasis. The numerous aristocrats were disproportionately concentrated in the Guards units and in the cavalry, while the line infantry officers were often men of humbler stock. Nevertheless in the 1750s some two thirds of officers were drawn from the landed gentry and this proportion would rise in coming years as *roturiers* (commoners) were steadily squeezed out. This was largely because it was widely regarded as unacceptable that someone of noble blood, however impoverished, should go into trade and therefore for the likes of Alexandre Dumas' Gascon adventurer 'D'Artagnan' the only resort was the Army. Denying promotion to commoners was not direct snobbery as such but rather reflected what was perceived to be the absolute necessity of reserving places for the otherwise unemployable minor gentry.

Infantry

French battalions normally comprised a small staff consisting of a lieutenant colonel, two majors and two ensigns (carrying the colours) and thirteen companies of which twelve were designated as fusiliers and one as grenadiers. Fusilier companies were generally forty strong with two commissioned officers – a captain, and a lieutenant as his second in command. The non-commissioned officers were two sergeants, three corporals, three lance-passadoes or lance corporals and a drummer. Grenadier companies were very slightly larger with forty-five men, a captain and two lieutenants. Most regiments had just one battalion, but a number of the more senior regiments boasted two or even more battalions. There was no apparent consistency in this, but on the other hand the French did employ, or at least tried to employ, a standardised four-battalion brigade organisation. In the Allied armies brigades were generally identified by the name of the officer commanding, but French practice was to identify each brigade by the name of the senior regiment irrespective of its other constituents. At Minden for example the *Anhalt* Brigade comprised two battalions of the Regiment *Anhalt*, one battalion of *Saint-Germain* and one of *Bergh*.

As in other armies the grenadier companies were normally detached from their parent units and formed into consolidated grenadier battalions, but although available for detached operations they also appear to have been deployed organically to their brigade. This was possible because the French also maintained two grenadier corps. The first was the *Grenadiers de France*, a four-battalion regiment originally formed from the grenadier companies of regiments disbanded at the close of the last war in 1749. While Metropolitan French regiments otherwise invariably wore white coats, this corps was distinguished by blue coats and fur caps. The second was the slightly more transient white coated *Grenadiers Royaux*, formed from the grenadier companies of Militia regiments.

A major element of the French Army was its foreign regiments, accounting on paper at least for some 48,000 men and their internal organisation could vary quite considerably. There were ten red-coated regiments of Swiss mercenaries, possessed of a considerable reputation and twelve companies apiece – they had no grenadier companies. However the establishment of each Swiss company was 120 men – three times that of an ordinary French company. While this number would inevitably have been depleted on active service, Swiss units were consequently always much larger than their French counterparts. So-called German regiments varied in number and in nationality. While the majority of the rank and file were German mercenaries, they were also comprised of Flemish, Walloon, and Dutch recruits as well as substantial numbers of men from Alsace, Loraine and Luxembourg. Generally speaking they comprised eight companies to a battalion albeit with a notional strength of about eighty men. There were no grenadier companies, but like many other German units six men in each fusilier company were designated as such and consolidated as and when required. Most, but not all, German regiments were distinguished by wearing blue coats and usually of a notably lighter shade than that worn by the Hessians and Brunswickers. Also serving in Germany was an Irish brigade comprising five red-coated Irish regiments and two blue-coated Scottish ones, which were unusual in that their establishment was exactly the same as ordinary French units with twelve companies of fusiliers and one of grenadiers.[2]

Cavalry

French cavalry were accorded a confusing variety of designations. All regiments of Horse or heavy cavalry were rather paradoxically classified as *cavalerie legere* or light cavalry. They were nothing of the sort of course for the term was an archaic one originally used to distinguish them from the heavily armoured *Gens d'Armes* or *Gendarmerie*. Regiments tended to be large with four squadrons apiece. Most, like the infantry, wore white coats but the Gendarmerie were in red and royal regiments in blue or red. So too were a handful of others, and a number of mainly foreign units boasted bearskin caps rather than hats.[3] Equipment and doctrine were conventional enough but their performance was to be compromised both by the slow pace of their manoeuvring and an alleged unwillingness on the part of their colonel proprietors to take risks.

Dragoons were still regarded as mounted infantry in the French service and from time to time as at Hastenbeck and Ste. Cast were employed accordingly. Whilst their organisation was broadly the same as other cavalry, their equipment was rather different and reflected that role with sabres rather than heavy broadswords, muskets rather than carbines, and even entrenching tools[4]. Uniforms were either red or blue and although hats were officially prescribed, some units retained a preference for forage caps. Whilst not so prominent in the mounted role they would emerge from the war with a more professional reputation than the heavy cavalry.

The artillery, as in most armies, was the most professional arm, requiring a high degree of theoretical and practical knowledge in both officers and men. French gunners had a good reputation and the Lieutenant General of the Artillery Jean-Florent de Valliere had imposed a considerable degree of standardisation in both calibre and design. Just five calibres existed of which an 8-pounder and a 12-pounder were used as field artillery. A 4-

pounder was assigned to the close support of the infantry and as in the British service largely crewed by infantrymen rather than blue-coated artillery personnel.

From the very beginning French light troops were very numerous and as we saw in the Hastenbeck campaign effectively swamped their Allied counterparts. This was in large part due to the earlier work of the great *Marechal* de Saxe and other influential writers such as the Marquis de Folard. A considerable number of light troops had been employed and proved their worth during the last war, and at its end the best of them were consolidated and retained in service.

Exclusive of units serving in other theatres, in total there were in Germany four regiments of Hussars proper, and eight legionary corps in 1757. As time went on most were enlarged and joined by others. The organisation and strength of individual units varied somewhat and in the beginning of the war it was common to find mixed companies of about forty infantry and thirty cavalry apiece. As they grew in size this mixing was soon found to be impractical and by 1759 most corps were fielding eight discrete companies apiece of infantry and cavalry. Uniforms were generally blue, often with red facings, and with laced hats but the celebrated *Chasseurs de Fischer* were all in green, coats waistcoats and breeches, and the *Volontaires-Etrangers de Clermont Prince* in a very striking buff yellow uniform faced red. One notable feature was their head-dress. Most infantry wore cocked hats, and their grenadiers had fur caps, but Fischer's men having started out wearing a hussar-style mirliton cap, adopted a smaller and more practical dragoon-style forage cap. His mounted chasseurs were in hussar dress, but most other corps fielded dragoons who were often distinguished by the 'classical' styled helmets with horse-hair manes introduced by *Marechal* de Saxe.

The Saxons

Frederick of Prussia had followed up his victory at Pirna in 1756 by incorporating the Saxon Army into his own, only to find them deserting en masse – sometimes by whole regiments. Sufficient of these *Reverenten* did so for the army to be reconstituted in Hungarian territory, albeit on a reduced scale.

Some cavalry units which had escaped the debacle at Pirna were taken directly into Austrian pay and a total of twelve infantry regiments were raised or rather re-raised. Not surprisingly deploying the reconstituted infantry units against the Prussians was considered imprudent. While those cavalry units which had not been involved in the capitulation at Pirna continued to serve with the Austrian Army against the Prussians, all twelve infantry regiments transferred to the French service in 1758 and were there commanded by the Comte de Lusace.[5] They would therefore form a substantial part of the French army at Minden.

The composition and organisation of these regiments was interesting. Three of the regiments (Kurprinzessen, Prinz Friederich August and Prinz Xaver) had escaped more or less intact and retained their original establishment of two battalions with a total of eight companies of *musketiers* and one company of grenadiers. The other nine had just a single battalion of four companies of musketiers (each with a nominal strength of 125 men). However, the regiments Garde, Prinz Maximilian, and Prinz Joseph had a grenadier company apiece formed from the former Leibgrenadiergarde. Rather more eccentrically the grenadier companies for the regiments Minckwitz, Rochow, Prinz Clemenz and Brühl were formed from dismounted cavalry troopers[6], while the grenadiers of Lubomirski and Gotha were former artillerymen.

At first the reconstituted Saxon army had no artillery train as such, but on entering the French service each infantry regiment was provided with two 'Swedish' 4-pounders by way of integral artillery support and so the gunners reverted to their proper role.

Initially the reconstituted regiments must have presented a somewhat motley appearance when paraded with their ad hoc grenadier companies, but with the aid of French and Austrian subsidies they were soon properly clothed and equipped. Saxon infantry were dressed in white coats with various coloured facings displayed on collar, cuffs and linings, facing coloured waistcoats and white breeches. At first all wore tricorne hats with white lace but by 1761 if not earlier the grenadiers had fur caps. The artillerymen wore green coats faced with red and had buff waistcoats and breeches, with yellow lace on their hats.

References and Notes

Chapter 1: Hastenbeck and the Fall of Cumberland

1. Sir Reginald Savory, *His Britannic Majesty's Army in Germany During the Seven Years War* (Oxford, Clarendon Press, 1966), p.9.
2. Cumberland Papers; quoted in Savory, p.15.
3. Fusilier-Regiments Nr.44 (Jungkenn), Nr.45 (von Dossow) and Nr.48 (Hessen-Kassel), under *Generalleutnant* the *Erbprinz* of Hesse Kassel.
4. *The Volontaires de Flandres* and the *Volontaires du Hainaut* were both colourfully uniformed legionary corps each comprising six companies with forty infantry and thirty dragoons apiece. The *Volontaires de l'Armee* were presumably an ad hoc collection of volunteers from the line. None of them figure in accounts of the subsequent fighting on the Obensberg.
5. All three of the original brigades assigned to Chevert were *Vieux* or Old corps, boasting four battalions apiece and therefore each constituted a brigade in its own right. Otherwise, when brigades comprised two or more regiments they were named after the senior one. Chevert was subsequently reinforced by the Brigade *D'Eau*, comprising two battalions of that corps and two others belonging to the regiment *D'Enghien*.
6. Anonymous French account, published in *Neues militärisches Journal* 1, Hanover 1788, pp.220-36.
7. ibid.
8. ibid.
9. The *Erbprinz*, or Hereditary Prince as he is most frequently referred to in British sources, was Karl Wilhelm Ferdinand (1735-1806), the eldest son of the Duke of Brunswick and nephew to Prince Ferdinand of Brunswick, the soon-to-be commander of the Allied forces in succession to Cumberland. He served outstandingly throughout the war and commanded the Coalition forces at Valmy in 1792, before being fatally wounded at the battle of Auerstädt in 1806.
10. Cumberland Papers 55/4 quoted in Savory, p.36.
11. Anonymous French account, published in *Neues militärisches Journal* 1, Hanover

1788, pp.220-36.
12. Savory, p.38.

Chapter 2: Ferdinand of Brunswick and the King's Enemies

1. At this period there was not one Foreign Secretary but two; that is one to deal with southern Europe, which included France, and the other, in this case Holderness, dealing with northern Europe.
2. The Sachsen Gotha Regiment was taken into the Hanoverian army proper in January 1759 and so fought at Minden in red coats rather than its original white ones. Confusingly there was also a Sachsen Gotha regiment in the Austrian Army and its 3rd battalion served with the brigade attached to d'Estrees army at Hastenbeck and afterwards.
3. Saxe, Maurice de and Philips, T.R. (Ed.), *Reveries on the Art of War* (Harrisburg, 1944), p.41.
4. Hughes, B.P., *Firepower: Weapons Effectiveness on the Battlefield 1630-1850* (Arms and Armour, London, 1974), pp.127-33.
5. Saxe, pp.32-3.
6. Tomasson, K., and Buist, F., *Battles of the '45* (Batsford, London, 1962), p.106.
7. Macksey, Piers, *The Coward of Minden. The Affair of Lord George Sackville* (Allen Lane, London, 1979), p.28.
8. Savory, Sir Reginald, *His Britannic Majesty's Army in Germany During the Seven Years War* (Clarendon Press, Oxford, 1966), p.58, quoting Johan Wilhelm von Archenholz, *Geschichte des Siebenjährigen Krieges in Deutschland, von 1756 bis 1763* (1793).
9. In fairness to Ferdinand he had intended to get over the river short of the Dutch border, but at the last moment the bargees contracted to assemble the bridge flatly refused to cross into German territory. A courteous apology for the 'inadvertent' error followed.
10. The *Legion Royale* was typical of French light infantry of the period, being made up of a mixture of infantry and mounted infantry.
11. Although these brigades would each have comprised four battalions they were all of them very weak and the disparity in numbers may not have been as great as might at first appear. Back in March, Clermont had declared that companies were only twelve strong, which would imply about 150 men to each battalion, exclusive of officers and grenadiers, (Savory, p.58). No doubt there was an element of exaggeration in this and replacement drafts were subsequently sent up into the line, but there seems little doubt as to the continuing weakness of the French infantry.

Chapter 3: The British Army Goes Buccaneering

1. Griffiths, R., *A Genuine and Particular Account of the Late Enterprise on the Coast of France, 1758* (R. Griffiths, London, 1763). The 74th and indeed all other regiments numbered above the 70th were disbanded at the war's end and have no

connection whatsoever with any units subsequently bearing those numbers.

2. They were organised as follows:

Guards Brigade under Major General Alexander Drury

       1st Footguards

       2nd Footguards

       3rd Footguards

It should be noted that the Footguards were organised rather differently from ordinary regiments of the line in that the 1st Footguards comprised no fewer than twenty-four battalion companies and four grenadier companies, whilst the 2nd (Coldstream) and 3rd (Scots) Footguards had sixteen battalion companies and two grenadier companies apiece. Service battalions would then be formed on a temporary basis from amongst this pool of companies. It was not unknown for such service battalions to be mixed formations comprising companies drawn from all three regiments.

1st Brigade under Major General John Mostyn

       Bentinck's 5th Foot

       Home's 25th Foot

       Manners 36th Foot

2nd Brigade under Major General John Waldegrave

       Kingsley's 20th Foot

       Loudoun's 30th Foot

       Wolfe's 67th Foot

3rd Brigade under Major General George Boscawen

       Huske's 23rd Royal Welch Fusiliers

       Hay's 33rd Foot

       Lambton's 68th Foot

4th Brigade under Major General Granville Elliot

       Cornwallis' 24th Foot

       Effingham's 34th Foot

       Richmond's 72nd Foot

3. The experiment was obviously successful in that a number of light dragoon regiments were raised afterwards. However, the original light troops did not accompany their parent units to Germany but were instead employed on what was laconically termed 'the Coast duty', i.e. patrolling the coast to provide support for the Revenue service and as look out for unwelcome visitors ranging from smugglers to French spies moving in either direction.

4. Walpole, Horace, *The Letters of Horace Walpole* (Lea and Blanchard, London, 1842), p.365. The letter, to Horace Mann, is misdated to 10 February 1758, but was obviously written in May shortly before the generals embarked for Ste. Malo.

5. Griffiths, p.8.

6. ibid, pp.9-10. This provides a clear illustration of the draining effect of maintaining grenadier companies. Assuming the grenadier companies were

already up to their authorised establishment of seventy rank and file, an additional thirty men was demanded from the rest of the battalion to bolster the grenadiers before a shot had been fired. The two battalions were commanded by Major Peter Daulhatt, of the 33rd, and Sir William Boothby.

7. ibid, p.22. 'Lord Down' was Francis Stuart, Lord Doune, eldest son and heir to the Earl of Moray, serving as a volunteer. The unfortunate colonel of militia was the Comte de Landal.

8. Todd, William, *The Journal of Corporal William Todd 1745-1762* (Army Records Society, Stroud, 2001), p.47.

9. ibid, p.48. Todd was exaggerating or misinformed as to the garrison. Ste. Malo was defended by a single battalion of the *Boulonnois* Regiment, three companies of the *Marboef* Dragoons and about 2,000 *Gardes Cotés*, all under the command of the Marquis de la Chatre.

10. Griffiths, p.33.

11. Walpole, p.365 'Mr Pitt's friends exult on the destruction of the three French ships of war, and one hundred and thirty privateers and trading ships, and affirm that it stopped the march of threescore thousand men, who were going to join the Comte de Clermont's army. On the other hand, Mr Fox and company called it breaking windows with guineas, and apply the fable of the mountain and the mouse.'
A guinea was a gold coin with a notional value of £1.05 and used as the principal unit of currency in most transactions greater than £1.00 sterling.

12. Middleton, Richard, *The Bells of Victory: The Pitt-Newcastle Ministry and the Conduct of the Seven Years War 1757-1762* (Cambridge University Press, Cambridge, 2002), p.73.

13. Macksey, p.31.

14. The Guards, under Drury, were unchanged of course, but otherwise a complete re-organisation took place:
    1st Brigade under Major General John Mostyn
        Bentinck's 5th Foot
        Hay's 33rd Foot
        Wolfe's 67th Foot
    2nd Brigade under Major General George Boscawen
        Cornwallis 24th Foot
        Effingham's 34th Foot
        Lambton's 68th Foot
    3rd Brigade under Major General Granville Elliot
        Loudoun's 30th Foot
        Manners' 36th Foot
        Richmond's 72nd Foot
    The Light Troops belonged this time to the 1st, 3rd, 7th and 11th Dragoons.

15. These were two battalions of the Regiment *Lorraine*, one of the Regiment *Horion*

(a blue-coated Walloon or Belgian unit), and one of the Irish regiment *Clare*, whose red coats were particularly commented on by a number of eyewitnesses. In addition the *Languedoc* Dragoons and three battalions of the *Royal Vaisseux* were available in the local reserve.

16. Bomb ketches were specially designed warships intended for the bombardment of onshore targets. The fore-mast was replaced by a specially strengthened hold containing a bomb or mortar piece, manned by Royal Artillery personnel.

17. Anonymous, *A Compleat History of the Present War: from its commencement in 1756, to the end of the campaign, 1760* (W. Owen etc., London, 1761), p.287; Todd, pp.68-9.

18. Todd, p.72. The reference to Pandours is misleading, since there is no other evidence of light troops being present. However, as with his later references to hussars it would appear he was referring to them by *role* rather than origin.

19. ibid, pp.74-5.

20. *Compleat History*, p.289. The complaint of young gentlemen with no business giving orders appears to be a veiled reference to Prince Edward, the Duke of York, who was present with the expedition as a volunteer. Captain William Lindsey belonged to the 11th Dragoons, and there had been an interesting piece about him in the *Weekly Journal* for 23 May 1758: 'The hussars of the 9 regiments are now preparing to go on the expedition. The flower of these Hussars is the Troop commanded by Capt. Lindsay quartered at Maidenhead where they have been practising the Prussian exercise and for some days have been digging large trenches and leaping over them, also leaping high hedges with broad ditches on the other side. Their Captain on Saturday last swam with his horse over the Thames and back again and the whole Troop were yesterday to swim the river'; Lawson, C.C.P., *A History of the Uniforms of the British Army,* Vol.II (Norman Military Publications, London, 1941), pp.148-9.

21. In all, d'Aiguillon assembled battalions from the regiments *Royal-Vaisseaux* (three battalions); *Bourbon; Brissac; Penthievre; Bresse; Quercy;* and *Volontaires Etrangers* (two battalions); to which were added the regiments *Brie* and *Boulonnois* from Ste. Malo. Then there were also the embodied militia battalions of *Marmande* and *Fontenay-le-Comte*, and the *Marboef Dragoons*. He also had ten guns and some mortars.

22. Todd, p.96. Todd identifies him as a deserter from the Irish Brigades in the French service, but as none of its regiments were present with d'Aiguillon, he may therefore have come from the *Volontaires Etrangers* – a mainly German foreign legion.

23. *A New Military Dictionary: or, the Field of war. Containing a particular ... account of the most remarkable battles, sieges, bombardments, and expeditions, whether by sea, or land, such as relate to Great Britain* (J. Cooke, London, 1760). Frustratingly the *Military Dictionary* is un-paginated but includes a lengthy, well researched essay on Ste. Cast under CAS.

24. ibid.

25. Mackinnon, Daniel, *Origin and Services of the Coldstream Guards* (London, 1883), p.401.

26. *A New Military Dictionary*.
27. Todd, p.291.

Chapter 4: Highe Germanie

1. The *Waldner* Brigade (four battalions of Swiss); *Royal Bavière* Brigade (three battalions of Germans); *Rohan* Brigade (four French battalions); and the *Royal Deux-Ponts* Brigade (three German battalions). Cavalry support comprised two squadrons apiece of the *Royal Allemand; Nassau-Sarrebruck; Wurtemberg* and *Cavalerie Liegeoise* (all but the latter being Germans) and four squadrons of the *Apchon* Dragoons. The light troops were the *Chasseurs de Fischer* and the *Royal-Nassau* Hussards – again both were predominantly German.
2. Isenberg had the Regiments Isenburg and Canitz and two squadrons of the *Reiter* Regiment von Prüschenk. Those units scraped together by the Landgraf were a very mixed bag, comprising three battalions of militia, five companies of garrison grenadiers and two of invalids, three companies of *Jäger*, and a squadron each of the Prinz Friederich Dragoons and the *Husaren Korps*.
3. Chevert was something of an oddity. It was rare for *roturiers* or commoners to rise beyond the rank of captain in the French Army, and would be well-nigh impossible under the post-war reforms, yet through bravery and sheer competence he had risen from the ranks to become a lieutenant general.
4. This again was a very mixed bag indeed, comprising two battalions apiece of Hanoverians (including the Sachsen Gotha Regiment), Hessians and Brunswickers, besides a couple of detached grenadier companies. Cavalry support amounted to four squadrons of the Hanoverian Buchse Dragoons and the fifty-strong Buckeburg *Karabiniere* – a rather exotic light cavalry unit wearing seventeenth century half-armour.
5. His two regular brigades were those of *Reding* and *Brancas*, the first largely being made up of Swiss and German units. The light troops comprised two troops of hussars, three small free-companies, and four regular grenadier companies taken from the Köln garrison.
6. The French Army was in the habit of mobilising the country's militia in wartime for a variety of purposes, including the provision of reinforcement drafts for regular units. Some, as we have seen were employed in local defence, particularly in coastal areas. Where this was not necessary they could be employed in the field on line of communications duties and even to serve as garrisons for fortresses well beyond France's borders. The *Grenadiers Royaux* were consolidated battalions made up of the grenadier companies of militia regiments. Ordinarily, they had a fairly good reputation, although they signally failed to live up to it at Mehr.
7. The best account of the battle is Chevert's own *Relation of the Combat of Mehr*, published in 1758, in which he was understandably bitter about the behaviour of the militia.
8. Born in 1721, Granby was the eldest son of the Duke of Rutland. His entry into

the army was a touch unorthodox in that in 1745 his father raised a provincial regiment for service against the Jacobites and young Granby was placed in command of it. The urgency of the emergency had seen the officers of the various provincial regiments reluctantly granted permanent rank in the Army. Granby made the most of this and political expediency saw him promoted to major general in 1755 and made colonel of the Horse Guards (Blues) in May 1758. He followed them to Germany, arriving on 21 August.

9. Once again it might be worth emphasising that with the coastal expeditions then still underway all six regiments had left their light troops behind. Although some individual officers subsequently made their way out there by way of replacements, none of the light troops ever served in Germany.

10. These were intended to replace the 51st Foot as the garrison of Emden, but also served as a repository for those soldiers belonging to the expeditionary force rendered unfit by wounds, sickness or other causes, to serve with the six battalions in the field. Originally ranked as the 82nd Foot, it survived the war as the 72nd Foot only to be disbanded in 1768.

11. Duncan, Francis, *History of the Royal Regiment of Artillery* (Murray, London, 1879), Vol.I, pp.207-14.

12. J.A. Oughton, *By Dint of Labour and Perseverance ... A journal recording two months in northern Germany kept by Lieutenant-Colonel James Adolphus Oughton, commanding 1st battalion 37th Regiment of Foot, 1758*, Society for Army Historical Research Special Publication No.14, (London, 1997), pp.44-5.

13. These were Breidenbach Dragoons and *Infantrie* regiments Diepenbroick and Block. Oddly enough, although their commander was a Hessian officer, all three regiments were Hanoverian, which serves to illustrate the degree of integration in the Allied army, at least at a command level.

14. It was probably regarded as a good omen that the arrival of the British contingent coincided with news of the capture of the French fortress of Louisburg, in Canada, and on 24 August Oughton recorded: 'A Feu de Joye of all the Army and Detached Corps for the taking of Louisburg beginning with 42 guns of the Hanoverian Park of Artillery, then the Battalion Guns, and lastly the small Arms beginning with the Cavalry on the right of the 1st. Line & ending with those on the right of the 2d. repeated 3 times, Drums beating & Trumpets sounding, and Solemn thanks-giving order'd to be returned for this great and important Event. The Cavalry fired their Pistols only; it Thundered Lightened & rained excessively hard the whole time.'

15. Savory, p.101, quoting Ferdinand's military secretary, Westphalen.

16. Oughton, p.51.

17. ibid, p.52. Yet a little contrarily, Oughton's diary for 30 August recorded: 'Severe orders from D. of Brunswick agst. Marauding, the British not included in the Reprimand.'

18. Mackesy, p.37.

19. ibid, p.25.

20. The dukedom was thus inherited through his aunt Henrietta, the 1st Duke's elder daughter, but until 1744 his enjoyment of the title was blighted by the continued existence of his great aunt Sarah, the Dowager Duchess of Marlborough. In order to propitiate her and assure his inheritance he found it necessary to align himself with the opposition in Parliament, thus alienating the King, although marriage in 1738 gave him the courage to effect a reconciliation with the Court. This enraged his great aunt but made it possible to launch a not particularly distinguished military career.

21. Pitt, William, *Correspondence of William Pitt, Earl of Chatham.* London, John Murray 1837, Vol.I, p.337, Marlborough to Pitt, 18 August 1758. The letter is worth reproducing in full:

'Sir: I wish I may not make you detest the sight of a letter from me, lest it should be filled with my distresses; but who should I address myself to when aggrieved but you, to whom I am already most obliged? I believe my present complaint may be called, in some degree a national one, though I have the misfortune to be the person most immediately injured. You may remember that, on Lord George Sackville's being permitted to come with the troops to Germany, major-generals Kilmanseg and Oberg were made lieutenant-generals, with their commissions ante-dated, lest they should be commanded by an Englishman, whom they had formerly had the *pas* of; which did not make the least murmur from him, or any one in the English Army.

'Judge then, Sir, how I must be astonished and afflicted to find, at my arrival here, lieutenant-general Spoken, whom I had commanded in this very country, just made a general of foot over my head! This is such a disgrace to me in the face of the whole allied army, that I most earnestly intreat you to lay my humble request at his Majesty's feet, which is, that he will either be so good as to give me a commission of general, dated from the time I was made master-general of the ordnance, from which moment I have, by his orders, the same orders and guards of a general, or permit me to retire from the army, and all employments for ever. I hope, if I am thought unworthy of that rank personally, I may be excused, as an Englishman, for not quite tamely submitting to so strong a mark of the English being thought fit for nothing, but to be cleavers of wood and drawers of water to the Hanoverians.

'If I have said anything too strong forgive me; for my heart is so full and so sore, it would burst if I was not to open it to you, whom I sincerely esteem and honour; and believe me to be, with great truth, your most sincere and humble servant. Marlborough.'

22. The Saxons were something of a nasty surprise for the Allies. At the very outset of the war Frederick of Prussia had trapped the Saxon Army at Pirna and contrary to the normal usages of war had incorporated it within his own at its surrender. Since that time sufficient men had escaped from the Prussian service to allow the army to be partially reconstituted under Austrian patronage and, in order to avoid complications in fighting the Prussians, most of it was transferred to the Western Front.

23. Oughton, p.48 and pp.52-3. This had little effect and another order stated that if the bread wagons were used for men with dysentery they were to be filled with straw and cleaned out before being reloaded with bread!

Chapter 5: Spring 1759

1. HMC, Stopford-Sackville, p.53 (Newcastle to Sackville, 31 October 1758).
2. HMC, Stopford-Sackville: pp.53-4 (Ligonier to Sackville, 31 October 1758). The reference was to the third clause in these instructions attached to Sackville's commission as General and Commander-in-Chief:

   1. WHEREAS We have thought fit to appoint you, by the Commission herewith transmitted to you, to be Commander in Chief of out British Forces employed on the Lower Rhine; you are, upon the Receipt of these Our Instructions and Commission, to give due notice thereof to Our good Cousin Prince Ferdinand of Brunswick, Commander in Chief of Our Army now assembled upon the Lower Rhine.
   2. WITH regard to Marching, Counter-marching, Attacking the Enemy, and all Operations whatsoever, to be undertaken by Our said Troops, you are constantly to put in Execution such Orders as you may receive from Our said Good Cousin Prince Ferdinand of Brunswick, or such other Person as may hereafter be Commander in Chief of Our said Army, according to the Rules of War.
   3. IN CASE of the Vacancy of any Commission in Our said British Forces, You are to give Us immediate Notice thereof, in order to your receiving Our further Pleasure thereupon, recommending to our Favour such Officers as shall, in your Opinion, best deserve to be advanced.
   4. DURING your Continuance in this Service, you are to send, or cause to be sent to Us, by one of Our Principal Secretaries of State, constant Accounts of all that passes; and you are to follow all such further Orders and Directions as We shall send you, either under our Sign Manual, or by one of Our Principal Secretaries of State [Court Martial: 9-10].

3. Mackesy, p.41.
4. Typically, on 15 April 1759, Sackville wrote to Lord Barrington, the Secretary of War, to advise that as Captain Hicks and Captain Burton had been appointed aides de camp to himself and Lord Granby he recommended that Peter Chabert of Napier's and Captain Richard Callis of the 1st Dragoon Guards should be appointed to replace them as majors of brigade. At the same time, noting that Ensign Thomas Clements, of Napier's, was too young to serve, he recommended that a volunteer named Arthur Ward be appointed in his place. Likewise, another named Mulcaster was recommended to the vacancy in Home's 25th Foot caused by the promotion of Ensign Gunning. At the same time, however, he regretted what while 'everyone' is pleased with the promotion of Colonel Whitley, he regretted that Major Robert Hepburn of the Inniskillings and some others 'have not been thought worthy of His Majesty's favour'. Sackville's powers were

indeed very much less than those enjoyed by his predecessor, or for that matter by his own father when in Ireland. See HMC, Stopford-Sackville, pp.305-6.

5. The Army List for 1740 confirms that this was his first commission and that as the son of the viceroy he was spared the ordinary necessity of first serving as a cornet and then a lieutenant. Cathcart's Horse was then carried on the Irish establishment and as the King's viceroy Dorset had an entirely free hand when it came to making appointments and approving promotions in the regiment. Although he was no longer viceroy in 1740, when the aged Lieutenant Colonel Hutcheson of Bragge's 28th Foot died, Philip Bragge was a close family friend, so appointing the then Captain Sackville to the resulting vacancy was easily arranged. As a measure of the close personal connection between them it is worth noting that when Bragge died in June 1759 he left the bulk of his £7,000 estate to Sackville.

6. Order dated 27 June 1743. By convention this brevet also conferred the appointment as Aide de Camp to the King. The promotion is universally attributed in secondary sources to Sackville's good conduct at Dettingen, but the 28th Foot did not fight there, and when the Bishop of Kildare wrote to congratulate Sackville's father on 14 July, he commented, 'it was a cruel misfortune to him [Sackville] not to have been at Dettingen'. HMC Stopford-Sackville, p.37.

7. As Cathcart's Horse this was the same regiment in which Sackville received his first commission. At that time it had been ranked 7th in seniority but became the 3rd in 1746.

8. Strictly speaking the set had originally been formed around King George's elder son Prince Frederick ('Poor Fred'). However, following his unexpected death in 1751 the group continued to meet at Leicester House under the leadership of the Marquis of Bute, nominally as adherents to the future George III.

9. Mackesy, p.30.

10. HMC, Stopford-Sackville p.53 (Ligonier to Sackville, 12 January 1758).

11. De la Warre MSS. in *Hist. MSS. Comm.* 4th Rep. p.282.

12. Guy, Alan, *Oeconomy and Discipline; Officership and Administration in the British Army 1714-63* (Manchester University Press, Manchester, 1985), p.20. Strangely enough the King's black book quite literally existed and may indeed have been the origin of the expression.

13. Pitt, Vol.1, p.337.

14. No sooner was Sackville gone than Granby discovered pressing personal business at home and had his father, the Duke of Rutland, pull strings at court to grant him leave. That left Waldgrave in command of the infantry and Whitefoord in charge of the cavalry.

15. HMC, Stopford-Sackville, p.302 (Ferdinand (in French) to Sackville, 31 December 1758).

16. HMC, Stopford-Sackville, p.302 (Sackville (in French) to Ferdinand, 19 January 1759).

17. The letter is a touch ambiguous as to whether Sackville thought Bedford might be obstructive or whether the King himself was expressing frustration at the prospect. In either event it is worth noting that although no British soldiers had as yet been killed or wounded in action during the five months since they landed, some hundreds of replacements were already required for those men dead or incapacitated through the ordinary attrition of service in a foreign country.

18. HMC, Stopford-Sackville, pp.303-4 (Sackville to Ferdinand, 23 February 1759).

19. The dismounted element of the Buckeburg Carabiniers were so converted, while the Hessians manned their new guns by taking men from the militia.

20. In his new role as a cavalry officer it is important not to confuse Major General Granville *Elliot* with the subsequently more famous Colonel George Augustus *Eliot* of the 15th Light Dragoons.

21. *The Operations of the Allied Army: Under the Command of His Serene Highness Prince Ferdinand, Duke of Brunswick and Luneberg, During the Greatest Part of Six Campaigns, Beginning in the Year 1757, and Ending in the Year 1762. By an Officer who served in the British forces* (T. Jeffreys, London, 1764), pp.69-70.

22. Notwithstanding his victory at Lutterberg, Soubise reckoned Kassel too far forward to maintain and had withdrawn southwards. However, it was still necessary to establish a proper base of operations and so Frankfurt am Main, then a Free city, was seized by treachery: 'On the 2d of January, the regiment of Nassau presented itself before one of the gates, demanding permission to pass through the city. This liberty was granted, and they were accordingly conducted by a detachment of the garrison, as is the customary ceremony on such occasions, as far as the Saxenhausen gate. When they arrived there, instead of proceeding forward, they halted, seized on the grand guard and took post.' Soubise himself was soon afterwards recalled to take command of the forces being assembled for the threatened invasion of England and handed over to Broglie on 4 February, *The Operations of the Allied Army*, p.74.

23. Ferdinand to Holderness, Münster, 21 March 1759, quoted in Savory, p.121. Frederick was also copied into the correspondence.

24. *The Operations of the Allied Army*, p.70. Of the remainder two squadrons were Hanoverian and two Hessian.

25. That is, his two regiments of dragoons, two squadrons of the Malachowski (Yellow) Hussars and one of the Reusch (Black) Hussars – the other two squadrons of the latter were with the Erbprinz.

26. *The Operations of the Allied Army*, pp.77-8.

27. The German regiments *Royal-Suédois* and *Royal Deux-Ponts*, and the Swiss regiments *Waldner* and *Planta.*

28. Interestingly the fifth battalion of the brigade was 1/Royal-Roussillon, whose second battalion was at the time serving in Canada.

29. He also had four squadrons of the Brunswick *Lieb Dragooner*, but they were obviously of little use in storming the orchards.

30. These were the grenadier companies of the Hanoverian *Füss-garde*.

31. *Rohan-Monbazon Infantrie* and *Beauvoisis Infantrie*, with two battalions apiece.

32. The *Piedmont* Brigade, the two battalions of *Alsace*, and the Swiss brigade comprising two battalions apiece of *Castalla* and *Diesbach*.

33. Savory, p.468. There are no further details, but as the British cavalry were not actively engaged, the circumstances suggest an unlucky shell burst.

34. Savory, pp.125-34; *The Operations of the Allied Army*, pp.79-80; Mackesy, p.53.

Chapter 6: Approach March

1. *The Operations of the Allied Army*, p.93. This battalion was presumably formed at the same time the brigades were re-organised, but although it came down from Münster with the rest of the British infantry it would soon be detached to join a quite separate grenadier brigade under Prinz Bevern as part of Wangenheim's corps.

2. HMC, Stopford-Sackville, p.307 (Sackville to Holdernesse, 16 June 1759).

3. *The Operations of the Allied Army*, pp.94-5.

4. Mackesy, p.61.

5. Summarised in Mackesy, p.62.

6. Notwithstanding, Fischer is a curiously elusive character. As a German protestant and a *roturier* (his father was a clerk in a tobacco factory) he had enemies enough on his own side and eventually fell from grace in 1761, supposedly on account of financial irregularities. Exactly what was really going on is hard to determine for while his corps was taken over in April 1761 by Louis Gabriel d'Armentière, Marquis de Conflans, Fischer himself remained in operational command as its lieutenant colonel. Significantly Conflans was the son of Fischer's old employer, Lieutenant General Louis de Conflans, Marquis de Armentiéres. Notwithstanding an exciting report that he was killed in action when Colonel Harvey of the Inniskillens struck his head off with a single blow, Fischer's death in or near Kassel in June 1762 was variously attributed to a duel or a fever, although the former rests on a very insubstantial legend.

7. A hornwork was a fortification, in this case an earthwork, protecting a bridgehead with bastions projecting on either side, which in plan view resembled a pair of horns, hence the term.

8. This was of course *Generalmajor* Georg Ludwig von Zastrow, and not to be confused with his uncle *Generalleutnant* Ludwig von Zastrow, the commander of the Hanoverian Army at the outset of the war, or with his brother Christian von Zastrow, the commandant of Münster. Although unquestionably gallant, Georg Ludwig was decidedly unlucky. He had been captured at Lutterberg in 1758 but although subsequently exchanged he had been badly wounded in the face there and was not yet ready for service in the field, hence this rear area posting. Exchanged once again, he was captured at Leimsfeld, near Ziegenhain, in March 1761, and captured again at Wolfenbuttel in October that year.

9. *The Operations of the Allied Army*, p.96. The author was understandably confused

between the Duc de Broglie and his brother the Comte de Broglie. The discrepancy between the 800 men assigned as a garrison and the 1,500 taken prisoner is probably accounted for by the presence of administrative personnel, sick, wounded and stragglers. There is also some confusion as to the date with this and some other accounts placing the capture on 9 July.

10. Grose, Francis, *Advice to Officers of the British Army* (G. Kearsly, London, 1782), pp.6-7.
11. HMC, Stopford-Sackville, p.305 (Sackville to Holdernesse, 14 April 1759).
12. HMC, Stopford-Sackville, p.310 (Sackville to Lord Bute?, 18 July 1759). For the sake of clarity, Sackville's written answer to Ferdinand of 11 July (a copy of which was in fact enclosed with the letter) is interpolated at the appropriate point and distinguished by italics.
13. HMC, Stopford-Sackville, p.309 (Sackville to Ferdinand, 11 July 1759).
14. Mackesy, p.69.
15. ibid, p.71.
16. HMC, Stopford-Sackville., p.306 (Sackville to Ferdinand, 29 April 1759 (draft)).
17. Ferdinand to King George, 26 July 1759, quoted in Savory, p.154.
18. Ten squadrons, seven battalions and possibly sixteen guns.
19. A very typical mercenary unit formed of both infantry and cavalry, rather startling dressed in buff yellow coats with red facings. The cavalry element consisted not of hussars but of dragoons further distinguished by brass helmets with horsehair manes.
20. *The Operations of the Allied Army*, pp. 98-9.
21. Linstrow (Hanoverian); Prinz Karl (Hessian); 1/Behr (Brunswick). In addition there was a mixed detachment of 300 dragoons drawn from a number of different regiments under Lieutenant Colonel Harvey of the Inniskillings, and two squadrons of the Reusch *Hussaren* (Prussian).

Chapter 7: The Battle of Minden
1. The very comprehensive orders, captured in Contades' baggage, were eventually transcribed in Westphalen's history and I have relied here upon the summary presented in Savory, pp.160-2. For Kingsley's admiring comment see HMC, Stopford-Sackville, p.320.
2. Now Maulbeerkamp.
3. Savory, p.162.
4. 'On Strategy', as translated by Daniel J. Hughes and Harry Bell in *Moltke on the Art of War: Selected Writings* (Novato, Presidio Press, 1993), p.92.
5. This was the solitary Sachsen-Gotha Regiment.
6. Sackville, Lorde George, *The Trial of the Right Honourable Lord George Sackville at a Court-Martial held at the Horse-Guards, February 29, 1760, for an enquiry into his conduct, being charged with Disobedience of Orders, while he commanded the British Horse in Germany. Together with his Lordship's Defence* (W. Owen, London, 1760), p.2. Considerable stress would be laid during the court martial on the fact

similar orders had been issued before and apparent omission of any specific instruction alerting commanders that Ferdinand was satisfied that the French were now about to come out in a few hours. Afterwards Kingsley would privately make the same complaint. Whilst true, the fact remains the point of the orders was that that they were to hold themselves in readiness to be called forward at as yet unknown point in time.

7. *The Operations of the Allied Army*, p.96.

8. Anhalt was certainly culpable of failing to ensure his piquets were close enough to have detected the French movement earlier, but Ferdinand had an unpleasant tendency to seek scapegoats and on this occasion there may have been a fair degree of exaggeration. Afterwards it was claimed that the deserters were picked up by Anhalt as early as 22.00 hours, but General Kingsley put the resulting delay at two hours, not five. Seee HMC, Stopford-Sackville, p.320.

9. *Großer Generalstab* map (1904). There is no record of how the three battalions were individually disposed, but it is likely that Anhalt's own blue-coated Hessians acted as the reserve while the red-coated Hanoverian and British piquets were the two working forward. While sadly anonymous, the latter were therefore the first British troops to be seriously engaged in Germany.

10. The term *debouchers* was used by the witnesses at Sackville's court martial in referring to the pre-prepared passages through the village and other obstacles to the line of march.

11. TNA, SP 87/37/56. ff. 122, 123, Statement by Count von Taube as to what orders he carried from Prince Ferdinand of Brunswick at Minden – dated at headquarters at Paderborn 12 February 1760. Given the date it is likely that the statement was solicited by way of possible evidence to be used in Lord George Sackville's court martial which commenced on 23 February. However, if so, his testimony was not used during the trial since he had carried no orders to Sackville.

12. HMC, Stopford-Sackville, p.320. So far as is known Kingsley did not leave a connected account of the battle, but in December 1775 an acquaintance of Sackville (or Lord Germain as he was then become) acquired a copy of Entick's *Compleat History of the Late War* – in Calcutta of all places – which had once belonged to Kingsley and was heavily annotated by the late general with a series of often splenetic remarks in the margins, throwing some very useful light on the attack by the infantry.

13. *The Operations of the Allied Army*, p.101. Sackville, p.69 and p.123. Both the unknown officer (Boyd?) and Lord Granby explicitly state that Scheele was 'detached from the center of the army by order of his Serene Highness to support the piquets in the village of Hahlen'. However, all the witnesses found Scheele's battalions drawn up in a single line on the north side of the woods, covering the gap left by Spörcken's advance. Captain Forbes Macbean of the Royal Artillery certainly testified that Scheele was 'in our rear at a distance' and commented on his apparent reluctance to come forward.

14. TNA, SP 87/37/56.

15. Wylly, H.C. et al, *History of the King's Own Yorkshire Light Infantry* (P. Lund, Humphries, London, 1926), p.48.

16. Sackville, p.110 and p.289. The transcript of Sackville's court martial is an astonishingly rich source of information as to how the British guns were moved and handled. None of the general officers sitting in judgement were gunners or seemingly had any notion of artillery matters and therefore required to have it all explained to them in very great detail!

17. ibid, pp.116-8. It was perhaps not surprising that the general officers comprising the court martial seemed bemused by this democratic way of proceeding or that the Advocate General should admit that he could not be supposed to know anything of artillery matters.

18. ibid, p.117 and p.122. Kingsley on the other hand huffily declared that the French artillery was not silenced until the end of the battle.

19. According to secondary sources they were eleven squadrons strong but in fact the two brigades together totalled fourteen squadrons.

20. Wylly, p.48. The officer of the 12th taken prisoner was either Captain Peter Chabert or Captain Robert Ackland, both of whom were afterwards returned as missing. Chabert was certainly serving with the regiment again afterwards and promoted in the following year, but Ackland went to an Invalid Company where he was breveted major in 1762. The artillery officer was presumably Lieutenant Carden, also returned as missing.

21. Savory, p.169. They were not the only trophy hunters. Lieutenant Montgomery of Napier's 12th Foot recounted that his spontoon or half-pike had been cut in two by a musket ball just below his hand, and that he was now doing duty with a French one!

22. Wylly, p.48.

23. HMC, Stopford-Sackville, p.322.

24. Notionally the regiment was 507 strong, but as with Napier's regiment at least sixty and perhaps as many as eighty officers and men should be deducted to allow for the detached grenadiers and piquets. So bad were the casualties that the regiment was excused duties afterwards, before resuming its place in the line, at its own request, three days later.

25. *The Operations of the Allied Army*, pp.101-2: 'In this attack the regiments du corps and Hammerstein (Hanoverian horse), the regiment of Holstein (Prussian), and the Hessian horse and battalions of grenadiers, signalised themselves prodigiously.'

26. Sackville, p.287. The cannon fire on the right which wakened him was, of course, the French diversionary attack at Eickhorst.

27. ibid, p.286: 'I attended at head quarters all the morning of the 30th, and remained there till I went in the afternoon to relieve Lieut. Gen. Imhoff in the command of the picquets of the army. The next day in visiting the posts of the picquets I reconnoitred the ground as far as an officer of my command ought to

have gone. The Prince of Anhalt relieved me about five in the evening, and in my return to head quarters to make my report, I sent off Col. Watson, Deputy Quarter-master General, and Capt. Smith, with directions to reconnoitre the avenues from the camp into the plain of Minden, that I had no opportunity of visiting.'

28. ibid, p.289.
29. Savory, p.71.
30. It is particularly disappointing to note that the map of the battle used by Savory to illustrate the crisis of the battle is fairly closely based on the definitive *Großer Generalstab* plan of 1904, yet egregiously omits the woods.
31. This appears to have originated in the youthful Fitzroy's excitement getting the better of him and offering to bring up the British cavalry, without realising (or forgetting) there were German ones as well.
32. Sackville, p.177.

Chapter 8: Afterwards
1. Savory, p.171.
2. See Mackesy for a very comprehensive account of the business.
3. Savory, p.474.
4. If there was any redeeming factor in this squalid affair it was the extraordinary wealth of eyewitness testimony which emerged at the Court Martial, not just pertaining to the immediate controversy over the orders, but shining unprecedented light on other events on the battlefield.
5. Royal Anglian Regiment (Napier's 12th Foot); Royal Regiment of Fusiliers (Kingsley's 20th Foot); Royal Welch Fusiliers (Huske's 23rd Fusiliers); Royal Regiment of Scotland (Home's 25th Foot); Princess of Wales Royal Regiment (Stuart's 37th Foot); the Rifles (Brudenell's 51st Foot). Whilst all six regiments have since gone through a series of amalgamations it is perhaps remarkable that none have been merged with each other.

Appendix I: Orders of Battle at Minden, 1 August 1759
1. Basic orders of battle for both sides are relatively easy to find in a variety of sources. Conversely it is surprisingly difficult to identify a great many of the individual officers referenced as brigade commanders. Blanks have only been filled through *very* extensive research using all available sources.
2. Mostyn (1709-1779), sometimes known as 'Jolly Jack', was a very experienced soldier who disguised his competence by an ostentatious dislike of paperwork and the intellectual aspects of his profession. Mackesy provides an entertaining pen-portrait.
3. Summaries of uniform details are again based on a variety of sources. A quick modern quick reference for Allied units is the author's *Frederick the Great's Allies*, Osprey Publishing, Oxford, 2010, while French units may be found in Rene Chartrand's multi-volume study of *Louis XV's Army*, same publisher 1996-7.

Details of Saxon units are taken from the Kronoskaf website.

4. Ordinarily the regiment would have been commanded by Lieutenant Colonel Edward Harvey (or Hervey) but he had been sent to join Gilsa with a detachment of 300 cavalry comprising an equal number of men drawn from each of the dragoon regiments on the right wing, (Savory, p.158).

5. Elliot (1713-1759) had a colourful career as a professional soldier, latterly in the Dutch service, before entering the British service and taking part in the St. Malo expedition. Afterwards he went to Germany, and died there of wounds on 10 October 1759, although the circumstances are obscure.

6. Macbean (1725-1800) was the son of the Rev. Alexander Macbean of Inverness, all of whose sons and stepsons entered the Army. He was a career Royal Artillery officer who died a lieutenant-general and colonel-commandant, Royal Invalid Artillery.

7. Sporcken (1698-1776). Seemingly regarded as a dependable, well-liked but undistinguished officer, Spörcken's action at Minden was undoubtedly the highlight of his career. At the end of the war he oversaw the demobilisation of the Allied forces and was afterwards C-in-C of the Hanoverian Army.

8. Waldgrave (1718-1784) was the youngest son of James 1st Earl Waldgrave, succeeding his elder brother as 3rd Earl in 1763. He commanded a brigade at Ste. Malo and afterwards in Germany with great distinction throughout the war.

9. Figures are taken from a return compiled on 25 July 1759 and printed in Westphalen, and refer to rank and file exclusive of officers. Although there would not have been any appreciable difference between those cited and the number of men actually present that day and those fit for duty a week later on 1 August, it is clear from the numbers of officers listed that the men of the grenadier companies serving with Wangenheim's corps are included as well as those men on piquet duty making up the equivalent of a battalion and taking part in Anhalt's action over at Hahlen. Lieutenant Montgomery of the 12th explicitly states that 'We actually fought that day not more than 480 private and 27 officers'; a difference of sixty rank and file which might justifiably be applied to the other five battalions as well.

10. Kingsley (1698?-1769) spent the early part of his career in the Footguards but was appointed colonel of the 20th Foot in 1756 and, unusually, took active command of the regiment both then and afterwards as a brigade commander. He was recalled, as a lieutenant general, in 1760 to command a secret expedition, which was aborted on the death of King George II.

11. Lent by Frederick,Holstein-Gottorp (1719-1765) was a formidably competent Prussian cavalry officer. He was also uncle, by marriage, to Catherine the Great of Russia and entered that service as a Field Marshal after the war.

12. Wangenheim (1706-1780). A battalion commander in England in 1756, he was regarded as one of Ferdinand's more reliable subordinates and fit to be entrusted with independent commands. Had family connections in England, where he lived for some years.

13. Bevern was a former Prussian officer who had been given command of one of the Saxon regiments taken at Pirna. When it promptly deserted shortly afterwards, Frederick blamed Bevern, hence his transfer to the Hanoverian service. Shortly after Minden he moved on once again, this time to settle down in the Danish service.

14. Schaumburg-Lippe (1724-1777) was born in London and reckoned an illegitimate son of King George I. Commissioned in the Lifeguards in 1742 and at Dettingen, but then with the Imperial army. Succeeded as Graf in 1748, studied under Frederick of Prussia and was appointed to command Hanoverian artillery in 1756. Went to Portugal as field marshal in 1762 and returned to Buckeburg to found a military academy.

15. Wounded and captured – contemporary reports of his death are exaggerated.

16. Per Chartrand 4:18-19, noting a different source suggesting a quite different red uniform with buff facings.

Appendix II: British Casualties at Minden 1759

1. Per *The London Gazette* 7-11 August 1759, with corrections and Christian names from regimental histories etc.

2. Captain Peter Chabbert at least was afterwards serving with the regiment, becoming major on 24 November 1759. When our old friend Corporal William Todd was subsequently posted into the 12th as part of a replacement draft he served in Chabbert's company. Ackland, however, went to an Invalid Company where he was breveted major in 1762.

3. Also noted as Adjutant – significantly he and the major were the only officers required to be mounted in action. He was wounded again at Kloster Kamp in 1760.

4. Died of wounds.

5. Adjutant.

6. First commissioned in 1737, he served at Culloden and was the author of a celebrated letter describing the battle.

7. Again noted as Adjutant.

8. Subsequently killed at Korbach in July 1760.

Appendix III: Lord George Sackville's Account of Minden

1. *The Trial of the Right Honourable Lord George Sackville at a Court-Martial held at the Horse-Guards, February 29, 1760, for an enquiry into his conduct, being charged with Disobedience of Orders, while he commanded the British Horse in Germany. Together with his Lordship's Defence*, (London, W. Owen, 1760).

2. Lieutenant Colonel Charles Hotham, (1729-1794) Adjutant General of the British forces at St. Malo and in Germany.

3. Captain Henry Stubbs, Horse Guards (Blue) Major of Brigade to the cavalry.

4. Graf Emmerich Otto August von Estorff, (1742-1796) a Brunswick officer who afterwards carried Ferdinand's dispatch to King George

216

5. Carl Gabriel Heinrich von Malortie (1734-1798) A Hanoverian officer on Ferdinand's Staff.
6. Lieutenant James Sutherland, 23rd Fusiliers (1728-1789).
7. Wilhelm Levin Ernst von Wintzingerode (1738-1781). A Hessian captain on Ferdinand's staff at Minden and later in a colonel in command of Hessian light troops.
8. Sackville's Hanoverian ADC. He testified on Sackville's behalf at the Court Martial and as a result found his career ruined – on learning of this Sackville offered to purchase a commission for him in the Danish service.
9. Assistant Quartermaster General.
10. Lieutenant Colonel Robert Sloper (1729-1802), commander of Bland's Dragoons at Minden and a very hostile witness indeed.
11. Edward Ligonier (1740-1782). Illegimate son of Francis Augustus Ligonier, the brother of John, Lord Ligonier. As a captain in the Footguards he is indiscriminately referred to in Sackville's narrative as a Captain and as a colonel since Footguards' captains ranked as lieutenant colonels in the Army.
12. Charles Fitzroy (1737-1797). Another Footguards officer on Ferdinand's staff.
13. General Adjutant von Derenthal – a Prussian staff officer.
14. Lieutenant Colonel William Augustus Pitt, (1728-1809) commanding officer of Mordaunt's 10th Dragoons
15. William Roy (1726-1790). An engineer and map-maker of some distinction, as engineers at this period were appointed, not commissioned, his substantive rank was a Lieutenant in the 53rd Foot.

Appendix IV: Contemporary Accounts of the Battle of Minden

–

Appendix V: Testimony of Royal Artillery Officers at the Sackville Court Martial

1. Unfortunately none of the maps or surveys referred to were reproduced in the account of the Court Martial. There is reason to believe however that the definitive *Großer Generalstab* plan of 1904 may have been based in part at least on the Graf's survey.

Appendix VI: The British Army in the Seven Years War

1. It should be pointed out that in ethnic terms the Irish Establishment was nothing of the sort. It was primarily conceived and maintained as a garrison for the country and intended to uphold the Protestant ascendency. Consequently, regiments serving on the Irish Establishment were actually forbidden to enlist men in that country until the 1790s and instead had to find their recruits in Scotland or in England. Conversely, of course, regiments serving on the British Establishment were allowed to recruit in Ireland – providing those they enlisted declared on oath they were Protestants. This stipulation did not, however, apply to officers, and Irish gentlemen were perfectly at liberty to obtain commissions in 'Irish' regiments.

2. So-called 'Additional Companies' were routinely authorised in wartime to serve as a temporary depot for the receiving of recruits, and at the beginning of the Seven Years War some units were allowed to expand these into second battalions. This, however, was merely an expedient to evade Parliamentary restrictions on the number of units entertained on the British Establishment and as soon as the necessary authority was obtained for the augmentation of the Army, the second battalions were hived off and taken into the line as new regiments in their own right. The 68th Foot for example (later the Durham Light Infantry) actually began life as the 2/23rd Royal Welch Fusiliers and apparently went buccaneering in France still wearing the uniform of that corps.

3. One company in each battalion serving in North America at this time was converted into a 'light' company, but this was a local arrangement and not duplicated in Germany until 1761 when volunteers were sought to serve in a temporary light battalion; Fraser's Chasseurs. Nor is there any suggestion that Fraser's men adopted any of the sartorial peculiarities of the American companies – such as peaked caps.

4. One exception was of course Major General William Kingsley, Colonel of the 20th Foot, who accompanied his regiment to Germany – but as its brigade commander and another was the Marquis of Granby, the colonel of the Blues, once again serving in a staff appointment rather than in direct command of the regiment.

5. Confusingly the four remaining regiments of Horse were then numbered accordingly before reverting to their original seniorities on becoming dragoon guards. Thus Sackville's original regiment, the 7th Horse, first became the 3rd Horse in 1746 and then the 6th Dragoon Guards in 1788.

6. Guy, p.210.

7. Bulloc (1914), pp.34-5.

8. TNA WO120. This example however appears to have been untypical in that Tovey was also recorded as having been 'born in the army'.

9. Razzell (1963), pp.248-60.

10. *Register of Madras Mayoral Court,* Vol.61, 7 July 1759.

11. Hayes (1956), pp.43-6. An example is provided in text where Sackville recommended two volunteers to vacancies as ensigns, but sadly had no power to appoint them himself.

Appendix VII: His Britannic Majesty's Army in Germany

1. For a fuller description of the Hanoverian and other contingents making up the army see the author's *Frederick the Great's Allies 1756-63* (Osprey, 2010). Regrettably Appendix 2 of Savory (1966) is inaccurate in a number of areas.

2. Not to be confused with the state of Hesse-Darmstadt which aligned itself with the Imperial forces.

3. This had begun life as a consolidated grenadier battalion, but when their parent units were disbanded at the end of the War of the Austrian Succession, the grenadier companies were retained in service and the battalion turned into a regiment of the line. It still retained its grenadier distinctions and judging by a

painting by David Morier in 1748 the men sported particularly ferocious moustaches. The regiment should not therefore be confused with the two temporary grenadier battalions.

4. Frederick II. As Erbprinz of Hesse-Kassel he had been a *Generalleutnant* in the Prussian service and commanded the three Prussian fusilier regiments which began the war as the garrison of Wesel, hence his keen-ness to reform the Hessian Army, at least outwardly, on Prussian lines.

5. They were certainly dark blue in the 1740s and straw-coloured by the end of the war. While an earlier change-over cannot be ruled out, the most likely occasion would have been the 1760 re-organisation which saw a number of other uniform changes closely modelled on Prussian lines.

6. Although illustrated by nineteenth century artists such as Knotel it is not entirely certain that they acquired armour.

Appendix VIII: The French Army and its Allies in the Seven Years War

1. As with so much else this comparison is slightly misleading in that while service in the British Army was theoretically unlimited it was relatively easy for a soldier to obtain his discharge except in time of war.

2. A sixth Irish regiment, *de Lally*, served in India.

3. Again there was no real consistency here, and while fur caps were generally worn by foreign units, the *Cuirassiers du Roi* had them too. Their designation incidentally came about through wearing a full cuirass comprising both back and breast plates, while all other heavy cavalry (including the Gendarmerie) only had breastplates.

4. Unlike the *cavallerie legere* they had only one pistol, which was balanced on the other side of the saddle bow by an entrenching tool. The theory was that they should be able to range ahead of the army, seize key points such as bridges and then dig in to hold on against superior numbers until the rest of the army caught up.

5. Otherwise Prinz Xavier of Saxony, (1730-1806) second surviving son of Fredrick Augustus, Elector of Saxony and King of Poland. He was also brother-in-law to the Dauphin of France, hence his title when serving with the French army.

6. The surviving cavalrymen were eventually found horses in 1761 and formed into a provisional *Karabiniere* regiment. At the same time, all twelve infantry regiments were placed on a standardised footing with just four companies of *musketiers* and one of grenadiers – which were in turn consolidated into three grenadier battalions.

Bibliography

Primary Sources

The National Archives (TNA), Kew

SP 87/37/56. ff. 122, 123, statement by Count von Taube as to what orders he carried from Prince Ferdinand of Brunswick at Minden.

WO120, Royal Hospital, Chelsea: Regimental Registers of Pensioners.

Printed Sources

Anonymous, *A Compleat History of the Present War: from its commencement in 1756, to the end of the campaign, 1760* (W. Owen etc., London, 1761).

Anonymous, *A New Military Dictionary: or, the Field of War. Containing a particular ... account of the most remarkable battles, sieges, bombardments, and expeditions, whether by sea, or land, such as relate to Great Britain* (J. Cooke, London, 1760).

Anonymous, *The Operations of the Allied Army: Under the Command of His Serene Highness Prince Ferdinand, Duke of Brunswick and Luneberg, During the Greatest Part of Six Campaigns, Beginning in the Year 1757, and Ending in the Year 1762. By an Officer who served in the British Forces* (T. Jeffreys, London, 1764).

Bulloch, J.M., *Territorial Soldiering in North-East Scotland* (Aberdeen University Press, Aberdeen, 1914).

Chandler, David, *The Art of War in the Age of Marlborough* (Batsford, London, 1976).

Chartrand, Rene, *The Army of Louis XV*, 5 volumes. (Osprey, 1996-1998).

Duncan, Francis, *History of the Royal Regiment of Artillery* (Murray, London, 1879), Volume 1.

Fortescue, J.W., *A History of the British Army* (MacMillan, London, 1899).

Griffiths, R., *A Genuine and Particular Account of the Late Enterprise on the Coast of France, 1758* (R. Griffiths, London, 1763).

Grose, Francis, *Advice to Officers of the British Army* (G. Kearsly, London, 1782).

Großer Generalstab (Ed.), *Die Kriege Friedrich des Großen, Dritter Teil: Der Siebenjährige Krieg 1756 – 1763* (Verlag Mittler und Sohn, Leuthen, Berlin, 1904).

Guy, Alan, *Oeconomy and Discipline; Officership and Administration in the British Army 1714-63* (Manchester University Press, Manchester, 1985).

Higgins, R.T., *The Records of the King's Own Borderers or Old Edinburgh Regiment* (Chapman and Hall, London, 1876).

Houlding, John, *Fit for Service: The Training of the British Army 1715-1795* (Oxford University Press, Oxford, 1981).

Hughes, B.P., *Firepower: Weapons Effectiveness on the Battlefield 1630-1850* (Arms and Armour, London, 1974).

Lawson, C.C.P., *A History of the Uniforms of the British Army*, Volume II (Norman Military Publications, London, 1941).

Mackinnon, Daniel, *Origin and Services of the Coldstream Guards* (London, 1883).

Mackesy, Piers, *The Coward of Minden: The Affair of Lord George Sackville* (Allen Lane, London, 1979).

Middleton, Richard, *The Bells of Victory: The Pitt-Newcastle Ministry and the Conduct of the Seven Years War 1757-1762* (Cambridge University Press, Cambridge, 2002).

Pitt, William, *Correspondence of William Pitt, Earl of Chatham* (John Murray, London, 1837).

Reid, Stuart, *Frederick the Great's Allies 1756-1763* (Oxford University Press, Oxford, 2010).

Savory, Sir Reginald, *His Britannic Majesty's Army in Germany during the Seven Years War* (Clarendon Press, Oxford, 1966).

Sackville, Lorde George, *The Trial of the Right Honourable Lord George Sackville at a Court-Martial held at the Horse-Guards, February 29, 1760, for an enquiry into his conduct, being charged with Disobedience of Orders, while he commanded the British Horse in Germany. Together with his Lordship's Defence* (W. Owen, London, 1760).

Saxe, Maurice de and Philips, T.R. (Ed.), *Reveries on the Art of War* (Harrisburg, 1944). Note that although originally published in 1757, the *Reveries* actually appear to have been written or dictated in December 1732.

Todd, William, *The Journal of Corporal William Todd 1745-1762* (Army Records Society, Stroud, 2001).

Tomasson, K. and Buist, F., *Battles of the '45* (Batsford, London, 1962).

Walpole, Horace, *The Letters of Horace Walpole* (Lea and Blanchard, London, 1842).

Wylly, H.C. et al, *History of the King's Own Yorkshire Light Infantry*, Volume 1 (P. Lund, Humphries, London, 1926).

Published Studies

Hayes, J., *The Social and Professional Background of the Officers of the British Army, 1714-63*, a MA thesis (London, 1956).

Historical Manuscripts Commission (HMC), *Report on the Manuscripts of Mrs Stopford-Sackville of Drayton House, Northamptonshire* (HMSO, London, 1904).

Oughton, J.A., *By Dint of Labour and Perseverance ... A journal recording two months in northern Germany kept by Lieutenant-Colonel James Adolphus Oughton, commanding 1st battalion 37th Regiment of Foot, 1758*, Society for Army Historical Research Special Publication No.14, (London, 1997).

Razzell, P.J., *Social Origins of Officers in the Indian and British Home Army 1758-1962*, British Journal of Sociology 14 (1963), pp.248-60.

Index

227